Poor Women's Lives

Poor Women's Lives

Gender, Work, and Poverty in Late-Victorian London

Andrew August

Madison • Teaneck
Fairleigh Dickinson University Press
London: Associated University Presses

Associated University Presses
440 Forsgate Drive
Cranbury, NJ 08512

Associated University Presses
16 Barter Street
London WC1A 2AH, England

Associated University Presses
P.O. Box 338, Port Credit
Mississauga, Ontario
Canada L5G 4L8

The paper used in this publication meets the requirements
of the American National Standard for Permanence of Paper
for Printed Library Materials Z39.48-1984.

Library of Congress Cataloging-in-Publication Data

August, Andrew, 1962–
    Poor women's lives : gender, work, and poverty in late-Victorian
London / Andrew August.
        p.   cm.
    Includes bibliographical references and index.
    ISBN 0-8386-3807-4 (alk. paper)
    1. Poor women—England—London—Social conditions. 2. Poverty-
-England—London—History—19th century. 3. Working class—England-
London—History—19th century. 4. London (England)—Social
Conditions. I. Title.
HQ1600.L6A93   1999
305.48'96942—dc21   98-54806
                                                                           CIP

For Barbara

Contents

List of Maps and Figures

Maps

Figures

List of Tables

Acknowledgments

This project had its origins as a doctoral dissertation at Columbia University. As a graduate student in New York, I was fortunate to find a community of scholars notable for the quality of their ideas and the extraordinary generosity with which they greeted my requests for help. Michael Hanagan, Ellen Ross, Charles Tilly, and Louise Tilly all played crucial roles in stimulating my thoughts and directing them in productive ways. In its formative stages, the project also benefited from the advice and criticism of Martha Howell, Robert Paxton, Isser Woloch, and the Columbia Social History Group.

While doing research in London, I enjoyed the intellectual and social community at the Institute of Historical Research, where I was always made to feel at home. I am also grateful to Anna Davin for her advice and the opportunity to visit the treasure trove of resources in her office.

As the project began to take shape, I was most fortunate to meet David Cannadine, who became my thesis advisor and friend. His enthusiasm and encouragement complemented his intelligent suggestions and criticisms and kept the thesis and the author on track. Betsy Blackmar, Michael Hanagan, Louise Tilly, and Deborah Valenze joined him on my dissertation committee, enriching the project through insightful comments and stimulating discussions.

Their direction shaped the revisions that transformed this work from dissertation to book, a process that also benefited immeasurably from Ellen Ross's careful reading and helpful recommendations and from discussions with Andrew Plaa and Clif Hubby. Janet Fink patiently edited the dissertation and manuscript, correcting numerous flaws. Errors that persist despite their efforts are, of course, the responsibility of the author.

I am also grateful to the staffs of the local history libraries of the Swiss Cottage, Tower Hamlets, and Marylebone libraries, as well as that of the Greater London Record Office. Jeannette Ullrich at the Penn State Abington College Library provided indispensable and efficient assistance. One chapter of this work appeared, in somewhat different form, in *Journal of Family*

History, whose publisher gave permission to use the material here. Thanks are also due to the publisher of *The A–Z of Victorian London,* Harry Margary, Lympne Castle, Kent, for permission to use its very helpful maps. Barry Ableman's friendship over the years has never wavered, and his advice on mapping issues was essential. He and Peter Brown prepared the maps. Peter Sandler proofread the manuscript and prepared the index.

Work on this project was supported by a Stephen Koss Memorial Fellowship, a Columbia College Chamberlain Grant, and a Penn State Abington Scholar award. Timely support from my parents, Jim and Doris August, and grandparents, Harry and Helen August, kept the work moving forward. Over the years, I have also enjoyed the encouragement of my family, in-laws, and friends. I thank them.

But my greatest debt of gratitude is owed to my wife, Barbara, who read early and late drafts of each chapter and strengthened the arguments through her patient questions. More importantly, her love and support made the production of this book possible.

Introduction

On a late spring evening in 1879, Mary Lawrence used a fire poker to smash two panes of glass, windows belonging to the owner of a local beer shop. The police arrested Lawrence, who lived in the Globe Town area of Bethnal Green, a poor neighborhood in the heart of working-class London. The image of a woman smashing shopwindows calls to mind those more famous glass-breakers, the militant suffrage activists, who embarked upon a widespread campaign of breaking shopwindows in London some three decades later. But Mary Lawrence did not break her local beer shop's windows to make a point about national politics or even to take a stand against restrictions on women. She took this dramatic action to warn the proprietor against encouraging her husband, who, she thought, spent far too much of his wages in the shop.[1]

Mary Lawrence and women like her in late-Victorian poor neighborhoods had little in common with the middle-class suffrage activists of the West End. When London suffrage militants stepped into the streets to press their claims, they invaded "male space," broke down barriers, and entered "contested terrain."[2] Mary Lawrence and her neighbors spent much of their time in the streets; public spaces in their neighborhoods belonged as much to them as to their husbands. Poor women asserted their interests aggressively and publicly, whether bargaining with street sellers or shopkeepers, arguing with their husbands, or battling the police. They also participated in the "public" realm of paid work, earning wages through most of their lives. Breaking a shopwindow represented an extraordinary step for a middle-class woman—moving into forbidden space, adopting the unlady-like attitude of a militant protester, and defying the code of behavior appropriate to her class and gender. For Mary Lawrence, smashing the fire poker through the panes of glass was unusual only in its destruction of property and resultant arrest. Acting assertively in the streets of their neighborhoods was business as usual for poor women in late-Victorian London.

The middle-class house reflected and reinforced the gender conventions influencing suffrage workers. Suburban homes created realms of privacy, associated with female space and with domesticity.[3] Working-class

15

housing lacked this distinction. Shared facilities and stairs, open doorways, and crowded conditions conspired to break down barriers between home and street.[4] Poor women moved in and out of their homes, congregated at the shared water tap, or simply stood in the doorway or at the window, occupying space that was both in the house and in the street. John Blake recalled that in his Poplar neighborhood, the doors of every house were open all day, and "anyone feeling lonely only had to stand at the door and in a short time someone would come along and have a chat."[5] Charles Booth's investigators reported finding "front doors always open" and "women at doors" in Lisson Grove, a poor neighborhood in Marylebone.[6] These two settings—the home and the neighborhood, the household and the community—formed the fundamental contexts for the lives of poor London women.

According to Charles Booth, 30.7% of late-Victorian London's 4.2 million residents lived in poverty at the moment of his inquiry. Booth classified the majority of the rest just above poverty at that time, and most of them likely fell into poverty at other points in their lives.[7] Yet this vast population exerted limited influence on national politics, as even its men often failed to meet the suffrage criteria established in the 1884–85 parliamentary reform. Employed in short-term and seasonal jobs, the London poor seldom joined unions or organized strikes.[8] Perhaps this absence from traditional political activity or union organization, the squeaky wheels that have attracted social historians' attention, helps explain why historians have rarely focused on the London poor.[9]

The almost three million London poor accounted for around one-tenth of the English population, and half of this often-ignored multitude were women.[10] Despite the growth of social and women's history in recent years, these women have escaped historians' attention, with the notable exception of the work of Ellen Ross. Ross's pathbreaking efforts have cast light into some important areas of poor women's hidden history, including the importance of their roles as mothers.[11] This study uncovers other hidden aspects of poor women's lives: their experiences as workers in local labor markets, as managers of household economies confronting potential shortfalls from week to week, and as creators and victims of gender roles in their households and communities. It reveals the challenges, burdens, and often heroic struggles that characterized these poor women's lives.

Communities, Households, and Gender

Poor Londoners inhabited the largest city in the West, the showplace of imperial glory, the glittering center of world capitalism. Greater London stretched fifteen miles in each direction from Charing Cross. The late-Victorian metropolis housed nearly one of five people in England. Its streets extended 7,000 miles and supported 11,000 cabs and 750,000 cats.[12] Yet the experiences of most residents of this vast metropolis focused on more circumscribed worlds. A particular group of streets defined the neighborhood, beyond which lay outsiders. A set of steps running over the railway line marked the edge of Edward Ezard's Battersea district, serving as "both our gateway to the big outside world and, on return, the entry to our cosy parish life."[13] A dock bridge formed the boundary of Grace Foakes's Wapping neighborhood; beyond it, "they were a community on their own and so were we."[14] There was even an expectation that one would find romance within this prescribed community. Ezard recalls hostility on the part of peers and parents toward those who went courting beyond their neighborhood.[15] Within these districts, residents knew one another well and established concentrated networks of interdependence and mutual aid, as well as rivalry and hierarchies.[16]

The value poor Londoners placed on this feeling of community is evident in their tendency to remain in particular districts even when moving house. High rents and unstable earnings made it necessary for poor families to pack up their meager belongings and relocate, often under pressure from landlords who hadn't received rent. But their house search would focus on the area with which they were familiar and in which they felt comfortable. John Blake's family moved a number of times during his childhood, always in the neighborhood of St. Leonard's Road, Poplar. As an adult, Blake moved further afield for a short time, but did not like it, and returned to his old neighborhood.[17] David Green and Alan Parton have documented the pattern of frequent moves all within a short distance as typical of residents in poor districts; "working-class households frequently remained in the same area for lengthy periods of time despite the frequency of residential shifts."[18]

Emotional bonds attracted these people to the communities in which they knew the neighbors and seemingly everyone knew them. Grace Foakes looked back nostalgically: "There was poverty, disease, dirt and ignorance, and yet to feel one belonged outweighed all else."[19] Long-term residence had important economic benefits as well. Neighbors helped one another in times of crisis, as George Acorn's Bethnal Green neighbors did when his father could not work. Friends and relatives held a "friendly lead," in which items were donated and raffled, raising £9 for his family.[20] Information about local job opportunities passed through networks of neighbors, kin, and friends, while casual work required residence nearby to be on hand whenever it became available. A clergyman in the Somers Town area of St.

Pancras noted this pattern at the nearby railway stations, which "employ[ed] a considerable amount of casual labour, the men being taken on early in the morning for the day and about midnight for the night shift."[21] These factors encouraged poor Londoners to remain in close-knit, stable communities. A survey of working-class men from various districts around the metropolis revealed that over 92% of respondents had lived in their neighborhood for over a year.[22] As a solicitor for the St. Pancras vestry observed in a hearing on housing conditions in Somers Town, residents "lived there for generations, and had local trades and local connections."[23]

These communities exerted powerful influences over those who lived in them, providing the basic framework of life for poor Londoners. Within these districts, though, individuals ate, slept, had sex, and made decisions about their lives in particular households, the fundamental building blocks of the communities. Most poor households in London were built around families, usually a parent or parents and their children. At times these "nuclear" families expanded to include kin, lodgers, or even servants. One crucial role of the family was economic; households shared living quarters and paid a single rent, shared meals, and generally purchased clothing and other necessities from a single household budget.[24] Thus, the individual's economic position and standard of living reflected that of his or her family. To a great extent, individuals made major decisions within the context of these family units, pursuing what some historians have described as "family strategies."[25]

Though family strategies can help us understand the motivations and decisions of the late-Victorian poor, a narrow focus on them obscures tensions and conflicting interests within families. Discord between husbands and wives simmered in poor households. Generational differences also impacted decisions and caused strife between parents and children. These conflicts become most apparent when husbands abandoned wives and children, or young men and women moved out of their parents' households against parental wishes. These ruptures were exceptional, but individual interests clashed within families all the time, particularly over the distribution of resources and responsibilities.

A rigid family-strategies approach also misses the permeability of boundaries between the family and the community. Just as working-class housing eliminated the frontier between home and street, so the distinction between family members and neighbors was not always sharply drawn. Mutual aid extended beyond family and kin to neighbors, and could even include the informal adoption of children.[26] The complexity of such boundaries among the London poor becomes evident in an anecdote related by George Acorn. When the police came to investigate, suspecting one of his neighbors of theft, another neighbor (who was also the landlady) hid the stolen goods to protect the guilty family. The police were thwarted, but the offending family was asked to move out.[27] Keeping in mind the importance of relationships beyond the household and of competing individual interests within it, this study will examine the household as the crucial terrain on which poor Londoners confronted the challenges of their lives.

Powerful notions of proper gender roles conditioned individual lives, family strategies, and neighborhood relations. In examining relationships within households, for example, the gender-blind term "spouse" is nearly meaningless, as husbands and wives approached their lives and relationships with widely differing expectations and choices. Similarly, sons and daughters received different treatment and faced sex-specific expectations.[28] Gender determined individuals' places in their communities and in local labor markets. This does not mean that men and women never did things like go to the pub or stroll in the streets together. But it does mean that they had different opportunities and approaches to their work, leisure, home, and community.

But these gendered expectations did not face poor Londoners as external forces imposed by a stifling elite culture. Rather, they grew out of poor men and women's daily activities. In struggles to make ends meet and to pursue their interests in families, they carved out and implemented gender roles. Networks of leisure, mutual aid, and gossip in neighborhoods built and reinforced sexual difference. As workers and small masters, men and women contributed to the persistent division of labor in local economies that provided the economic underpinning for gender inequality in households. Ideas about gender and the cultural prescriptions that followed from them developed in poor neighborhoods and did not simply mimic middle-class notions.

Poverty

Poverty cast a wide net in late-Victorian London. Most people faced impoverishment as a very real and threatening possibility at some points in their lives. Yet the historian faces a difficult challenge, as did contemporaries, in defining poverty. The standards by which individuals may be classified as poor are relative; poverty must be measured with reference to time and place. The poor in late-twentieth-century Western cities have access (in some cases) to more comfortable clothing and more varied diets than those enjoyed by comfortable peasants of previous centuries. But this does not make contemporary poverty less troubling for those who suffer it or less disgraceful for the societies that perpetuate it. Its relative quality does not make poverty a less useful or valid concept for understanding past societies or our own.

In studying the poor in a past society, we should focus on those whose food, housing, and clothing were inadequate by their contemporary standards. Very few people in late-Victorian London actually faced starvation; there was no famine in late-nineteenth-century Britain. But persistent hunger was widespread. George Acorn recalls eating so poorly as a child that he often felt fatigued.[29] While some people lived on the streets, far more resided in crowded, poorly ventilated quarters, without adequate provision for waste. They enjoyed only intermittent, often unsafe, water supplies. These were the London poor that Charles Booth set out to study, launching the social survey that ultimately would produce seventeen volumes of description and analysis of London life at the turn of the century. He sought to document and quantify poverty, and assumed that his sources and investigators knew what poverty was and could recognize it.[30]

Based on interviews and observation, Booth and his team classified households and streets in London in eight categories, ranging from the poorest, "A," to the most affluent, "H." These categories fit into four larger classifications—very poor, poor, comfortable, and well-off—and Booth presented detailed figures for the population fitting each category. These numbers offer a useful starting point for the study of the London poor, yet we must approach them with some skepticism. It is hard to imagine that Booth's investigators were able to distinguish accurately between those in classification "D" (poverty) and "E" (comfort). Booth himself acknowledged the difficulty: "E passes imperceptibly into either the irregular position of C or the base remuneration of D."[31] But Booth's figures offer at least a general sense of the prevalence of poverty and the general social structure of late-nineteenth-century London.

Another complexity confronting Booth lay in the constantly shifting economic situations facing most Londoners. Individuals moved in and out of poverty. Work opportunities did not provide stable, long-term employment on which they could build a stable family economy. Rather, wages fluctuated seasonally and many worked at short-term (casual) jobs. Household structure exerted a huge influence on people's likelihood of suffering in poverty at a particular time. A couple with young children might find themselves unable to afford adequate food or decent space, but once these children grew up and contributed to the household economy, the family might achieve relative comfort. Far more London residents experienced poverty at some point in their lives than snapshots such as Booth's survey indicate. Thus the historian John Gillis observes, "[A]ll but a minority of working-class people would experience real scarcity at some point in their lives."[32]

Contemporary observers and modern historians have posited a clear distinction between the solid, comfortable working class and "the residuum," which allegedly did not participate in the broader trends in Victorian culture and society.[33] But the boundary between the "poor" and the "stable working class" shifts as we try to define it. At any particular moment, it would be extremely difficult to classify individuals as poor as opposed to comfortably working class, as these conditions shaded into one another.[34] Over time, individuals moved back and forth through this gray area at the edge of poverty. Despite Booth's impressive efforts, the "London poor" is an inexact category, and efforts to count this group must be seen as broad estimates. Though the numbers actually in poverty at any particular moment may be impossible to determine exactly, poverty offers a meaningful category for analyzing the lives of those segments of the working class inhabiting inner London districts where local labor markets and housing conditions made it endemic.

Studying Poor Women

The experiences of poor women can best be understood in the context of the households, neighborhoods, local labor markets, and gender definitions within which they lived. Throughout their lives, poor women devoted themselves to their households and families. As young single women, they helped their mothers and looked forward to forming their own families. Wives and mothers did anything they could to maintain their families and the welfare of children and husbands. But this endeavor can only be understood within the framework of close-knit communities in poor neighborhoods. Women helped each other out, gossiped about the neighbors, and enforced ideas of propriety in their districts. The way of life in each poor neighborhood grew out of conditions in the local labor market. The kinds of work available to men and women drew economic limits around their lives, enforced the poverty that continually threatened them, and supported gender inequality in households. These patterns of gender, work, and poverty in households and communities formed the fabric of poor women's lives in late-Victorian London.

Thus, a focus on households and communities forms a useful framework for the study of poor women. Only by studying particular districts can we gain insight into the impact of local labor market conditions on household structures and relationships. To that end, case studies of three

London neighborhoods—Somers Town, Lisson Grove, and Globe Town—form the core of this work, but particularly valuable sources for other London neighborhoods have been used to supplement these local studies.

David Green has identified two distinct geographic patterns in which poor neighborhoods developed in nineteenth-century London.[35] In some cases, poor neighborhoods grew in pockets surrounded by more affluent districts. Just behind major streets, around the corner from the spacious squares, one could find the crowded, unsanitary conditions in which poor Londoners lived. In contrast, in the East End and much of London south of the Thames, poor neighborhoods stretched almost endlessly. Here working-class districts grew up cheek by jowl, each with its own sense of community and often dependent on particular industries.

Somers Town and Lisson Grove represent the first type of poor neighborhood. Somers Town, in southern St. Pancras, abutted solid middle-class areas in Bloomsbury and along the southern and eastern edges of Regent's Park. Lisson Grove, in Marylebone, was nestled among the comfortable areas of Paddington to the west, St. John's Wood to the north, and the impressive squares and shopping districts of southern Marylebone to its south. Both neighborhoods grew in part as service annexes to these more affluent areas, housing servants, building, and transportation workers. On the other hand, Globe Town, the eastern portion of Bethnal Green, lay in the heart of the East End, an expanse of poor and working-class districts. In every direction, neighborhoods filled with manual laborers in manufacturing, dock work, and other trades extended around Globe Town.

Somers Town, Lisson Grove, and Globe Town were chosen in part because they represent the different types of poor neighborhoods and in part because of the quality of the most important source for the study of labor markets and women's employment, the manuscript census enumerators' books from 1881. Enumerators' books list all residents of the neighborhoods, their age, sex, occupation, position within the household, and birthplace. This allows a detailed study of household, family, and occupational structure. It places individuals in the context of their life course and family positions in ways other sources cannot.

However, a number of difficulties complicate use of the census as a source for information on women's employment.[36] Men defined as household heads generally filled out the census schedules. They were ignorant of their wives' efforts on behalf of the household, which often included wage earning. Some husbands who were aware of their wives' employment may have hidden this from the census because they were embarrassed at being unable to support their families without the contribution of their wives. In addition, some enumerators who compiled information from individual schedules into the manuscript census books ignored reported employment by wives, listing them as not occupied, or defined them according to their husbands' occupations. Fortunately, these inaccuracies due to enumerator bias are obvious, as some enumerators' districts in poor neighborhoods, surrounded by streets in which many married women were employed, show almost no married women's employment. Though aggregate census data include the reports of these enumerators, this study has eliminated "bad enumerators" in its choice of neighborhoods.

Women in poor neighborhoods earned cash in a number of ways that did not appear in the census records. Women minded children, took in laundry, and offered aid during childbirth to their neighbors, often receiving some cash payment.[37] However, unless this work was constant enough to be reported on the census schedule, we have little record of it. Other kinds of earning that escaped the census enumerators include many occupations that authorities frowned upon. Prostitution is the most notable example, and some women in the three areas certainly worked, at least occasionally, as prostitutes. Begging and stealing likely contributed to household economies of some residents. It is impossible to quantify the impact of this type of work, but it was common in working-class neighborhoods.

Most jobs in poor London neighborhoods offered only irregular employment. Many residents of the three neighborhoods, male and female, worked on jobs that were seasonal, often dovetailing different occupations during slack seasons. The census reflects the occupations of people on 4 April 1881, and the jobs taken on in the winter or midsummer months are underrepresented. Finally, many jobs in these areas offered only casual employment. Underemployment was the common status of residents of the neighborhoods. But out-of-work men were likely to report themselves as occupied in whatever job they last performed. Women who were out of work may have been more commonly listed as unoccupied.[38]

Nonetheless, the census does provide a great deal of information on women's employment available in no other source. Thus, we are presented with the choice of discarding a valuable but not flawless source, or using the source while keeping its limitations in mind.[39] This study takes the latter course.

Using the census and a range of other sources, chapter 1 of this study examines the development of each neighborhood and patterns of household formation in them. The neighborhoods grew in response to localized demand for labor but had stabilized by the last decades of the century. Chapter 2 then analyzes the causes of poverty among residents of the areas, locating the origins of poverty in local labor markets and household structures. The powerful division of labor that confined women in poor neighborhoods to poorly paid jobs forms the subject of chapter 3. Women's employment is then, in chapter 4, placed in the context of their life courses, uncovering a pattern of wage earning throughout women's lives. Even married women commonly sought employment, except when the domestic work demanded of them grew too burdensome. Chapter 5 explains the ways in which women's welfare suffered, despite their contributions to household economies. The division of labor that denied them economic independence and the close-knit communities that enforced gender roles created powerful frameworks for these women's lives.

The case studies show a number of specific differences among the three neighborhoods. Each grew in response to particular market and geographic forces, and different trades were concentrated in each. But the general structures of the labor markets were quite similar, particularly in the pervasiveness of casual and seasonal employment and the strict division of labor by sex. Common patterns of household formation existed across all three neighborhoods. The dynamics of women's employment and of gender relations within households reveals a common way of life in the neighborhoods and apparently throughout inner-London poor areas. In all of them, tremendous burdens of work, powerfully restrictive gender ideologies, and crushing poverty presented women with massive challenges, to which they responded with energy and determination.

Map 1: Somers Town and Environs

Source: The A to Z of Victorian London
Harry Margary, Lympne Castle, Kent
1987

26

Map 2: Lisson Grove and Environs

Source: The A to Z of Victorian London
Harry Margary, Lympne Castle, Kent
1987

Map 3: Globe Town and Environs

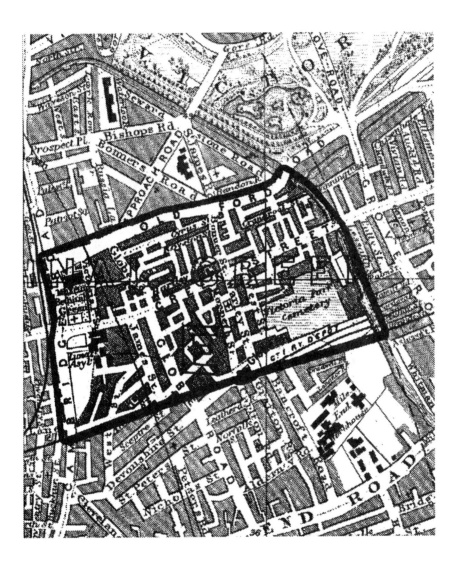

Source: The A to Z of Victorian London
Harry Margary, Lympne Castle, Kent
1987

Map 4: Somers Town, Lisson Grove and Globe Town in Late-Victorian London

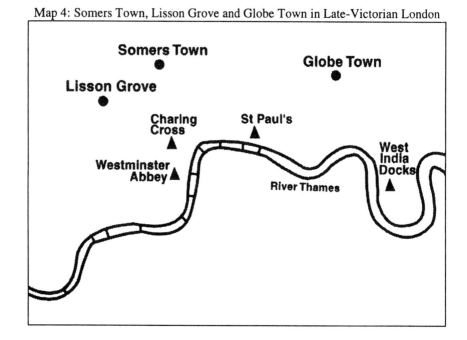

Poor Women's Lives

1

Little Communities:
Neighborhoods and Households

When Grace Foakes, born in Wapping just after the turn of the century, recalled her impoverished London district, she said, "This was a little community which lived almost entirely within itself."[1] In her neighborhood, she "found comradeship and happiness."[2] Many of those who grew up poor in London near the end of the last century recall such powerful feelings of community. To outside observers like G. R. Sims, poor Londoners lived in a uniform mass; "The story of one slum is the story of another."[3] Despite the unawareness of Sims and other middle-class observers, poor Londoners' strong sense of place reflects the importance of particular local conditions shaping their lives.

London's poor communities did not randomly fall into indistinct slum masses. Rather they grew in response to specific historical processes and individual decisions over the course of the century. The populations of London's poor areas in the last quarter of the nineteenth century represented legacies of decades of migration, driven by employment opportunities in particular local labor markets. Thus, an understanding of the lives of poor Londoners in the late-Victorian period begins with the stories of the settlement and development of their neighborhoods. Somers Town, Lisson Grove, and Globe Town had all grown rapidly earlier in the nineteenth century, but by late century, they formed stable communities typical of inner-London working-class areas.

Legacies of Growth

SOMERS TOWN

The earliest phase of Somers Town's growth began in the last decade of the eighteenth century, when Lord Somers planned an affluent New Town

31

on his land north of the New Road. But the location of the land and the quality of its soil made Somers Town unappealing to its intended middle-class market. Instead, demand for labor attracted workers and tradesmen into the new development. Construction work on housing developments such as the Skinners Estate and on the Regent's Canal (begun in 1812) drew many workers to the northern reaches of London. The brickfields in and around Somers Town required a large labor force, and many of these building workers settled in the area. The already established neighborhood of Bloomsbury, south of the New Road, attracted traders and service work-ers to Somers Town. The growth of poorer neighborhoods nearby to sup-port wealthy populations was a common pattern in the metropolis.[4] Many men and women who made their living by providing goods and services to the residents of Bloomsbury settled in the cheaper neighborhood.[5]

In the two decades following the end of the French wars these trends intensified. The thriving market along the southeastern edge of the neigh-borhood attracted many people to Somers Town. In Chapel Street, Brill Row, and Skinner Street (beyond Somers Town on the Skinners Estate), shop-keepers offered their wares, street traders shouted to attract customers, and shoppers congregated. These merchants sought housing nearby, and many of them crowded into the oldest streets in the southeast portion of the neigh-borhood. Continued construction in North London sustained demand for building workers in the area. In this period, perhaps as many as half of the employed men in the neighborhood worked in trades connected to building.[6]

Beginning in the 1830s, Somers Town's population expanded dramati-cally as a result of railway construction that employed many workers and demolished housing nearby. In 1837, the London and Birmingham Railway opened its Euston terminus, just west of Somers Town. The Great Northern station at King's Cross opened in 1852, serving both the Great Northern and Midland Railways. Increased traffic soon led Midland to open a third sta-tion, adjacent to King's Cross, in 1867. These developments created a new market for labor in Somers Town. The construction of railway lines at-tracted a population of navvies, and the stations and buildings employed large numbers of building workers. Once opened, railway stations required a variety of workers, from porters to clerks, and carriage cleaners to rail-way guards. In addition, passenger and freight traffic at the stations pro-vided opportunities for porters, carmen, cabmen, etc., to handle the goods and people brought to London on the rails.[7] As will be discussed below, many of these occupations offered casual work, paying unsteady wages and requiring workers to settle near employment sites. One observer told Booth's investigators that these workers "must live near their work, partly because the work is irregular and partly because the working hours are abnormal."[8] The impact of railway construction can be seen in population figures for these decades. The area's population grew rapidly until the 1860s (table 1-1).[9] But by the end of the railway boom in the 1860s, Somers Town ceased to attract large numbers of migrants. The destruction of a significant part of the neighborhood in 1875, to make room for the Midland Railway goods depot, explains the decline in Somers Town's population in the 1870s.

LISSON GROVE

Similar factors explain the growth of Lisson Grove in the first decades of the nineteenth century. Wealthy residents settled in areas of Marylebone south of the New Road late in the eighteenth century, creating demand for goods and services nearby. With the construction of the Regent's Canal, the same demand for laborers that drew a growing population to Somers Town attracted migrants to Lisson Grove.

Also analogous to the situation in Somers Town, innovations in transportation in and around Lisson Grove exerted important influences on the area. Around 1820 transportation between the City of London and outlying residential districts expanded rapidly. Lisson Grove lay at the heart of this development; "Many more coaches ran to Paddington than to any other single destination" in 1825.[10] In 1829, a key innovation in London transportation began at the Paddington Green, just beyond Lisson Grove. George Shillibeer opened omnibus service to the Bank via the New Road, the first such service in London. By 1833, coaches and omnibuses ran every five minutes between Paddington and the City. In 1854, the Great Western Railway opened Paddington Station, less than a half-mile west of Lisson Grove. In 1863, the first major underground line, the Metropolitan Railway from Paddington to Farringdon Street, also opened in this area. The underground's Edgware Road Station lay along Chapel Street in Lisson Grove. Later, in 1894, the Great Central Railway opened Marylebone Station, just to the east of the neighborhood.[11]

The transportation industry in Lisson Grove offered growing opportunities for employment. The area was an important center of the coach building industry, linked to its position at a major intersection of the New Road and the Edgware Road.[12] The growth of coach and omnibus travel to and from Paddington created demand for coach and carmen, as well as for the keepers of the horses upon which this industry depended. The construction of railway lines and stations employed other Lisson Grove residents. Perhaps the most important impact of the transportation industry on Lisson Grove was indirect, having to do more with the development of the neighboring districts of Paddington and St. John's Wood. With the expansion of short-stage coaches, the institution of regular omnibus trips from Paddington to the City, and the later expansion of transport along this route, Paddington and Marylebone became more convenient for middle-class families whose breadwinners worked in the City.

Services for these more affluent neighbors drove growth in the Lisson Grove labor market from the 1820s on. For example, William Tayler, raised in Berkshire, worked as a footman in Marylebone beginning in 1837. His family lived in Exeter Street and Earl Street, Lisson Grove.[13] In 1830 the Portman Market opened just across Church Street from Lisson Grove. This covered market provided space for "100 loads of hay, and for carts and waggons, all sheltered from the weather, with stabling, storehouses, and separate abattoirs for slaughtering Beasts, Sheep and Pigs; and pens for the sale of livestock."[14] Demand for labor serving affluent neighboring household, staffing transport on road and rail, or hawking food and goods at the Portman Market drew many of the new residents of Lisson Grove in this period.

The growth of Marylebone in the decades from 1821 to 1861 reflects these patterns (table 1-2). Though it slowed toward the end of this period, in these forty years the population expanded by 68%. Beginning in 1841, it is possible to trace the population of a part of Marylebone that contained Lisson Grove: the Christchurch subdistrict.[15] As in Somers Town, the population in Christchurch district grew from 1841 to 1861, then declined slightly in the following decades.[16] This follows the demand for railway construction labor and for builders and service workers for the surrounding areas, which were completed and themselves stabilized by the last quarter of the century.

GLOBE TOWN

In contrast, Globe Town owed its early development to the silk industry, centered from the seventeenth century on in Spitalfields, just to the west. By the end of the eighteenth century, Spitalfields silk workers spread eastward, the poorest among them settling as far east as Globe Town. After 1800, the silk trade experienced an upswing, and the Spitalfields area concentrated on the luxury fashion market in the capital. The boom attracted new weavers to the trade, and in the 1820s, more people worked in Spitalfields silks than at any other time, operating some twenty thousand looms.[17]

In that decade, however, a shift in economic policy brought a swift end to prosperity in the Spitalfields silk industry. With the rise of liberal economic ideas, regulations protecting the English silk trade by barring imports came under attack. Beginning in 1824, French silks could be legally imported, with a 30% duty. Even with this tax, French competition severely damaged the English industry. In the downturn that followed the implementation of the new policy, up to half the looms in the Spitalfields area were idle, and earnings of silk weavers halved.[18]

Population dynamics in Bethnal Green through these decades reflect the vicissitudes of the silk industry. Each decade from 1801 to 1831 saw dramatic population growth in the parish (table 1-3). From 1801 to 1821, the population more than doubled, and over the first three decades of the century, it nearly tripled. After 1831, growth slowed somewhat as the silk boom ended. But new industries soon fueled growth in Bethnal Green.

Despite slack periods and severely reduced earnings in the silk industry beginning around 1824, many workers continued to weave silk.[19] Other industries gradually expanded in London's East End, providing needed opportunities and even attracting migrants to Globe Town. These trades, including boot and shoe, furniture, and clothing manufacture, located in the East End for two main reasons. First, the proximity of wholesalers located in the eastern parts of the City of London made the East End a logical place for consumer goods manufactures. Second, the pool of labor made available by the decline of the silk industry (and later the shipbuilding trades) offered a supply of labor, male and female, for these new East End trades.[20]

The East London furniture trade developed in the Curtain Road area of Shoreditch and gradually extended into Bethnal Green. Boot and shoe production was concentrated primarily in Shoreditch and Bethnal Green as well. The clothing trades developed around the Whitechapel district, particularly near Commercial Road. The rapid expansion of these trades around Globe Town continued through the 1860s, corresponding to the years of decline in the silk industry.[21]

Thus, despite the decline of the silk trade, Globe Town's population grew through most of the nineteenth century. Population figures for the Green subdistrict of Bethnal Green, including Globe Town, reveal rapid rates of growth from 1821, when the district was first recorded in the census, to 1871, after which the rate of growth declined (table 1-3). The district nearly doubled in population from 1821 to 1841, and again from 1841 to 1861.[22] As the century drew to a close, population growth slowed in the area, and the community of Globe Town stabilized.

This relative stability contrasts sharply with other parts of the metropolis. Overall, London continued to grow rapidly for nearly a half century after 1871. Annual growth rates for Greater London remained high through the first decade of the twentieth century. But migration to London and growth in the metropolis focused in newer, more outlying areas.[23] The "inner industrial perimeter" no longer attracted job seekers from elsewhere in England, though foreign immigrants continued to settle in certain parts of East London. Manufacturing concentrated in this inner zone, which included northern districts such as Clerkenwell, East London (including Globe Town), and much of inner South London.[24] Though Somers Town and Lisson Grove lay outside the core districts of this industrial zone, they shared many of its characteristics. In these districts, population either grew slowly or decreased in the decades around the turn of the century.

Though the areas no longer attracted numerous migrants, many of the children and even grandchildren of the migrants drawn to Somers Town and Lisson Grove by transport, service, and retail opportunities, and to Globe Town by silk and other manufacturing work, remained in the neighborhoods into the twentieth century, discouraged from leaving by a number of conditions. The casual nature of many local jobs, particularly those in road transport, building, general labor, small-scale manufacture, and domestic service, required workers to seek employment on a daily or weekly basis. By remaining in the areas, workers could cultivate relationships with foremen, subcontractors, cab proprietors, and other employers of casual labor.[25] Many also benefited from networks of kin in the area. Long-established residents could also count on their neighbors for aid and support in times of crisis.[26] Poor households could often survive only with the provision of credit by local merchants. Such credit was most likely to be offered to customers whom the merchants had known and served for long periods.[27]

Thus, even as housing conditions deteriorated and rents rose along with overcrowding, many of the descendants of those who had come to these neighborhoods in the middle years of the century stayed put. The main sources of employment continued to offer jobs. These work opportunities were overwhelmingly unsteady and poorly paid, but they offered enough of an economic base to maintain the impoverished populations. The inner-London working class settled into established, tightly knit communities in the last decades of the century.[28] This stability is reflected in the common household structure and demographic patterns in the neighborhoods, which differed from those of the metropolis as a whole, or of other dynamic urban environments in the nineteenth century.[29]

Demographic Patterns

BIRTHPLACES

Because substantial migration to the three areas ceased before 1880, the vast majority of those living in the neighborhoods were born in London.

Excluding those born in unspecified parts of Middlesex, Kent, and Surrey, 75.1% of the Somers Town, 69.1% of the Lisson Grove, and 82.9% of the Globe Town populations were London-born.[30] Throughout London, 63.0% of the population were born locally.[31] Each of the neighborhoods included a smaller percentage of migrants from every region of England, and of foreign immigrants, than did the overall London population (table 1-4). Overall, 48.6% of the Somers Town population specified that they had been born in the parish of St. Pancras, while 41.1% of those living in Lisson Grove listed Marylebone as their birthplace and another 3.5% originated in Paddington, next door. In Globe Town, 52.7% of residents gave Bethnal Green as their birthplace, and an additional 6.8% first saw the light of day in Mile End Old Town.[32] Though part of the prevalence of the London-born in Globe Town can be attributed to the large number of children in the neighborhood, even among adults 82.3% were born in London or the adjacent counties.

The regional breakdown of those born outside the metropolitan counties reveals the dynamics of migration into the areas in their decades of great growth. For instance, more than a third of migrants in Globe Town came from the eastern counties of Essex, Suffolk, and Norfolk.[33] This region appears to have been an important source for migrants into the neighborhood in the decades around 1860.[34] In Somers Town, no single non-London area contributed as significant a proportion of migrants, but 16.3% of non-London-born Somers Town residents were born in the South Midlands.[35] This region also contributed 15.0% of Lisson Grove migrants. In Lisson Grove, one out of five migrants came from Ireland, and this Irish-born population made up 4.7% of the neighborhood. These patterns offer clues about migration streams into these particular neighborhoods earlier in the century, and may reflect networks of labor recruitment and chain migration.[36]

The age distribution of these migrants reinforces this picture of formerly active migration streams that slowed to a trickle by the 1870s. Most migrants to London moved between the ages of fifteen and twenty-five.[37] But only 17.5% of migrants to these three areas were between the ages twenty and twenty-nine (the most likely ages of recent migrants) in 1881. In contrast, 22.7% were between thirty-five and forty-four years old, and 35.6% were forty-five or older. Thus, most of them probably came to the area decades before 1881. Some groups of migrants were even older. For example, among the Irish-born population of Lisson Grove only 14.2% were aged twenty to thirty-four, while over 40% were between forty and fifty-four. While in-migration had not completely ceased, and many migrants from previous years had certainly moved on, the populations of these three neighborhoods settled into a period of relative stability.[38]

Throughout England and Wales in 1881, women outnumbered men in a ratio of 95 men per 100 women. In London, this pattern was even more extreme, with only 89 men per 100 women. The metropolis acted as a magnet for young women, coming to work as domestic servants in the homes of affluent Londoners. But in poor neighborhoods, the sex ratio was far different. Across Somers Town, Lisson Grove, and Globe Town, the sex ratio was 101 men per 100 women.[39] Live-in service was not common in poor neighborhoods, and in fact the areas probably supplied some young women who served as live-in domestics in richer areas of the metropolis.[40]

Among the three poor neighborhoods, Lisson Grove had the greatest preponderance of men, with a sex ratio of 104 men per 100 women. This reflects the presence of seven significant lodging houses or dormitories that housed 235 men and only 20 women. Globe Town's ratio (102 men per 100 women), while not as high as that in Lisson Grove, was still greater than that of Somers Town (98 men per 100 women). This may reflect the younger population of Globe Town, discussed below. Mortality rates for men were generally higher than those for women, and a younger population would likely have a higher male proportion than an older population.[41]

AGE

In a population unaffected by crises of mortality, dramatically shifting birth rates, or significant migration, we can expect a distribution of ages that reflects the deaths of certain numbers of people in every age group. Thus, there should be a larger population at younger ages, and gradually decreasing population of older residents. The population of England and Wales in 1881 reveals this kind of pattern, with population gradually decreasing at succeeding age levels (fig. 1-1). But the age distribution of the London population does not fit the "natural" pattern. Instead of declining in succeeding age groups, the London population aged fifteen to nineteen is *larger* than that aged ten to fourteen; that aged twenty to twenty-four is again larger than the younger group. This shows the importance of migration. Young men and women coming to London to seek work swelled the ranks of fifteen- to twenty-four-year-olds. Stable, inner-London working-class neighborhoods were not destinations for large numbers of migrants. Instead, the age structures in Somers Town, Lisson Grove, and Globe Town resemble the "natural" pattern present in the national population, with fewer survivors at each successive age level (fig. 1-2).

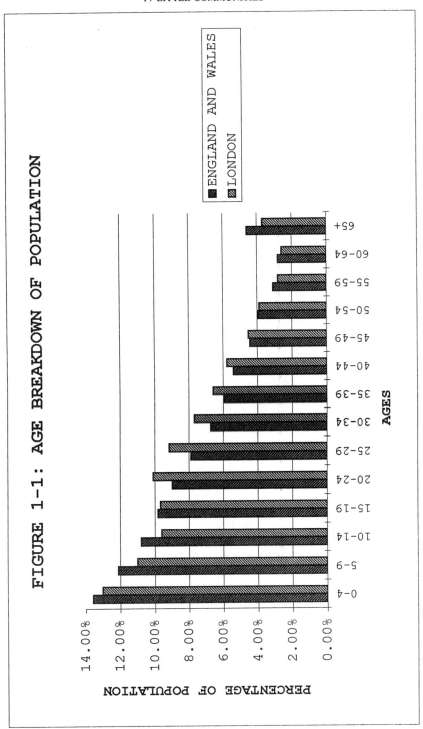

FIGURE 1-1: AGE BREAKDOWN OF POPULATION

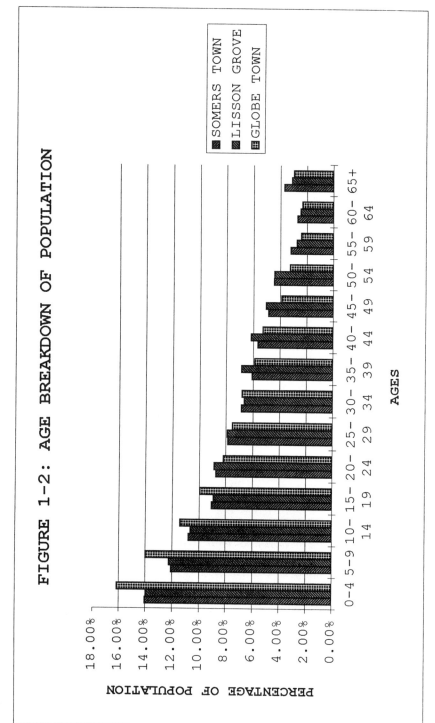

FIGURE 1-2: AGE BREAKDOWN OF POPULATION

However, age patterns in the three neighborhoods were not identical. The population of Somers Town most closely resembles the natural pattern. In Lisson Grove, there were more thirty-five- to thirty-nine-year-olds than thirty- to thirty-four-year-olds. The increase is almost entirely made up of women. This demographic anomaly may reflect women who returned to Lisson Grove after periods as live-in servants in other London neighborhoods. Also, opportunities for women's employment in and around Lisson Grove may have attracted single women or widows to the neighborhood in these age groups.[42]

The age structure of the Globe Town population, while sharing the general shape of the "natural" population curve with those of Somers Town, Lisson Grove, and the nation as a whole, is distinctive in an important sense. A higher proportion of the population of Globe Town was under ten years old (30.4%) than was the case elsewhere (26.1% in both Somers Town and Lisson Grove and 25.7% throughout England and Wales). This abundance of children is reflected also in the "fertility ratio," the number of children under five living in households with married women (table 1-5).[43] Compared with the other poor neighborhoods under study and with the nation as a whole, Globe Town was crawling with children.

The preponderance of children in Globe Town could be due to different nuptial behavior. If women married younger in the neighborhood, they would have longer periods of marital fertility, and thus more children. But marital behavior in Somers Town and Lisson Grove was remarkably similar to that in Globe Town. The mean age at marriage for women in Globe Town was 23.2, while in both Lisson Grove and Somers Town the age was 23.1.[44] Percentages of adults ever married in the three areas are also quite similar (table 1-6). Thus, the abundance of children in Globe Town does not appear attributable to lower marriage age or higher marriage rates.[45]

A more intriguing possibility is that women in Lisson Grove and Somers Town controlled their fertility more actively than did Globe Town residents. By the end of the nineteenth century, English working-class women did seek to restrict their fertility, despite lacking safe or reliable birth-control technology.[46] The evidence suggests that women in Somers Town and Lisson Grove more frequently resorted to the often dangerous techniques used by poor women to limit childbirths. Rents were higher and crowded conditions appear to have been more serious in these two neighborhoods than in Globe Town; families may have limited their fertility in response to the more cramped circumstances. Conversely, the types of occupations common in Globe Town, many involving the participation of children in home production, may have encouraged residents of this neighborhood to have larger families. These are mere guesses, however, as detailed information on the number of annual births in these districts is not available.[47]

Infant mortality rates may have been higher in Lisson Grove and Somers Town than in Globe Town. In this case, even if the same number of children were born to women in the three neighborhoods, more would survive in Globe Town. The overall mortality rate appears somewhat higher in Globe Town than in the other areas, which makes sense, given its younger population.[48] Unfortunately, available statistics on age-specific mortality rates are neither comprehensive nor broken down for each of the three neighborhoods, making it impossible to compare infant death rates. Thus, less active birth-control practices and possibly a lower infant mortality rate may explain the higher number of children in Globe Town.

Household Structure

Household formation reflects decisions of individuals influenced by the legacies of prior conditions and contemporary pressures. Decades of development and migration into these areas shaped the population and the physical environment, including housing stock. Opportunities for work and the structure of housing markets created key contexts for individual choices that determined household formation. Cultural forces also influenced these decisions. For example, expectations of proper behavior might encourage an eldest daughter to remain single and live with her father if her mother died. Household structures also reflect particular circumstances, the place of individuals and family members in their own life courses, and their personal histories of marriage, reproduction, illness, and death.

To illustrate common household structures in poor London areas, it is useful to focus on a single ordinary street. Bridgewater Street, in the northern part of Somers Town, housed 464 people in 111 households. Booth's descriptive map classes Bridgewater as a "poor" street (colored light blue on the map). It was built in the 1820s and probably attracted a typical Somers Town population: building workers in its early years, and increasing numbers of railway workers and those in related trades as the decades passed.

A large majority of the households in the three areas included only family members; relatively few people lived with nonrelatives. Across the three neighborhoods, 87.6% of households included only relatives of the household head.[49] The vast majority of the nonrelatives were either lodgers or servants.[50] But compared to other nineteenth-century urban environments, these neighborhoods housed few lodgers and few servants.

In Bridgewater Street, only eleven people were not related to the heads of their households. Typical of this small group was William Stretton, who described himself to the census enumerator as a "sanitation engineer." A twenty-three-year-old single man, Stretton had been born in Poplar and lived as a lodger with James and Rachel Francis at no. 25. But the Francis household was atypical in including a man like Stretton, as only seven other households included people who were not related to all of the others.

In many working-class areas, lodgers provided common sources of household income, and living with established families offered a useful housing alternative, particularly for young migrants.[51] However, fewer than one-twelfth of Somers Town, Lisson Grove, and Globe Town households included lodgers or boarders. In contrast, better than one in five York and Preston households in 1851 included them. In Bradford, 17.4% of households had such residents in 1881.[52]

The vast majority of Somers Town, Lisson Grove, and Globe Town households with these residents included only a single lodger.[53] Many lodgers were young adults; half were between the ages fifteen and twenty-nine. They were mostly men (71.9%), and were more likely to be migrants into London than others living in the areas.[54] These figures fit with the notion that lodging was typically a strategy of young male migrants to cities. Yet even among those lodgers between the ages fifteen and twenty-nine, 72.7% were born in the London area. Out of the almost forty-seven thousand residents of the three areas, fewer than two hundred were young migrants living as lodgers. This reinforces the general picture of these stable neighborhoods without many migrants. Most lodgers in these areas left their parental households in London to live as lodgers for reasons that are not clear. Perhaps their original households were broken apart by the death of the mother, or personal tensions drove the young men out. But lodging was exceptional in these areas.

In Bridgewater Street, only a handful of households took in lodgers. James and Rachel Francis, discussed above, housed William Stretton; Henry and Eliza Attwood at no. 21 also housed a single lodger. At no. 8, a forty-six-year-old widow, Annie Atwood (perhaps Henry's sister or sister-in-law despite the slightly different spelling), had two single men as lodgers. Only one other Bridgewater Street household included lodgers or boarders: the unusually large household of James and Sarah Posford, which included nine children, aged one to twenty-two, and three boarders.

Taking in a lodger could offer a viable strategy for bringing resources into the household economy. This was particularly true for households headed by women, usually widows. While 19.3% of households in the three areas had female heads, women were in charge of 26.6% of households that included lodgers.[55] Nonetheless, nearly 90% of female-headed households did not include lodgers, probably because these areas were simply not the right environments for widespread lodging.

It is less surprising that few households in the three neighborhoods included servants.[56] In Somers Town and Globe Town, these servant-holding households were concentrated in a few streets that were more affluent than the rest of the neighborhoods (table 1-7). In Somers Town, five streets that accounted for 29.5% of the total households included 60.5% of those with servants.[57] Three Globe Town streets accounted for better than 70% of those including servants in the neighborhood.[58] Servants were even rarer in Lisson Grove and servant-holding households were concentrated as they were in the other areas. While three of the four Lisson Grove streets that accounted for half of servant-holding households had mixed poor and comfortable populations, only 2.8% of households in these streets held servants.[59]

The patterns of servant holding in Globe Town and Somers Town, and to a lesser extent Lisson Grove, reflect the existence of more comfortable populations in the areas. Clustered along commercial streets with many shops and pubs, and surrounded by severe poverty, it is likely that these were not hawkers and street sellers, but the proprietors of more established businesses. In poor neighborhoods, businesses and shops were concentrated along large through streets. These commercial streets were the sites of the small-scale shopping that formed such a central part of poor women's attempts to make the most of their domestic budgets. The street sellers and hawkers who congregated in the commercial streets during the day lived in homes in the smaller and poorer surrounding streets, but the owners of established shops often resided above the shops, forming a resident lower-middle class. In Globe Town, Globe Road and Green Street typify this pattern. It was this retailing class that accounted for most servant holding in these areas.

Many of those listed as live-in servants in their households were not domestics.[60] The more comfortable residents whose households included servants carried on businesses such as pubs, bakeries, or butcher shops.[61] These retail food trades appear to have been organized along traditional craft lines, at least as far as the employment of assistants who lived with their employers is concerned. These trades account for a large portion of the more comfortable populations that lived among their customers in these poor neighborhoods (table 1-8), and many of the servant-holding households.

At the other end of the household-formation spectrum from these households that took in nonrelatives were individuals who lived by themselves. In Somers Town and Lisson Grove, about 12% of households were comprised of an individual living alone, which resembles the overall London figure of 11% of households in 1851.[62] But in Globe Town, individuals living alone accounted for only 7% of households.[63] One explanation for this difference lies in the age structures in the areas. In all three neighbor-hoods, older people, particularly older women, were most likely to live alone.[64] Higher proportions of the populations of Somers Town and Lisson Grove were aged fifty or over than was the case in Globe Town (14.1% in Somers Town, 12.7% in Lisson Grove, and 11.0% in Globe Town). This reflects the earlier decline of migration and growth in the two North Lon-don neighborhoods and the higher fertility in Globe Town.

In Bridgewater Street, twelve people lived on their own, accounting for just over a tenth of households on the street. Most of those who lived alone on this street were women aged fifty or over who were either wid-owed or had never married. Typical of these was Carry Angell, a widow who lived at no. 23 Bridgewater Street. She lived alone, and worked as a washerwoman. Angell had been born sixty-two years before in St. Pancras, probably in Somers Town itself.

But neither individuals living alone nor households swelled by the tak-ing in of lodgers, servants, or other nonrelatives typified households in poor neighborhoods. The vast majority of poor Londoners lived with their families. More than three-quarters of households in the three neighbor-hoods included only related people.[65] Four out of five people in the areas lived in these family-based households (79.0% in Somers Town, 80.6% in Lisson Grove, and 82.0% in Globe Town).

About one out of ten households included kin beyond the nuclear fam-ily of parent(s) and children. In Somers Town, 10.9% of families included such kin, compared with 8.7% in Lisson Grove and 10.9% in Globe Town, and about three-quarters of these families included only one extended rela-tive.[66] This contrasts sharply with figures from Preston and York in 1851 and Bradford in 1881, which show that more than 20% of all households included kin.[67] The most common pattern of extended households involved the inclusion of grandchildren, who accounted for over a quarter of kin in the neighborhoods. Siblings of household heads were the next most com-mon kin relation (table 1-9). Many of these kin were young adults, in age groups most likely to boost the viability of the household economy. Slightly over a quarter were between the ages fifteen and twenty-four. Also some-what common were older kin; around a tenth of the kin were sixty-five or over, and nearly 80% of these were women. These women likely contrib-uted to their households by performing domestic work.[68] But most families in these neighborhoods were nuclear families, consisting either of child-less couples or a parent or parents and children (table 1-10).[69]

Bridgewater Street households followed these patterns as well. The vast majority included only people related to one another, and most of these were nuclear families. Among the unusual families that included kin was that of Charles Hales and his wife Eliza, who lived at no. 7. Charles, aged sixty-seven, worked as a shoemaker, and Eliza, who was sixty-four, was not employed. They shared their home with their nineteen-year-old grandson, also named Charles Hales and also a shoemaker. The younger Charles was born in St. Pancras, as was his grandmother, and the elder Charles came to Somers Town from nearby Holborn.

As mentioned above, marital patterns in the three areas were remarkably similar. The average female resident of these neighborhoods was married around age twenty-three. The mean age at marriage for men was higher, around twenty-five.[70] Before marrying, the majority of young single adults remained in their parental families. Among single men between the ages of fifteen and twenty-nine born in the London region, 75.7% in Somers Town, 68.1% in Lisson Grove, and 77.9% in Globe Town lived with their parents.[71] The figures for young women are even higher: 80.3% in Somers Town, 82.1% in Lisson Grove, and 80.8% in Globe Town.

As sons and daughters, these young people were in a position to contribute to the stability of their household economies and ease the burden on their mothers. Many young people were proud to be able to help their mothers in this way, and they turned over their wages to her. Mothers allowed their employed children pocket money, and devoted the rest to the household budget.[72] Grace Foakes exemplifies this attitude. Rather than leave home for a job in service upon reaching school-leaving age, Foakes remained at home to help her mother.[73] Parents expected their sons and especially their daughters to remain at home during this period when they could significantly ease the economic burden. George Acorn, who grew up on Bethnal Green, near Globe Town, defied convention and moved out of his parents' home as a young man. This angered his parents, even though he still ate his meals with them and paid for this (thus contributing to their household economy).[74]

At no. 10 Bridgewater Street, Henry and Margaret Boult's family shows the advantages of the normal pattern. Henry and Margaret were fifty and forty-seven years old, respectively, and they appear to have moved to the Somers Town area in the late 1850s. In 1881, Henry worked as a cabman, and Margaret and the oldest daughter (also named Margaret) worked as machinists, probably in the clothing industry. Five other children lived at home, including three sons between the ages of seventeen and twenty-three, another daughter, aged fifteen, and the baby of the family, thirteen-year-old Herbert, who was still in school. The five older children were all single, all employed, and all lived at home. The Boults must have had one of the most stable family economies in the area, as seven of the eight family members were employed.

But once they married, few young adults remained in their parental households. Though the young couple, particularly if both were employed, would likely be in a position to benefit their parental domestic economies, it appears their marriages effectively ended the expectation that children would remain in their parents' household and help support their parents and siblings. Across the three neighborhoods, only 2.0% of married women and 1.8% of married men under age forty-five lived with their parents or those of their spouse.[75] The childless young couples would likely find themselves in relatively stable economic straits, commonly enjoying two incomes (irregular though they likely were), without the economic pressures of supporting nonearning children.

Philip and Bridget Holland lived at no. 20 Bridgewater Street. Both had been born in the parish, and they had probably married recently. He was twenty-six, and worked as a "brewer's man." She was twenty-five and worked in day domestic service. Rather than remain in one of their parents' households, this young couple struck out on their own. With their two incomes and no children, the Hollands probably could maintain a degree of economic stability.

The relative stability of the household economy in this stage would be disrupted with the arrival of young children. The family with young nonearning children faced a difficult challenge. As will be seen below, mothers of young children generally withdrew from employment, just as the financial burdens on the family increased.

As the oldest children grew up, they became more capable of earning a few shillings to add to the family income, and, especially in the case of girls, of helping with the housework and allowing their mothers to earn money.[76] Households with a number of employed children could even partially neutralize the irregularity of jobs in the areas by "diversifying" in a number of trades. While the father might be out of work, the family could support itself if other household members were earning something.

Once the children grew up and left the parental household, the couple would enter a stage that mirrored their first years together. Both husband and wife were often employed, and, as long as their health held out, they remained in a relatively solid economic position.

Of course, this schematic outline of a family cycle does not take into account those families ruptured by separation and death. Nearly a quarter of the households in these neighborhoods were headed by men and women whose spouses were not present. Even when individuals living alone are excluded, 19.1% of households of more than one person were headed by an incomplete couple. While most of these household heads were widowed, about a fifth of them were married, but their spouses were not present.

Thus, the outline of a family cycle needs to be revised, as many families did not include a married couple at their head.

The number of household heads who were married but whose spouses did not live in their households reflects the fluidity of domestic relations in poor neighborhoods. Though unable to obtain legally sanctioned divorces because of the expense, men and women in poor neighborhoods did separate from one another. Within the neighborhoods, these separated individuals were free to form new relationships and even have children with new partners. These unofficial second marriages were accepted, and appear to have been common. John William Page, a bricklayer living in Highworth Street, Lisson Grove, claimed that his wife Catherine had deserted him, taking along their young son. He remained in the neighborhood and soon began living with another woman.[77] In Charles Street, Lisson Grove, Dennis Sullivan lived for twelve years with a woman named Barron. She already had four children by her husband, and then two more with Sullivan. The couple was described as living "as husband and wife."[78] In Globe Town, Eliza Harriet Baker married James Baker in 1876. After her husband was convicted of burglary and sentenced to five years of penal servitude, she took up with another man, John Swinton. She claimed, "There was nothing before me but starvation or the streets," noting that Baker had told her that he did not intend to work when he got out of prison.[79] Yet the number of widows without domestic partners and separated married men and women heading households indicates that it was not always easy to find a new partner upon death or separation.

These patterns of household formation combined to create a relatively small average household size, particularly in Somers Town and Lisson Grove. Somers Town residents lived in households that averaged 3.95 members, and households in Lisson Grove averaged 3.86, but those in Globe Town averaged 4.60 (table 1-11). Around two-thirds of the households in the two North London neighborhoods included one to four members. Somers Town and Lisson Grove households were smaller than those of England and Wales as a whole, estimated by Peter Laslett to average 4.54 in 1881.[80] Anderson's data on Preston and Armstrong's for York also show larger mean household size (5.4 and 4.7) in 1851.[81] Lees found that Irish migrant families in London in 1851 lived in households that averaged 3.7 members, a number similar to that of Somers Town and Lisson Grove.[82] The relatively small size of these households reflects the rarity of extended kin, lodgers, boarders, or live-in servants. The larger Globe Town households show the higher fertility in that neighborhood and the generally younger population.

Conclusion

These patterns of household structure reflect a particular demographic and familial regime in these areas that responded to economic and cultural pressures and reflected the legacy of previous decades. The areas had ceased their dynamic growth and no longer attracted large numbers of migrants. By the late nineteenth century, they had settled into a relatively stable, family-based pattern. The prevalence of small nuclear families reflects the pressures of high rents and crowded conditions, especially in Somers Town and Lisson Grove. These patterns emerged as individuals and households made choices and developed strategies within the economic, cultural, and physical constraints of their environments.

Though it is impossible to know for certain, it appears that many of the children born in the areas in the 1870s and 1880s stayed there, pulled by the economic advantages of established relationships with employers, merchants, neighbors, and relatives, and by cultural expectations that enforced their ties to their parents. As single young people, they usually stayed in their parental households. Many young married couples, though they moved out of their parents' houses, probably remained in the neighborhood due to the advantages of living in these communities. Despite the poverty that confronted residents of these areas, the strong ties between neighbors and relatives and the real economic advantages these links afforded kept many of their children in the vicinity, leading to the persistence of what became "traditional" London working-class ways of life.[83]

2

"I Often Want Bread":
The Causes of Poverty

Looking back on the findings of the first phases of his monumental social survey, Charles Booth reiterated the inescapable conclusion of his work: "[T]he actual poverty disclosed was so great, both in mass and in degree, and so absolutely certain, that I have gradually become equally anxious not to overstate."[1] Overall, he found nearly a third of London residents in poverty and most of the rest just beyond it.[2] Booth and others suspected that poverty in London was far worse than that in other cities.[3] Similarly, within the metropolis poverty was concentrated in certain areas. London's poor neighborhoods could be found in two kinds of locations, the broad stretches of proletarian areas in eastern and southern districts, and pockets of poverty surrounded by more affluent areas.[4] In both types of poor neighborhood, though, two fundamental determinants shaped poverty: the local labor market and household composition.

Booth's sensitivity to the localized nature of poverty drove an attempt to calculate poverty rates in particular neighborhoods through a classification of residents in school-board blocks and divisions (table 2-1). These figures show that 53.2% of those in part of Somers Town lived under conditions of poverty, and 43.6% in an area including Lisson Grove were poor. In Globe Town, 55.0% were classified as poor or very poor. Many of the other residents were classified in category "E," living on "ordinary standard earnings." People in group "E" were just above Booth's poverty line at the time of his survey, and many of them fell into poverty at other points in their lives.

The Booth notebooks provide results of an additional survey of the conditions under which children ages three to thirteen lived in parts of Somers Town and Lisson Grove. Though the study covered only about half of Lisson Grove, 68% of those surveyed lived in poverty, including 52% in the "very poor" category. Another 24% fell into class "E."[5] A similar study included nearly the whole of Somers Town. Of 3,192 children ages three to thirteen, 63% lived under conditions of poverty. Another 30% fell into category "E," just above poverty, requiring only an illness or loss of work to become poor.[6] In Bridgewater Street, described in the previous chapter, Booth found 147 children, 47 of whom were in category "B," among the very poor, and 30 more were classified in group "C," among the poor. The remaining 70 children lived just above the poverty line, in category "E."[7]

Economic conditions, particularly the kinds of employment available in local labor markets, caused much of this poverty. Among households with an employed male head, low wages and casual or seasonal underemployment left many in poverty.[8] Opportunities for regular employment uninterrupted by seasonal fluctuations or casual employment practices were rare in or near the three areas. But even for the few with steady employment, wages were often less than £1 per week.[9] In a survey of four thousand poor families from various London districts, Booth found that 20% of those in categories "C" and "D" ("poor," but not "very poor"), had regular earnings but made too little to escape poverty.[10]

But opportunities in local labor markets only partially explain why families suffered poverty. Household structure played an equally central role in determining whether residents suffered from want or could satisfy their basic needs. Ruptured families, missing an adult male earner or a woman who could manage the domestic budget, would likely fall into poverty. But even among families with an adult man and woman present, poverty was far more likely when families included only young children than when children could earn and contribute.

Local Labor Markets

Recent studies of industrialization have called into question the predominance of large-scale, steam- and coal-powered factory production in the British economy.[11] Small-scale, fragmented patterns of production characterized British capitalism well into what has traditionally been considered the era of monopoly capitalism.[12] While historians have recently discovered the persistence of hand technology in many industrial districts in the nineteenth century, in London decentralized production dominated manufacture. As the century wore on, competition from the provinces and the unforeseen consequences of government regulation drove production into smaller workshops and workers' homes.[13] As David R. Green notes, the "fragmentation of work and the development of small-scale manufacturing reached its utmost limits in nineteenth-century London."[14] Gareth Stedman Jones concurs: "The effect of the Industrial Revolution upon London was to accentuate its 'pre-industrial' characteristics."[15] The London economy was driven by the production of consumer goods, construction of homes and buildings, transportation, storage and sale of goods, provision of services, and management of finance and business. All but the last of these industries were dominated by the working class and poor. In addition, many London general laborers worked at whatever unskilled tasks they could find.

Employment figures for the metropolis reflect these patterns. The largest industry in London in 1881 was the building trade, employing 10.4% of adult men, followed by general unskilled work, accounting for 8.3% of men fifteen and over. Other common occupational categories for men included business and finance, which also occupied 8.3% of adult men, few of them working-class or poor; food processing and selling (6.6%); and road transport (5.5%).[16] Among women, domestic service employed 22.5% of adults in the metropolis. Clothing manufacture ranked a distant second among women's jobs (8.8%). Education, textiles, and institutional service round out the top five occupations in London, but each of these categories accounted for less than 2% of adult women.

The instability of work opportunities inherent in London trades, along with low wages when work was available, left in poverty a large proportion of the workforce upon which the metropolis' prosperity depended. In a detailed inquiry into the causes of this poverty in four thousand London families, Booth found nearly two-thirds suffered poverty due to "questions of employment," including irregular work and low pay.[17] The Royal Commission on the Poor Laws concluded, "[O]f all the causes or conditions predisposing to pauperism the most potent, the most certain and the most extensive in its operation was this method of employment in odd jobs."[18] But the London labor market did not operate as a single, unified entity. Rather, labor markets developed around distinct centers of industrial or service work opportunities. London workers, particularly those lacking highly desired skills, found work in their neighborhoods or in those immediately surrounding them. As Eric Hobsbawm notes, "[A]ll that lay beyond a tiny circle of personal acquaintance or walking distance was darkness."[19] P. L. Garside concurs that job seekers "depended largely on hearsay and personal tips, so that from the individual worker's point of view the metropolitan ideal faded before the reality of a much more localized pattern of employment."[20] Thus, residents of Somers Town, Lisson Grove, and Globe Town sought work in the narrowly defined labor markets of these areas.

MEN'S OCCUPATIONS

Employment opportunities in the three neighborhoods shared some common characteristics of the London economy, but each local labor market also reflected distinctive conditions. A large proportion of men in all three neighborhoods were general laborers. They performed a variety of unskilled manual jobs in whatever industry offered work. The building trades also formed an important sector of the labor market in all three neighborhoods. Other leading male occupations in the three areas included food processing and selling and road transport, also common London occupations.[21]

Even in these common trades, however, a number of differences distinguish the three neighborhoods. For example, general labor and the building trades played a much larger role in the employment structure of Lisson Grove than of the other areas (table 2-2). Nearly one in three employed men in that neighborhood worked in either building or general labor, compared with just under one in five in Globe Town.

Each poor neighborhood in the metropolis grew in response to localized demand for labor, shaped by the wider London economy and its geographic and topographical position within it. Thus in Somers Town, the men's occupations common in London were supplemented by trades far more important in the local labor market than elsewhere (table 2-3). The demand for labor in road transport and on the railways can be traced to the railway stations around Somers Town. Passengers and freight on the rails required service and handling, and the trains needed drivers, brakemen, signalmen, and maintenance workers. Once arrived in St. Pancras, King's Cross, or Euston Station, passengers sought transport to other parts of London, while freight required unloading and carting to markets, workshops, or warehouses. This accounts for many of the cabmen, porters, and carmen who lived in Somers Town.

Two other related groups of occupations—furniture and musical instrument manufacture—were far more common in Somers Town than throughout London. The Tottenham Court Road area just south of Somers Town formed an important center for manufacturing ready-made furniture.[22] Furniture making began in southern St. Pancras around 1800, and by the 1880s was organized under a subcontracting system for large furniture stores, such as that run by John Maple. Maple's employed some two thousand people on its premises in Tottenham Court Road and gave work out to many small firms in the area.[23] This system demanded that the workers live near the large stores, and "a tightly-knit industrial quarter developed."[24]

Pianoforte making was the dominant form of musical instrument making in Somers Town. Proximity to railway transport may have played an important role in encouraging the first pianoforte factories to locate in Camden Town, just north of Somers Town, in 1851. Another attraction may have been the presence of experienced furniture makers, able to transfer their woodworking skills to the making of cabinets for the musical instruments. Small workshops made parts for the instruments, which were then assembled in a few large factories.[25] Kelly's Directory for 1881 lists fourteen musical instrument makers in Somers Town and its border streets (Euston Road and Seymour Street).[26]

In Lisson Grove, too, common London trades coexisted with jobs particular to the local economy (table 2-4). Occupations connected to transportation on roads, including road transport, carriage and coach building, and servicing and caring for animals, were more than twice as common in Lisson Grove than in the metropolis as a whole.[27] The area around the intersection of the Edgware and New Roads (later Marylebone Road) was the single most important site for omnibus, cab, and coach transportation in London.[28] Though one might expect the construction of railway lines to and under the metropolis to cause a decline in horse-pulled transport, the opposite was the case. Increased rail traffic spurred growth in road transport, which in turn required large numbers of horses. This boom provided jobs for Lisson Grove residents as horse keepers, farriers (to shoe or treat horses), coach and carriage builders, cabmen, carmen, and porters.[29]

Globe Town had an occupational structure different from those of Lisson Grove and Somers Town. Here, the boot and shoe, furniture, and silk industries employed many men (table 2-5). The sweated system of production, in which manufacture was often carried out in small workshops or in workers' homes, was typical in Globe Town. Middlemen or wholesalers located in the City and the East End controlled these industries and subcontracted work to small producers. Sweated production paid low wages and demanded long hours on the part of its workers. Employment was often irregular, so subcontracting provided wholesalers and middlemen with a flexible workforce that was employed only when needed.[30]

Boot and shoemaking was concentrated in the East End, around Shoreditch and Bethnal Green, including Globe Town. The East End also formed the most important London center of cheap, ready-made furniture manufacture, chiefly organized in a system of subcontracting. Though the hub of this trade lay in the Curtain Road area of Shoreditch, as the century progressed furniture making expanded eastward through Globe Town to the Regents Canal. Workers toiled in their own homes or in workshops employing only a handful of workers. The raw materials for furniture production were provided by sawmills, in which sawyers and turners rented space as independent "tenants." The sawyers cut wood into the shapes needed by individual furniture makers and geared their trade to the small-scale customer.[31]

Despite its long decline following the change in trade policy in 1824, the silk industry still employed many Globe Town residents in 1881.[32] As the trade suffered during the middle decades of the century, and particularly following the establishment of free trade with France in 1860, the better-off weavers of Spitalfields left the trade and the area, and the remaining silk production was concentrated in the poorer sections of Globe Town. It is estimated that the number of looms declined from a peak of twenty thousand in 1824 to around nine hundred by the 1880s. The organization of production in the silk industry evolved during this period to resemble that of the sweated trades. Middlemen or "factors" controlled production in the trade, giving out work to impoverished weavers in the cottages of Globe Town.[33]

Another common London occupation, retail, particularly street marketing and the hawking of food and other items, played an important role in the neighborhoods. In Somers Town, retail activity concentrated in the commercial area in the southern part of the neighborhood; in Lisson Grove, in the nearby Portman Market, along the Edgware Road, and in Bell/Great James Street; and in Globe Town, along Green Street, Globe Road, and Old Ford Road.[34]

WOMEN'S OCCUPATIONS

In all three neighborhoods, as well as throughout London, the most common women's occupations were in domestic service. In Lisson Grove and throughout London, domestic work accounted for more than half of all employed women. In Somers Town, the portion so employed was 38.0%; and in Globe Town, 20.5%. However, domestic service was organized in different ways in various parts of the metropolis. In poor neighborhoods, few of the women doing domestic work lived with their employers. Large numbers of women in Lisson Grove and Somers Town worked as laundresses and charwomen, both forms of day work. But in London as a whole, the largest group of domestics were general servants (table 2-6, figs. 2-1, 2-2, 2-3, 2-4). In many neighborhoods, the general servant was most often a young woman who lived and worked in a middle-class or wealthy home. In Lisson Grove and Somers Town, however, the majority lived with their

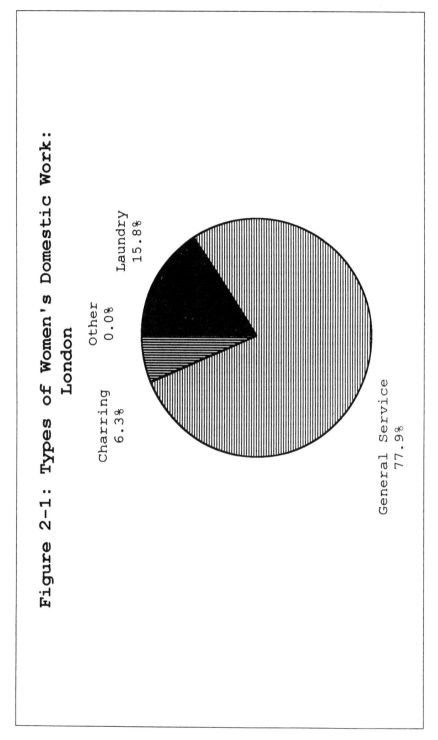

Figure 2-1: Types of Women's Domestic Work: London

Charring 6.3%

Other 0.0%

Laundry 15.8%

General Service 77.9%

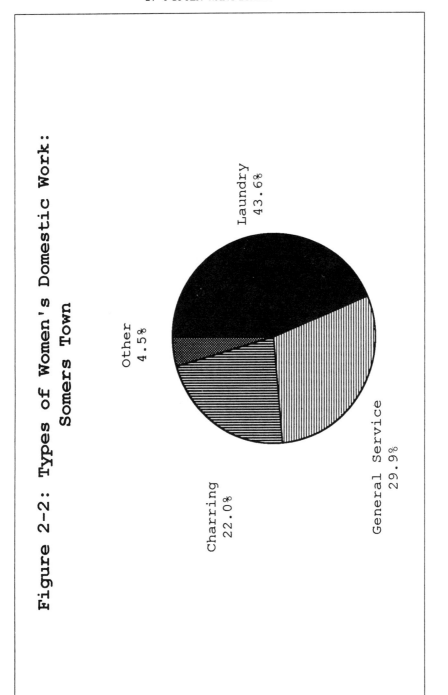

Figure 2-2: Types of Women's Domestic Work: Somers Town

Other
4.5%

Laundry
43.6%

Charring
22.0%

General Service
29.9%

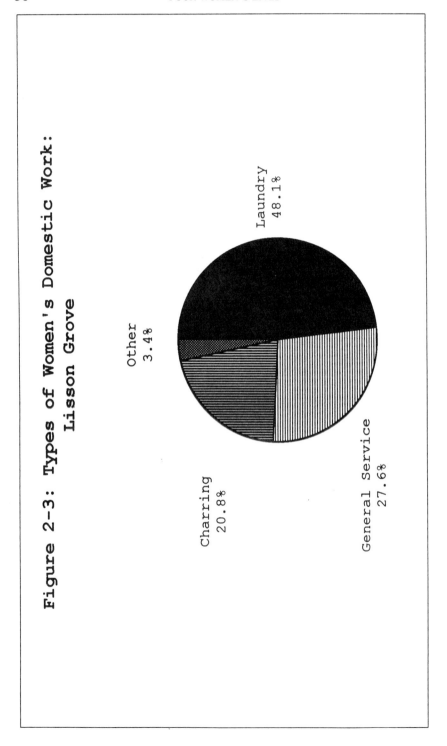

Figure 2-3: Types of Women's Domestic Work:
Lisson Grove

Laundry
48.1%

Other
3.4%

General Service
27.6%

Charring
20.8%

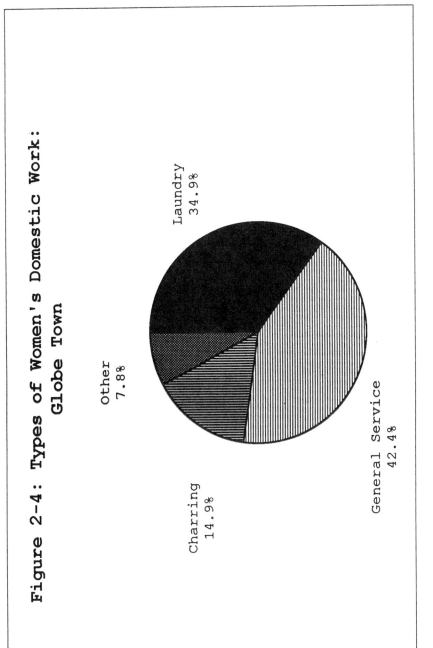

Figure 2-4: Types of Women's Domestic Work: Globe Town

Other 7.8%

Laundry 34.9%

Charring 14.9%

General Service 42.4%

own families and did day work in the wealthier areas nearby.[35] Many Lisson Grove women cleaned and washed for households in affluent parts of Marylebone and Paddington, while those living in Somers Town served their neighbors in Bloomsbury and other proximate middle-class areas.

In Globe Town, domestic work accounted for a far smaller proportion of female employment than in the other two poor neighborhoods. Because surrounding areas housed working-class populations, Globe Town women's opportunities to work as day servants, charwomen, and laundresses were far more limited. This geographic distinction exerted a significant impact on the female labor market in poor neighborhoods in the East End, and in expanses of working-class South London. Instead of performing day domestic work for more affluent neighbors, these women were likely to find employment in manufacturing.

Outside domestic service, the female labor markets of Lisson Grove and Somers Town also resembled one another (tables 2-7, 2-8). In both areas, sweated industries—particularly clothing manufacture, but also other sewing and artificial-flower making—employed significant numbers of women (table 2-9).[36] Other jobs serving affluent neighbors or institutions were common in the two North London neighborhoods. There were many nurses (categorized as "other professions") in the areas, but it is impossible to distinguish how many worked in neighbors' homes and how many in local medical institutions.[37] Hospitals and other institutions in the area also employed many Lisson Grove women as servants.[38] Women retailers proliferated in the marketing districts of both areas, as did sellers of food products.[39]

In Globe Town, sweated industry commanded the female labor market. Though domestic service was the most common single female occupation in Globe Town, the next six highest ranking occupations, including 61% of employed women, were in manufacturing (table 2-10). Many Globe Town women worked as clothing workers and machinists, silk workers, boot makers, shoemakers, paper box makers, and bag makers. Of these, clothing manufacture was significant in the two other neighborhoods and London as a whole; the concentration of other types of small-scale manufacture distinguished Globe Town.

Thus, from information in the census schedules, we can glean a detailed picture of the local labor markets (fig. 2-5).[40] Male employment in the three areas, as in London, featured large numbers of general laborers, building workers, and retail tradesmen. But each of these areas included particular trades that were unusually concentrated, reflecting the fragmented nature of London labor markets. Somers Town formed an important center of the furniture- and pianoforte-making industries, and the three nearby rail stations exerted a strong influence on its labor market. In Lisson Grove,

Fig. 2-5: Leading Occupations in the Three Neighborhoods
Over-Represented Trades in Boldface

SOMERS TOWN	LISSON GROVE	GLOBE TOWN
MEN:	MEN:	MEN:
Building	General Wkrs.	**Boot & Shoe**
Road Trans.	Building	General Wkrs.
General Wkrs.	**Road Trans.**	**Textiles**
Food Proc.	Food Proc.	Building
Furniture	**Animal Care**	Food Proc.
Iron, etc.	**Communicat.**	**Furniture**
Railroads	Boot & Shoe	Road Trans.
Printing	General	**Wood**
Musical Inst.	Dealers	Communicat.
	Iron, etc.	Printing
WOMEN:	WOMEN:	WOMEN:
Domestic Work	Domestic Work	Domestic Work
Clothing	Clothing	Clothing
General Wkrs.	**Food Proc.**	**Textiles**
Other Profs.	Other Profs.	**Boot & Shoe**
Paper	**General Wkrs.**	**Paper**
Textiles	**Home Fittings**	**General Wkrs.**
Home Fittings		**Hair Products**

road transport accounted for the peculiarities of the labor market. The area formed a center for building, operating, and caring for the coaches, carriages, omnibuses, and horses that packed the London streets and carried middle-class Londoners to and fro. The role of these districts as transportation hubs provided similar opportunities for men's labor in the two North London neighborhoods. Globe Town's male labor market reflects typical conditions in East End industrial quarters, which were dominated by sweated production in the furniture, boot and shoe, and silk industries.

Domestic service was the most important area of female employment in all three areas and across London. But service was more important in the two North London neighborhoods that bordered on more affluent areas, and day service was far more common than live-in service in all three neighborhoods. Clothing manufacture was a key occupation of women in these areas and in London. In Somers Town, women also commonly worked as street sellers, upholstery workers, box and bag makers, and artificial-flower makers. In Lisson Grove, the two leading female occupations, domestic service and clothing manufacture, dominated the female labor market to a greater extent than in Somers Town; and retailing, other service and sewing occupations, and artificial-flower making employed significant numbers of women. In Globe Town, sweated industries offered the most widespread opportunities for women's work, whether in clothing manufacture, silk weaving, footwear manufacture, or other trades.

The above description of occupation patterns in Somers Town, Lisson Grove, and Globe Town reflects localized labor market conditions, as most people in the areas worked near their homes. Mentions of individuals' residence and place of work in newspapers and other sources show that nearly everyone worked either within the neighborhoods or in the immediate surroundings.[41] A survey of residents in Devonshire Street in Lisson Grove cited the importance of the Edgware Road (food processing and selling, for example) and the "better class neighborhood round here" as the major workplaces for Devonshire Street residents.[42] In Globe Town, many workers in the sweated trades produced goods in their own homes.[43] Others worked in trades concentrated in the East End, particularly in Bethnal Green, Shoreditch, and Stepney.[44] Small workshop or home production in these trades was closely linked to middlemen and wholesalers or factories in the East End or in the eastern districts of the City.[45]

In 1913, a London County Council (LCC) study evaluated the relationship of home and work in poor London neighborhoods. It concluded that many working-class Londoners, particularly those with casual or irregular hours, had no choice but to live close to their places of employment. The trades requiring residence near the workplace included porters, carmen, cabmen, charwomen, daily servants, costermongers, and hawkers, all common occupations in these neighborhoods. The LCC study included a survey of residents of Bethnal Green, finding that 90% of those with a fixed place of employment worked either in the City of London or in the East End.[46] Because of the nature of local employment opportunities, residents of these three neighborhoods tended to work near their homes.

The common occupations in all three local labor markets provided only irregular employment, paying uncertain and intermittent wages.[47] Residents of the neighborhoods formed part of the "reserve army of labor," employed in casual work by the day or week.[48] Among the leading jobs of men in these areas, general labor, transport on roads, and some of the building, clothing, and food-processing trades employed casual labor. Unsteady work was the rule in the leading female occupations, including day domestic work and manufacturing.

The majority of sweated manufacturing trades, employing many men and women in Globe Town, offered similarly unreliable employment. Small manufacturers were dependent on orders from wholesalers, which were unpredictable. George Acorn's brief experience making furniture in his own workshop illustrates this phenomenon. Both Acorn and a friend with whom he shared space and rent worked in spurts when they could obtain orders. Eventually, the orders came too slowly, and Acorn was forced to find work in the shops of other manufacturers. In these jobs, as well, Acorn's earnings fluctuated, depending on the amount of work available, and he moved from employer to employer.[49] This slack was caused in part by the over-supply of labor in these trades. Silk manufacture had suffered from this problem for decades, and few looms were in steady production. Unsteady employment was typical in other East London sweated trades such as boot manufacture and box and brush making.

In addition to daily or weekly periods of inactivity, workers in many occupations suffered seasonal underemployment.[50] Perhaps the most severe seasonal rhythms were in the building trades, but clothing, furniture, and silk manufacture and many other trades suffered seasonal fluctuation in demand. William Swan, who worked as a baker in Stoke Newington, recorded the details of his seasonal employment in his journal. In 1877, the first year of this record, Swan noted that in January he spent "all the month out of work," and February was no better: "[O]ut of work all this month." In March, Swan had "a fortnight's work at the shop," and April similarly offered "part time in the shop." In May and June, Swan "had a good share of work," and July was "very busy at the shop." Steady work continued through August, but in September Swan was reduced to "only ten days work at the shop this month." In October, he "had some work during three weeks." But his records of November and December offer the same lament: "Had no work this month."[51] Swan's account continues for three and a half years, revealing steady work in the summer months, but little or no employment during the winter, a typical pattern in London labor markets.

Navigating these fragmented and unpromising labor markets required effort and ingenuity on the part of poor Londoners. One common strategy involved dovetailing various jobs during the course of the year. A man who worked as a coal heaver during winter months, for example, might seek work as a builder's laborer in the summer.[52] Pianoforte makers facing slack season in the summer could work in the furniture trades. Some local London labor markets offered particularly promising opportunities for dovetailing. In Battersea, for example, the gas works employed many men during the winter months, when other trades were slack. But in the summer, when the gas works were less busy, workers sought employment in the building trades.[53]

Opportunities for dovetailing by individuals varied, and were seldom as tidy as those apparent in Battersea. But households with more than one worker could dovetail wages from various jobs and enjoy somewhat more stable income. In some cases, men's and women's jobs in local labor markets complemented one another this way. Patricia Malcolmson describes a different pattern of dovetailing in Battersea and in North Kensington, in which women worked in laundries when their husbands had less work. Thus, wives of gas workers enjoyed a peak season in the laundries during June, while wives of building workers earned wages as laundresses during a smaller laundry season in October or November.[54]

But dovetailing did not often provide viable insurance against seasonality. As Stedman Jones notes, examples of dovetailing and other exceptions to seasonal patterns "provide a misleadingly harmonious picture of seasonal employment in London."[55] Perhaps the most important limitation on dovetailing was that the largest trades in most London labor markets had seasons that overlapped. Stedman Jones's extraordinary tables of seasonality show that the vast majority of important London trades were slack during the winter months. Builders enjoyed busy seasons from March to May and again in August and September, but were slack from November to February. Manufactures connected to the London aristocratic "season," such as coach building and artificial-flower making were busy between March and October and slack from November through February (artificial-flower making was also slack in June and July). Domestic work servicing the swollen affluent population in London during the "season" shared this pattern. Cabinetmakers' prime seasons occurred from April to June, though they enjoyed another peak in late fall. Of common seasonal trades in the three local labor markets under study here, only musical instrument making enjoyed a busy period that spanned January and February.[56] While individuals and households in poor London areas adopted dovetailing to try to mitigate the impact of seasonal irregularity, the correspondence of seasons in most common trades limited the efficacy of this strategy.

London labor markets demanded large numbers of workers who were paid low wages and could be employed and released on a daily or weekly basis, or employed during peak seasons and unemployed or underemployed during slack periods. This system had clear advantages for employers, who maintained the flexibility to respond to changing market conditions. While the economy of the metropolis depended on this labor supply, it provided these workers and their families with insufficient resources, denied them the benefits of rising real wages enjoyed by skilled and semiskilled workers in this period, and left them in poverty.[57]

Household Structure and Poverty

Household structure played an important role in determining whether a family would suffer from poverty or maintain a level of "working-class comfort." Many households depended on a woman as the major earner. These included families with invalid, drunk, or unemployed men as their heads and households with female heads.[58] Women's place in the London labor market made poverty nearly inevitable for these households. Women earned far less than men, and were subject to similar casual and seasonal work patterns.

In households with an employed male breadwinner, poverty was more likely during certain periods in the development of the family. Young couples with no children enjoyed a relatively strong economic position, while those with children too young to contribute to the household economy suffered the worst position. Households with children earning money more likely escaped severe poverty.[59] Depending on their health, older couples whose children moved out could also form viable economic units. Thus, poverty was not a static category; individuals moved in and out of poverty during their lives.

In evaluating links between household structure and poverty, it would be useful to determine a typical household budget in these neighborhoods. But "normal" levels of income and expenditure cannot be easily known in an environment of casual and inconsistent earning and fluctuating expenses.[60]

Women whose responsibility it was to maintain the family budget stretched and squeezed from week to week to make ends meet. Despite the difficulties, we can estimate household income and expenses in these areas for different types of families, the potential increase in resources offered by a wife's or child's employment, and the additional expenses accompanying the arrival of a new baby.

Charles Booth's survey presents budget data on London households in the 1880s, classified in categories ranging from very poor to well-paid working class. These examples illustrate the widely varied patterns of household expenditure among working-class families.[61] But Booth also offers averages for families in each category of economic status. Among the very poor, he found an average family to be composed of the equivalent of 3.44 "full adults."[62] The weekly income to the household totaled 17s. 5d.[63] This "average" family in the very poor category spent 4s. 4d. on rent and 12s. 2d. on food weekly. Thus, once food and rent were paid for, only 11d. remained for fire, light, clothes, and other items.

Among the poor, an average household included Booth's equivalent of 3.12 adults. In this case, the weekly income reached 23s. 6d., and weekly rent, 5s. 2d. Food expenditure totaled 12s. 11d., leaving 5s. 6d. for other expenses. The "average" comfortable working-class family listed by Booth included the equivalent of 2.5 adults, and received a weekly income of 25s. 2d. This family paid 4s. 9d. rent, and spent 13s. 5d. a week on food. This food budget, though only slightly higher than those in the "very poor" category, fed a significantly smaller family. This family had 7s. per week left for other expenses. From these examples, it appears that the major difference between the standards of living of the poor and the very poor lay in per capita spending on food, fire, light, clothing, and other expenses. Though these averages mask wide variation among the households enumerated in Booth's evidence, and his calculation of equivalent household sizes in "full adults" is questionable, the figures provide a starting point for the consideration of family budgets.

Maud Pember Reeves and the Fabian Women's Group undertook a detailed study of family budgets in Lambeth in the years 1909–13.[64] Though this study concentrated on households of regularly employed men earning around 20s. per week, it confirms the general patterns discovered by Booth and sheds light on specific expenses involved in managing a working-class household. Pember Reeves estimated that food for the male head of household might be 6d. per day, or 3s. 6d. per week. After rent and other expenses were paid, women and children in the households surveyed ate an average of 1s. 5½d. of food per week.[65] Additional expenditures included soap and washing expenses, clothing, medicine, and, perhaps, burial insurance.[66] Also, a larger family might, if possible, take two rooms instead of one, thus paying higher rent. As Booth's survey showed, food and other expenses aside from rent were likely to be the areas of greatest flexibility in the household budget, where a wife could save a few shillings in the course of the week.

These examples offer some sense for the financial constraints and demands involved in managing domestic economies. In attempting to determine how much a child added to the expenses of a poor household, we must rely on broad estimates and particular cases. Ellen Ross cites the example of a "professional nurse-mother" in the 1890s who complained that a ten-month-old child cost her more than 5s. per week. An infant also could require equipment such as a perambulator, if the mother did not already possess one, and the birth itself might be attended by a midwife, whose fee in 1910 would be about 10s.[67] After infancy, children cost somewhat less than this. A workhouse allotted 2s. 11d. per head for food.[68] Booth reports a child of three was "boarded out at 2s. 6d. a week to relieve the mother [a widow] for her work."[69] As the amount spent on food and other commodities varied greatly, it is impossible to determine the "normal" cost of raising a child, but these figures offer broad estimates.

Estimates of rent in the areas indicate that one room might be had for 3s. 6d. per week, while two rooms might range from a norm of 5s. in Globe Town, to 8s. 6d. in Lisson Grove.[70] Given the flexibility apparent from Booth's figures for expenditures on clothing, fire, light, and other expenses, it seems wise to estimate these conservatively at a minimum of 9d. per person weekly.[71] Various descriptive sources indicate that 14s. or 15s. per week served as an ordinary contribution by husbands in these neighborhoods to the household budget.[72] It would also be useful to estimate the amount a woman or employed child might contribute to the household income. Though this varied tremendously, depending on the job and regularity of work, women could earn from 3s. to 14s. per week, if they worked extended hours in typical women's jobs. A child's contribution might fit in the same range, depending upon the child's age, sex, and job.[73]

An attempt can now be made, despite the difficulties involved in such generalizations, to offer model family budgets for various types of families in Somers Town, Lisson Grove, and Globe Town (table 2-11). When first married, the young husband and wife lived together without children. Later, we find them with two young children, though this estimate does not take into account infants requiring extra expenditure. As the family grew to three children, and the children reached their teens, they entered the job market and contributed to the household economy. Eventually, the children moved out, and the couple again resided without offspring at home. The figures in this table reveal the financial difficulty faced by families with young children. Even without taking larger accommodations, this family of four would have great difficulty affording food, rent, and minimal household needs on the normal household income from the husband. Living in a single room, these families would be constantly on the brink of economic need, limiting their food consumption and relying on the wife's ability to stretch the household budget. But when the children could earn wages, their earnings gave the household a significant financial cushion, even if the family took larger accommodations. When the couple did not have children at home, even if the wife was not employed, 4s. 3d. remained in the family budget for additional food, clothing, burial insurance, etc. Couples in these households could also more easily live in one room. Thus, the economic position of families with coresident, nonearning children was clearly quite precarious, while those without such responsibilities might enjoy some meager surplus.

The relationship between earnings and expenses, the key determinant of whether a family fell into or escaped poverty, changed dramatically as households changed their composition. The same contribution by the husband to the domestic economy that allowed his wife and himself a small surplus early in their marriage left the family on the brink of want when they had small children. But when these children reached wage-earning age, their contributions again put the household on more solid ground. Wives' earnings also impacted this balance, but, as will be shown in chapter 4, married women's wage earning was shaped more by the domestic work demanded by the household than by narrow budgetary considerations. Of course, during slack seasons or periods of underemployment, the husbands' contribution might drop, and unless other earners could make up the slack, this reduction in household resources would throw the family into temporary poverty regardless of the number and ages of children.

Similarly, the rupture of the household structure, through death or separation, would cost the household dearly. Female-headed households faced almost certain poverty, unless they included a number of wage-earning children. Men without wives would see their domestic expenses soar, unless they had a daughter or another woman present who could take over the essential tasks of managing the domestic budget. Thus, the individual's economic condition was dynamic. One could make ends meet relatively easily at some moments and at other times face nearly certain poverty. Limited and unstable opportunities in local labor markets, combined with changing household structures, made it likely that the vast majority of residents of these areas would suffer in poverty at some point in their lives.

The Impact of Poverty

The material situation of residents in these neighborhoods who lived either in poverty or just above it had serious effects on their health. Financial need forced many to curtail their caloric intake. Even in cases of relative comfort, women and children generally ate less and poorer quality food than did their husbands and fathers.[74] Under extreme conditions, the whole family was forced to live on the most meager provisions. In Eastnor Place, Somers Town, a family of seven living in one room often "had hardly sufficient bread to allow each member one slice" per day.[75] A family named Bath, living in Lisson Grove, exemplifies the effects of such a reduced diet. Though the wife had given birth to seven children, only two survived, and the four of them lived in one room. In 1879, Mrs. Bath was pregnant again, but her child was stillborn. The authorities determined that the mother was weak due to lack of nourishment.[76] In Globe Town, an observer interviewed by Booth's investigator noted that the "young people [were] very anemic through bad food and insufficient nourishment."[77] George Acorn reports feeling fatigued due to his poor diet as a youth.[78] James Sales, a dairyman in Lisson Street, was intimately acquainted with the attempts by neighborhood women to save on food. Though he could not afford to sell milk for under 5d. per quart, his poor customers could not afford it. So he watered down the product and sold it for less.[79]

Poverty also forced residents of these neighborhoods to live in unsanitary conditions. Many families, particularly in Somers Town and Lisson Grove, occupied only one room. In some streets, an average of more than two people inhabited every room, sometimes ones without ventilation.[80] The medical officer of health for St. Pancras claimed that the southern part of Somers Town "contains houses, courts, or alleys, unfit for human habitation, and the narrowness, closeness, and bad arrangement and condition of the streets and houses or groups of houses within such area, and the want of light, air, ventilation, and proper conveniences and the presence of other sanitary defects are dangerous and injurious to the health of the inhabitants."[81] In September 1880, Robert Bailey Bird, a child of three and a half years, died in Christ Church Residences, Lisson Grove, of complications of diphtheria and scarlet fever. A doctor who saw the boy "unquestionably attributed the death to the unsanitary state of the house in which the parents lived."[82] In Grace Foakes's Wapping neighborhood, the litany of familiar diseases included scarlet fever, diphtheria, and smallpox, and "of course Tuberculosis was with us all the time."[83]

In addition to facilitating the spread of illnesses through the air, the most serious health hazard caused by crowded conditions was the impact on inadequate water supplies and provisions for sewage and waste disposal. During the construction of the areas, regulation of these matters was rarely a factor. The Bethnal Green vestry was notoriously inefficient, "noted for its corruption and negligence," and local commissioners of paving were "hardly any better than the vestry."[84] In St. Pancras, sanitary reform was impeded by the unwillingness of the vestry to raise rates for improvements. Though local government in St. Marylebone was somewhat more effective, progress in sewer construction after 1855 had only begun to rectify sanitary problems, and the medical officer of health found many examples of defective drainage in the neighborhood in the 1880s.[85] Landlords were reluctant to pay for improvements themselves, because their tenants could not afford increased rents.

Thus the poor were forced to live with accumulations of waste and sewage in their streets.[86] In 1848, Hector Gavin investigated Globe Town, and found many streets in unacceptable sanitary condition. Type Street, for example, "was in *the most filthy state possible*, the stagnant pools of foetid, and putrid mud with their green scum, presents [*sic*] an aspect as offensive to the sight, as the smell was repulsive." Nearby, Pleasant Place "is nothing more or less than an elongated lake or canal; only, in place of water, we have a black, slimy, muddy compost of clay and putrescent animal and vegetable remains."[87]

Many houses in the areas lacked a direct water supply, and the flow of water was often intermittent and of questionable quality.[88] In 1881, a typhus epidemic hit Charles Street, Lisson Grove. Nineteen residents were afflicted as the result of the contamination of their water.[89] The lack of water also made washing difficult. One of Booth's observers noted that because of the lack of washing facilities, many of the children in a Globe Town school "practically never wash their bodies."[90] Another local observer complained of the filth in the area, describing homes as "bug holes," adding, "[Y]ou could grow mustard and cress on the walls."[91]

One impact of the grinding poverty and poor conditions suffered by area residents that seldom receives notice is the psychological effect. In his study of an impoverished London neighborhood in the 1920s and 1930s, J. White examined the role of violence as a response to the powerlessness suffered by impoverished men.[92] In exceptional cases, resignation and depression followed unsuccessful attempts to earn a decent living or grew out of persistent hunger and unsanitary living conditions.[93] Henry Richard Kemp, a fifty-four-year-old cabinetmaker living in Globe Town, was out of work for six weeks. His wife reported that he "had been very desponding for some time," and one Saturday night Kemp hanged himself, "driven to the act of desperation, by being out of work for some time and having a family of ten children dependent upon him."[94] But most poor Londoners continued to fight to make ends meet, despite the stresses and challenges they faced.

Poverty, poor diet, and crowded and unsanitary living conditions inflated death rates in poor neighborhoods. In the year ending in March 1882, the death rate in the Somers Town subdistrict was 20.6 per thousand, slightly higher than that in the Christchurch subdistrict that included Lisson Grove (19.3 per thousand). The Green subdistrict in Bethnal Green that included Globe Town had a significantly higher death rate of 30.4 per thousand. The major reason for this large discrepancy is that these registration districts are significantly larger than the neighborhoods defined in this study, and the two North London districts include some of the more affluent areas surrounding Somers Town and Lisson Grove. The areas surrounding Globe Town were poor neighborhoods with high death rates. The impact of poverty on mortality is clear in a comparison with the comfortable residential districts of Hampstead, which had a death rate of 13.4 per thousand that year.[95] Even within poor neighborhoods, death rates could vary from street to street. In Burne Street, Lisson Grove, during the years 1876–83, the average death rate was 24 per thousand, while in nearby Devonshire Street residents suffered a death rate of 39. An analysis of these death rates concluded that they were "mainly due to the disproportion that working men's incomes bear to the rent demanded—forcing them to live in one room."[96] This exacerbated the impact of deficient drainage and sewers, inadequate water supplies, and poor nutrition. Poverty and the resultant living conditions caused the death of many residents of Somers Town, Lisson Grove, and Globe Town.

Responsibility for confronting the challenges of poverty and attempting to minimize its impact on their families fell to poor women. Their ingenuity and resourcefulness determined the ability of their families to avoid the equivalent of bankruptcy, the workhouse. Their efforts and skills stretched meager and unsteady household resources to feed, house, and clothe their families. Strategies for balancing household budgets included adjusting household income, consumption, and spending.

One common strategy for balancing the domestic budget involved seeking other sources of income to supplement the earnings of the household head. Often other household members, wives and children of the head, entered the labor force. Women also performed small chores for neighbors, or minded neighborhood children.[97] Though it was less common in these three neighborhoods than in many other areas, some took in lodgers to boost household income. Seeking charity from religious institutions or out-relief from the parish could supplement an inadequate household budget. When George Acorn's father went into the hospital with an injury, his mother received two loaves of bread per day in out-relief.[98] Finally, some residents augmented their household income by begging.[99] Through these various means, the women in charge of their household budgets added to inadequate incomes.

Expenses were also manipulated by cutting consumption, purchasing poor quality and cheaper goods, obtaining credit, and simply not paying. Under conditions of poverty, families reduced their food consumption and went hungry. Scarce funds might be conserved by purchasing adulterated or poor-quality food, which was widely available in neighborhood markets. One Globe Town woman noted, "I often want bread, and so do all of us."[100] Often such conservation fell disproportionately on the women and children, while the male "breadwinner's" diet was preserved.[101] Clothing could also be stretched by repeated mending.

Perhaps the most common form of household budgeting involved the manipulation of spending and borrowing. A resourceful wife could bargain with shopkeepers for lower prices. If she was trustworthy and known in the neighborhood, she could obtain credit from local shopkeepers and merchants. Pawning provided another source of credit essential to poor households. Networks of neighborhood sharing often made possible the borrowing of small sums of money or needed household goods from neighbors. However, some local residents charged their neighbors inflated interest rates.[102] Finally, spending could be curtailed by stealing goods from shops, stalls, employers, or even neighbors, or by moving out when rent was in arrears.

The impact of poverty fell disproportionately on women. Shortfalls in household budgets became wives' and mothers' problems. When food was scarce, women did without. When there was not enough money for a doctor, women faced health problems with stoic acceptance. In the face of shortage, self-sacrifice was expected of and accepted by women. They shielded their husbands and children from the ravages of poverty as much as they could by absorbing its costs themselves. Chapter 5 will examine these patterns in more detail.

Conclusion

Though the majority of late-Victorian London's population faced poverty at some point in their lives, London poverty was a local phenomenon, concentrated in particular areas. Yet its causes were similar in each poor neighborhood: local labor markets offering jobs that paid poor and irregular wages, and the impact of household composition, especially the ratio of earners to nonearners. Individuals operated in narrow, circumscribed neighborhoods, seeking employment, shopping, and pursuing leisure in the vicinity of their homes. Work opportunities in their local labor markets reflected the particular legacies of each area; but labor markets in different poor neighborhoods shared the fundamental characteristics that made them profitable for employers and left the residents confronting poverty and its effects.

3

"The Work Is Quite Different":
The Sexual Division of Labor
and Women's Jobs

Isabella Killick worked as a trouser finisher in London's East End for over twenty years beginning in the 1860s, probably sewing pockets, lining trousers, sewing on buttons, and making buttonholes. She earned very little, under 1s. per day, and the work required limited skill. From November through January her trade was slack, and she did a bit of charring or laundry to earn a few shillings. In many ways, Killick's work was typical of women's jobs in the London economy: poorly paid, irregular, and dismissed as women's work. As another tailor, Lewis Lyons, explained of women's as opposed to men's jobs in tailoring: "The work is quite different that they do."[1]

Throughout the three neighborhoods, the census recorded 44% of women aged fifteen or over as employed, including 43% in both Somers Town and Globe Town, and 47% in Lisson Grove.[2] Throughout England and Wales, the employed included 37% of adult women.[3] Despite the underestimation of women's employment in the census, it counted nearly half of all adult women in the neighborhoods as employed, and their jobs reflect a persistent sexual division of labor in local labor markets.

Sally Alexander, in her study of London women's work during the first half of the nineteenth century, discovered a tenacious sexual division of labor that distinguished men's and women's jobs.[4] Nearly half a century later these divisions persisted, determining women's wage-earning opportunities. Because of their sex, women were confined to specifically female occupations or distinct female portions of mixed trades. In both cases, this gendered division restricted women to the worst portions of labor markets.

Jobs open to women paid lower and more irregular wages, were considered less skilled than men's jobs, and manifested and reinforced sexual hierarchies.

Many women's jobs fit into categories consistent with traditional domestic work. Important areas of women's employment included caring for homes, children, and sick people; sewing; and making apparel. Exceptions included well-defined parts of established London trades reserved for women (e.g., bookfolding), and a significant sector of domestic manufacture that spread during the century. The latter category included box and artificial-flower making, which developed in part to exploit an available cheap source of female labor.

Female occupations could not be counted on to provide steady wages. Most jobs were interrupted by seasonal fluctuations, and the organization of manufacture along sweated lines allowed employers to offer work only during those times when they needed workers. In decentralized sweated industries, women worked in their own homes or small workshops. These work sites cost employers little or nothing when business slowed. Even in more centralized manufacturing jobs, such as upholstery or bookbinding, work was irregular and wages could fall to nearly nothing during slow seasons. Domestic work for day servants, charwomen, and laundresses was also episodic.[5]

Women's jobs were viewed as less skilled, and thus paid lower wages than those filled by men. However, gender-based cultural assumptions rather than objective criteria of difficulty or the necessity of extensive training often determined this conception of skill. Typically, "the classification of women's jobs as unskilled and men's jobs as skilled or semiskilled frequently bears little relation to the actual amount of training or ability required for them. Skill definitions are saturated with sexual bias."[6] Definitions of skill were manipulated by employers to enforce low wages, and, at times, by organized male workers to preserve men's positions in industries. Nevertheless, the reorganization of production into more complex divisions of labor did divide tasks into smaller, simpler components, diluting skills. Some men's work became unskilled female work through this process, and some formerly privileged and skilled women's jobs became unskilled and poorly paid.[7] Thus, even women who possessed genuine skills found their positions undercut through the definition of their work as unskilled or through actual de-skilling. As Alexander noted for the earlier period, "[I]n none of these trades and occupations were women's wages ever high enough to secure for them and their children economic independence from men."[8]

The Division of Labor

WOMEN'S JOBS IN MIXED TRADES

In Somers Town, Lisson Grove, and Globe Town, common trades that employed both men and women included boot and shoemaking, silk manufacture, tailoring, brush making, bookbinding, upholstery, and milk distribution (table 3-1). Though both men and women worked in these industries, women had well-defined, distinct jobs. Men worked in those portions of the trades viewed as requiring skill, where they earned higher wages. Women were limited to low-paying jobs categorized as unskilled.

Boot and shoemakers. Globe Town lay at the center of the London footwear trade, and boot and shoe manufacture employed many men and women in the neighborhood.[9] Nearly a tenth of employed women in the neighborhood worked in the trade, which was far less common in Somers Town and Lisson Grove (table 3-1).[10] The boot and shoe trade typified the sweated system of production, characterized by subdivided work processes, decentralized production, long hours of work (during the busy season), and low wages. In fact, one witness before the House of Lords Select Committee testified that the sweated system applied "most virulently" to the boot trade.[11]

The manufacture of footwear involved four major processes—clicking, closing, making, and finishing. "Clicking" referred to the cutting out of material for the boot or shoe upper. This was a male job. "Closing"—sewing together the pieces of the upper—employed most of the women in the trade. Closing was often subdivided into simpler processes: fitters or paste fitters put pieces together in preparation for sewing and machinists sewed them together. If the product had buttons, the buttons were attached and holes made during the closing process as well.[12] Of women in the footwear trade in the three neighborhoods, 58% were specified by the census as either fitters or machinists, subspecialties of closing.

The next process, "making," involved attaching the upper to the sole, using a last or model of a foot to shape the upper. Fewer women worked in the making phase than in closing, as they were confined to the preparatory process of attaching the inner sole to the upper part of the boot or shoe. Then, men fixed the outer sole and the heel. The boot or shoe might be sewn together (increasingly by machine), or attached using pegs or rivets. Riveted boots were a particular specialty of the Globe Town area.[13]

The final stage in boot manufacture was "finishing." This involved a number of processes, the most important of which, "knifing" (trimming the edge of the sole and surface of the heel into shape), was defined as a skilled job and reserved for men. Women worked in finishing primarily as "sockers" who inserted the lining for the insole. The subdivisions of boot and shoe manufacture meant that individuals specialized in specific parts of the trade.[14]

Though boot and shoe factories were not unknown in London, generally these processes were subcontracted to small workshops or home workers.[15] D. F. Schloss, who wrote the section on boot making in Booth's survey, describes two women who ran small-scale closing workshops. The first employed four other women, including her daughter and a shop girl who carried the work to and from the warehouse. She had three machines, one of which she worked herself. The second employed three women, including her sister and a shop girl, and also had three machines (she had work for only one at the time of the enquiry).[16] These examples show the small scale of organization in the trade. One needed only to hire a sewing machine to set up as an "independent" closer, and thus small-scale workshops proliferated.[17]

Clear distinctions between men's and women's jobs in footwear manufacture developed through the nineteenth century. Traditionally, men manufactured footwear with some help from their families. However, pressure from provincial competition undercut the position of skilled artisans, as seen in the failure of an 1812 strike. Employers imposed a more complex division of labor as a strategy to reduce wages and lower production costs, and the various processes in shoe manufacture became distinct stages, performed by separate workers. Closing had often been the task of the wife of a skilled shoemaker, and this stage became clearly defined as women's work and was increasingly given to outworkers in their homes or small workshops. The application of the sewing machine to closing, beginning in the 1850s, simplified this work, further depressing wages. In the last half of the century, finishing processes also incorporated the division of labor. Though "knifing" remained men's work, socking and other finishing tasks became low-paid women's jobs. Through these developments, skilled men lost control of production to employers, and wages throughout the trade decreased. The division of labor and the application of machines made some jobs easier, while others were simply redefined as unskilled; the jobs paying the lowest wages became women's work.[18]

Silk workers. Despite the long decline of the Spitalfields silk industry, almost one in ten employed Globe Town women still worked in the trade (table 3-1).[19] The northeast corner of Globe Town housed the last remnant of the proud Spitalfields silk industry that once employed up to fifty thousand people.[20]

The manufacture of silk in Globe Town was chiefly a domestic industry, with weaving done in home workshops on the upper floors of weavers' cottages. Workshops generally contained two looms, but sometimes three or four.[21] Silk weavers often worked in family groups, and silk work employed 291 men and 245 women in Globe Town. Of female silk workers in Globe Town who were not themselves household heads, 57% lived in households headed by silk manufacturers. Changes in the industry through the nineteenth century, however, deprived these weaving families of the autonomy enjoyed by traditional artisans. A. K. Sabin describes the decline of the silk craft: "It came about that the middleman—the factor—became the owner of the apparatus in numerous instances, lending it and supplying the raw silk to the weaver he chose to employ, and collecting it with the finished goods when the job was done. Then the weaver was poor indeed, for he had ceased to be his own master!"[22] Silk manufacture increasingly resembled other sweated trades in Globe Town.

The vast majority of female silk workers in the neighborhood were classed by the census as weavers' (81%) or winders (12%). Winding referred to two different processes. In the warehouse, silk thread was wound onto bobbins by machine. The other sort of silk winding occurred at the loom as a preparation for weaving. Silk threads were wound onto quills fixed to the shuttles of the loom. The latter process was generally done by a female relative of the weaver. Silk weaving itself involved working the looms, which varied according to the job. Plain work required smaller looms and was generally done by women, while men wove figured patterns on heavier jacquard looms. This specialization again placed women in the lower-paid portions of the trade. Weavers in patterned work could earn approximately 75% more than plain work weavers.[23]

Tailoresses. Tailoresses chiefly manufactured men's outerwear, coats, waistcoats (vests), and trousers.[24] London tailoring has traditionally been divided into a high-class, bespoke (custom) trade in the West End, and cheap, ready-made manufacture in the East End. But this distinction cannot be sharply drawn, as West End tailors subcontracted work to the East End, and some East End tailors made clothing of moderate quality. In both the East and West Ends, tailoring was commonly organized in sweated manufacturing, involving long hours, low pay, a complex division of labor, and often subcontracting.[25] Of the three neighborhoods under study here, tailoring played the largest role in the female labor market in Globe Town, where the trade accounted for 6.5% of employed women (table 3-1). Globe

Town lay near the center of the trouser and vest trade in the East End, while the focus of sweated tailoring in the West End lay around Soho, south of Lisson Grove and Somers Town.[26]

Of the three types of men's clothing (coats, vests, and trousers), women in these neighborhoods played the least significant role in the manufacture of coats. In the higher-class trade, coats were sewn by hand, a job reserved for men. Women made buttonholes for these high-quality garments, and sometimes felled (stitched in) the linings of the coats. Jewish immigrants dominated the manufacturing of cheap, ready-made coats in the late nineteenth century, and this trade was focused in the Jewish area of Whitechapel and its environs.[27]

Local women played a greater role in the manufacture of vests or waistcoats. A few women even made whole garments—the highest-quality, hand-sewn vests, requiring a skilled hand. In the lower-quality portions of the trade, the processes involved in making waistcoats were subdivided and contracted out to workshops and home workers. In one small East End workshop, a mother, father, and daughter, along with another man and a young woman, manufactured vests, probably of medium quality. Vests came already cut out by men at the warehouse, and the mother and daughter tacked the edges. The hired man then stitched the seams and edges, and the father pressed the garment and prepared it for buttonholing and lining. The young woman made the buttonholes, and the mother felled the linings. This shop took in work from wholesalers in the City and in the West End, and the tailor and tailoress's son carried the work back and forth from the warehouse.[28] Women performed all the tasks in the poorest sections of the trade: "As price and quality decline, so women take an increasing share in the shop work."[29]

High-quality trousers were manufactured by skilled male tailors, often with the assistance of their wives and daughters. In the medium-quality sections of this trade, the garments were generally manufactured in workshops with men pressing the trousers and women machine-stitching and finishing them. The lowest-quality trousers were usually given out to women for machining and finishing at home. Trouser finishing involved sewing pockets, lining the seat and top of the garment, sewing on buttons, and making buttonholes.[30]

The complex organization of the tailoring trade fostered the sexual division of labor along two axes. High-quality goods requiring the greatest skill (and paying the highest wages) generally boasted male handiwork, while women workers played a larger role in the production of medium-quality goods. Poor-quality clothing was often manufactured exclusively by women.[31] Thus as markets for cheaper goods expanded, so did women's role in the trade. Within the production of a particular garment, if men were involved they did the better-paid work. For example, although the manufacture of high-quality coats was dominated by men, women sewed buttonholes and sometimes stitched the linings.[32]

Brush makers. Brush making was a common women's occupation in Globe Town and in Somers Town, but few women living in Lisson Grove worked in the trade (table 3-1). Women in brush making were chiefly limited to the drawing and finishing processes. Brush drawers attached bristles to the brush itself by running them through a wire loop, which was then pulled through a hole bored in the brush. A wire at the back of the brush held the bristles in place. The drawer then trimmed the ends of the bristles with table-mounted shears, though some home workers returned them to the shop for trimming.[33] Finishing included hiding the wire work at the back of the brush by gluing a piece of wood or other covering on the back. Brushes also might require painting or polishing.

The organization of brush manufacture in London proceeded along three lines. Some enterprises employed brush makers in large shops or factories. Here women worked on the premises, particularly in the "heavy work" section of the trade in which bristles were fastened using pitch, rather than drawn through holes in brushes. Alternatively, brush-drawing women were employed as home workers who collected materials and returned the finished goods at a factory or shop. Finally, small-scale brush makers bought their own materials, manufactured the brushes, and sold them to retailers independently. Many of these makers employed a few workers in their small shops.[34]

Bookfolders and sewers. Proximity to the primary center of the printing and bookbinding trades in London—Holborn and Clerkenwell—explains the importance of bookbinding for women in Somers Town (table 3-1). Of women in these trades, the census specifies that 68% were bookfolders, 13% were described merely as bookbinders, another 12% were book sewers, and 7% were vellum sewers. It is likely, however, that those listed as bookbinders worked folding or sewing together pages, as the actual binding of books was reserved for men. Folding and sewing had been women's jobs since the eighteenth century.[35]

All printed material longer than a single page needed folding to put the pages in their proper order. Some bookfolding was done by machine, but many women folded pages by hand. The machine folder was a woman who fed the machine by placing the sheet in precisely the correct position. She might also be employed gathering the printed and folded pages, or checking the collating to make sure the pages were in order. Hand folders had to be careful to fold each sheet the same way.[36]

After the pages were folded, gathered, and collated if necessary, the book sewer took over. Better-quality books, whether sewn by hand or by machine, boasted threads sewn through tape to hold them together. Cheaper books or pamphlets were "sewn" on a machine that inserted a staple-binder. The woman working this machine would place the pamphlet into a trough and activate the machine, which passed a wire staple through the pages and pressed it flat. Folding and sewing books were jobs done by women, but formally bound books then passed into the hands of male bookbinders who would finish the process. Women were thus confined to the preparatory phases of the trade, which paid lower wages.[37]

Though the mechanized processes in bookfolding and sewing were done in workshops, hand folding, particularly of cheap materials, was often done by home workers. Some women who worked in the workshop during the day were given pages to fold at home by hand in the evening. Others never worked in the shop, but took work home when it was available. This was the favored arrangement for some women who worked in the shop before their marriage, but preferred to work at home as married women.[38] Other home workers were used at moments of peak demand for labor; these "job hands" worked for a few days each month. One employer described this system: "I have a number of hands that come regularly to me every month to do Bradshaw's Guide and magazine work. They take it home and bring it back again."[39] Knowing how much work was carried on in workshops and how much at home is difficult, but with the spread of mechanization in bookfolding, homework grew less common.[40]

Folding pages could be learned easily and quickly, while sewing was more difficult. However, many women in both parts of the trade were forced to undergo an extended training period. One survey found that over half the firms under examination required new bookfolders or sewers to serve as learners for one to two years, and 27% instituted training periods of two or three years. Observers criticized these patterns, as the work could generally be picked up in a matter of weeks, and even the more difficult sewing processes did not require a three-year training period.[41] Learners, however, were paid less than full-fledged workers, so employers could save money by extending the period during which each worker held this lower status.[42]

A long-established division of labor in the bookbinding trade placed women in the preparatory stages of the process, while the actual binding was the preserve of male workers. Early in the nineteenth century, female bookfolders and sewers were viewed as somewhat skilled, granting them status and respectability. These women, however, earned wages one-third

to half those paid male bookbinders. With the expansion and mechanization of the trade late in the century, the skills of many bookfolders and
sewers became obsolete; their position deteriorated in the face of the widespread practice of employing many learners in the unskilled and semiskilled
occupations. While some male bookbinders successfully defended privileged and relatively high-paid positions despite mechanization, women in
the trade suffered de-skilling and declining wages.[43] Male workers cooperated in restricting women's employment, defending their positions in the
better-paid jobs.

Upholsteresses. Upholstery work formed a notable female trade in
Somers Town, but not in Lisson Grove or Globe Town (table 3-1). The
presence of these workers in Somers Town reflects the proximity of large-
scale furniture makers and sellers in the Tottenham Court Road area.[44] For
example, Maple's, perhaps the largest of these firms, employed 391 female
workers, mostly in upholstery and carpet sewing. These large houses also
gave out work to workshops nearby, around the intersection of Euston and
Tottenham Court Roads, less than half a mile from Somers Town.[45]

Women were generally confined to that part of the upholstery process
involving sewing. Men cut out the covers and filled them with stuffing.[46]
As in many trades, machine work was spreading in the late nineteenth century, along with the manufacture of a cheaper class of furniture. One London upholsteress complained to the Royal Commission on Labour that a
growing portion of furniture was worked on machines, with simple
finishings, as opposed to more complex trimmings that required hand sewing.[47] This work was carried out in large businesses or small workshops,
though some work might be taken home for finishing after hours.[48]
Upholsteresses performed a traditional female task (sewing), and the skill
required in the job eroded with the spread of machine sewing.

Milk sellers. The late nineteenth century saw significant changes in the
distribution of milk, as traditional urban dairy production gave way to larger-
scale distribution of milk produced farther from London.[49] But in Lisson
Grove, the significant number of women employed in the milk trade suggests that the traditional pattern persisted.

The census specifies that most Lisson Grove women in the trade (58%)
were milk carriers, while another 31% were described less specifically as
milk women or milk girls. In the traditional system, women delivered the
milk produced in urban dairies from house to house.[50] William Collison,
who grew up in Stepney, recalled his first job, at age ten, of helping a milk

woman. She carried pails in "a common yoke fitting into the neck, and on to the shoulders. From each end of the yoke a strap and hook depended, from which a milk-pail hung, and as the milk-pails had to be put down each time a customer was served, milk-selling was not the easy job it is today."[51] Though in many areas, women hunched under yokes had been replaced by a system of distribution dependent upon rail lines and rapid, large-scale delivery in horse-drawn "floats," the Lisson Grove area appears to have been a center of the older system based on urban dairies. The most famous of these was Wellford and Sons, "Dairymen to the Queen," whose well-kept cow houses were in Maida Vale, just north of Lisson Grove.[52] Women in this trade required great strength but little skill, and were concentrated in a backwater of traditional distribution methods. In most trades, the application of new technology led to the replacement of male workers with women, but in areas outside Lisson Grove, the new floats drove women out of milk selling, replacing them with male drivers.

Summary: Women's roles in mixed trades. In trades employing many men and women, a rigid division of labor persisted in the late nineteenth century. Entrenched patterns defined those jobs open to female workers and those reserved for men. Women's occupations in these trades were defined as less skilled than those of men and paid poorer wages. This sexual division of labor reflected long-established traditions and expectations of proper women's work. Through the nineteenth century mechanization and the division of labor disrupted production processes in many trades. Some of the newly created jobs offered low-paid work and became women's jobs.

SPECIFICALLY FEMALE TRADES

While some women worked in well-defined female portions of mixed trades, other occupations employed predominantly female workforces. These trades included domestic work and a number of manufactures. As in mixed trades, these women workers earned low wages under poor conditions in work viewed as unskilled.

Domestic Trades

Five of the most common women's occupations in the three neighborhoods fit the category of domestic work (table 3-2). Cleaning, washing, cooking, and caring for children or the infirm were seen as proper female concerns and offered pay and conditions that male workers spurned.

Women's employment in domestic work did not draw opposition from observers who objected to "unfeminine" pursuits by women.[53] However, this work often involved long hours, difficult conditions, and low wages.

The late nineteenth century was a period of transition in the domestic trades. The move from live-in to day service began in these years, accelerating early in the twentieth century. This shift reflects changes in the attitudes and status of employers of servants (mostly middle class) and of domestic workers themselves, making live-in service less attractive to potential servants and to their employers.[54] Though fewer middle-class families wanted young working-class women living in their homes, they still sought to have domestic work done for them. The dominant form of domestic occupation in three neighborhoods exemplifies the new type of service: women living in their own homes and washing, cleaning, and doing other domestic tasks for employers on a daily basis. These jobs were particularly common in Somers Town and Lisson Grove, reflecting the impact of nearby middle-class populations on the local labor markets.

Laundresses. Doing laundry in the late nineteenth century was arduous and time-consuming, involving three major operations: sorting, washing, and ironing. "Sorting" separated items of different fabrics and colors requiring different treatments. "Washing" included pounding or scrubbing clothes in a tub of hot soapy water, rinsing the items, and then boiling them in a copper (a large vessel for boiling water) if the laundress had access to one. The clothes were then wrung out, using a combined wringer and mangle (if that machine was available), and hung to dry. Finally, the clean laundry was smoothed or ironed, using a mangle for flat linens and a hot iron for garments.[55] Though most of these processes required more effort than skill, ironing demanded a skilled hand, and some ironers specialized in this task.

In addition to the strain of lifting and wringing out heavy wet laundry and managing large containers of hot water, laundresses suffered under miserable conditions. Whether at home or employed in small-scale laundries, laundresses worked in extreme heat caused by the requisite boiling. The need to keep windows closed to avoid the soiling of clothes by soot in the air exacerbated the high temperatures and steamy conditions. As hanging clothes outside to dry was often impossible, they might be dried in the room in which a family lived. In this case the wet clothes dripped water on the workers and their families.[56] Grace Foakes described the atmosphere created by washing in her family's rooms: "Most of the time the washing was dangling on our heads. The place was damp and smelly, with steam running down windows and walls. Sometimes in bad weather the washing took two or three days to dry."[57]

Though laundry work fit accepted notions of "women's work," contemporary observers generally disapproved of laundresses' behavior. A medical officer in one London slum identified laundresses as the most immoral of all women workers.[58] Drinking was common among laundresses, and their pay in commercial laundries generally included the provision of beer.[59] Malcolmson observes: "The 'liquid lunch' was as much their habit as that of the modern executive."[60] Laundresses were known for their toughness and assertiveness, an approach that did not square with accepted female behavior. Nonetheless, laundry was by far the most common women's occupation in both Somers Town and Lisson Grove.

General servants. Domestic and general servants were common in all three neighborhoods, though they formed a higher proportion of employed women in Lisson Grove and Somers Town than in Globe Town. However, the census's categorization of women as general servants or domestic servants does not provide a clear picture of these women's occupations. The census category included women in four different positions. "Servants" included traditional live-in domestic servants, as well as day servants who worked in other people's homes during the day and returned to their own homes at night. The category also included women whose relationship to the household head was described as "lodger." Finally, the category included women who lived with kin and performed unpaid household domestic service for them.

Those servants classed as lodgers by the census remain a mystery. It is impossible to tell whether these women worked as servants in the households in which they lived, or whether they worked elsewhere as day servants. These women, called "out servants" by Higgs, resist categorization, but they comprised only 5% of all servants in the neighborhoods.[61]

A more interesting and problematic group of servants were relatives of their household heads, called "possible servants" by Higgs. These women included 62% of all servants, but it is impossible to know with certainty how many were day servants in other households and how many lived and worked in the same household. Higgs identified characteristics of these women and their households in Rochdale, indicating that most of them worked at home for their families.[62] However, the "possible servants" in Somers Town, Lisson Grove, and Globe Town do not share many of these characteristics with Higgs's sample. Most were probably employed as day servants (see appendix 2).

Higgs observes that "these women, if day servants, would have been employed in what was basically 'charring.'"[63] Perhaps the distinction between these women, called "servants" and "general servants" in the census, and those listed as charwomen is merely convention. Most charwomen were older, often widows or married women. These day servants, however, were mostly young and single.

Those whose relationship to the household head was "servant" fit the model of a traditional domestic servant, living in the homes of their employers. Twenty-seven percent of domestic servants in the three neighborhoods whose relationship could be determined from the census schedules were this type of servant, including 46% of those in Globe Town.[64] In the three neighborhoods, 67% of live-in domestic servants worked in households in which they were the only servant, and another 19% worked with only one other servant.[65] These women served as maids-of-all-work, the generalists among domestic servants.

Maids-of-all-work faced a daunting variety of jobs, due to the lack of other servants with whom they could share the domestic burdens. Their tasks ranged from heavy cleaning, such as scrubbing flagstones, to preparing and cleaning up after meals. They might also run errands and serve tea. As many heads of these households were employed in food trades, they probably helped with this work as well.[66] The types of work that might be demanded of these maids-of-all-work had no limit, as one domestic manual noted: "The mistress's commands are the measure of the maid-of-all-work's duties."[67]

A unique aspect of live-in domestic service involved the relationship between the servant and her employers. Living as subordinate members of their households, under the watchful eye of employers, these women were subject to interference in all aspects of their lives. Mistresses might dictate everything from the servants' dress to religious practices.[68] Sometimes, domestic servants faced sexual exploitation by their employers, as McBride notes: "The power which her employer exercised over her could easily be used to force sexual submission."[69]

Charwomen. The term "charring" refers to the performance of cleaning or other domestic tasks in another person's home, an office, or an institution. Charwomen's tasks covered the whole range of domestic jobs. Carl Chinn describes the daily routine of a charwoman in Birmingham, whose day's work included "washing and drying up the breakfast dishes; filling up the coal scuttles from the out-house; cleaning the fire irons with emery cloth; blackleading the fire-grate; dusting, cleaning and polishing cutlery and ornaments, and beating and shaking the carpets outside."[70] Because it required general domestic skills, charring offered what was perhaps the most convenient job for a woman seeking employment, particularly in areas like Somers Town or Lisson Grove, where residents of surrounding neighborhoods employed many charwomen.[71]

Nurses. The census enumerators' books list a significant number of women in the three neighborhoods as nurses. This category, however, refers to varied types of employment. Nurses providing "subordinate medical service" accounted for 11% of nurses in the three neighborhoods. Another 15% worked as monthly nurses, helping new mothers.[72] A further 12% were nursemaids, who cared for children. The majority (53%) were simply classed as "nurses," and may have done any of these jobs. As McBride notes, "[T]he use of the same term . . . tends to confuse their functions."[73]

Few of these general nurses worked as live-in nursemaids in middle-class homes, as is evident in their positions in households and the lack of young children living with them. Of general nurses whose relationship to the household head could be determined, 59% were household heads themselves, and another 9% were wives of the head of the household. Nearly half the general nurses lived in households without any offspring of the household head, and the households of 23% of these nurses had only one son or daughter living at home. Thus, the vast majority of general nurses were employed outside the households in which they lived. They may have cared for children on a daily basis, served the infirm in hospitals or homes, or helped new mothers.

Child-minders among the English poor developed a reputation for providing poor-quality care to their charges. It was alleged that the common pattern of child care among these nurses involved "children and old women left in charge of babies liberally [*sic*] dosed with such opiates as Godfrey's Cordial."[74] One historian offers a more optimistic view of young nurse-maids: "They were responsible for dressing and undressing the children, playing with them and taking them out for walks. Needless to say, the most ruthless were also accused of administering Godfrey's Cordial."[75] Child care was often provided by neighbors of mothers employed in other jobs. These neighborly "baby-sitters" fell into the category of nurses if their work was steady enough to be reported on the census.

Cooks. Women employed preparing food for others worked, as did laundresses, in a variety of settings. Some cooks lived in their employers' homes and worked as domestic servants. Others lived in their own homes and cooked either in other people's houses, in institutions, or in eating establishments. Cooks were most common in Lisson Grove, where they counted 1.9% of employed women. Most of the cooks in all three areas were listed by the census enumerators as "cook, not domestic," implying that they worked in pubs, restaurants, coffeehouses, or institutions. Nearly all the cooks in Lisson Grove fit this category.

Even the live-in cooks did not fit the model of a domestic cook on a large staff. In households with many servants, the cook held a privileged position and might oversee a kitchen maid and scullery maid, her assistants. However, in these three neighborhoods, those cooks who were live-in servants worked in smaller households, 80% of which had three or fewer servants. In Lisson Grove, all the live-in cooks were the only servants in their households. These cooks took on tasks not directly related to food preparation, such as sweeping and other cleaning tasks.[76]

All cooks, whether they lived with their employers or worked on a daily basis in various establishments or institutions, required some skill. Unlike the maid-of-all-work, who might be expected to learn her duties on the job, a cook brought some expertise to her employment. Perhaps these cooks had served as kitchen maids and learned their trade this way. It appears that this skill entitled cooks to higher pay than most women who did domestic jobs. Live-in cooks were among the most highly paid female servants, and this probably applied to those working as day cooks as well.[77] Like laundresses, cooks worked under difficult conditions. Kitchens were hot and often poorly ventilated, and food preparation could be hard work. Though their reputation for bad behavior was not as serious as that of laundresses, cooks were also known for drinking to excess.[78]

Summary: Women's work in domestic trades. Domestic work formed the largest category of employment for women in these neighborhoods, particularly in Somers Town and Lisson Grove. The vast majority of domestic occupations involved menial, unskilled labor. The two major domestic jobs requiring some skill, ironing and cooking, were done under extremely harsh physical conditions. Domestic occupations almost exclusively employed women, as their accordance with accepted female tasks and low pay made them unappealing to men.

Manufacturing Trades

Manufacture played an important role in the London economy of the late nineteenth century, and women dominated a number of manufacturing trades. For the most part, manufacturing trades employing predominantly female labor forces were consistent with traditional "female" pursuits (table 3-3).[79] Dressmakers, trimming makers, milliners, mantle makers, needlewomen, and machinists all manufactured clothing or footwear. Box making and artificial-flower making, less obviously linked to traditional female pursuits, grew in particular areas to exploit available female labor forces.

Most trades discussed in this section were organized in the sweated system. The decentralized nature of this system encouraged and was encouraged by complex divisions of labor. Isolation of parts of the production process and the substitution of machine for hand work caused a dilution of skill, making workers' expertise obsolete and offering lower pay for the simpler work. The women's manufacturing trades were particularly subject to such dilution.

Dressmakers. The manufacture of women's dresses occupied more than one in ten employed women in Somers Town and Lisson Grove, reflecting the fact that the center of dress manufacture in London was around Westminster and southern Marylebone. A significant, but far smaller number of women in Globe Town worked in the trade (table 3-3). They were likely connected to the secondary center of dressmaking in Stepney.[80]

Dressmaking can be divided into three major sections: bodice, skirt, and sleeve making. These three areas again involved two separate processes: machinists who sewed the seams and linings, and finishers. In a trend much criticized by workers and observers, workers increasingly learned only one section of the trade, specializing in sleeves, for example.[81] The intensified division of labor undercut the position of skilled and relatively well paid dressmakers in the last decades of the nineteenth century. Dressmaking increasingly came to resemble women's jobs in other sweated trades, involving long hours, poor conditions, and low pay.

Machinists and needlewomen. Women who made their living sewing often reported these general occupations to the census enumerators. A significant number of women in the three neighborhoods were listed by the census enumerators' books as "machinists," but this category was particularly important in Globe Town (table 3-3). It appears that most of these women worked on sewing machines in the clothing or footwear trades; boot and shoe machinists were probably the majority in Globe Town.[82]

Invented before the 1851 Great Exhibition, the sewing machine's impact increased through the 1860s and 1870s. In this period, most machines ran on foot power, and were used in homes and small workshops. Special machines were rapidly developed for particular tasks in the clothing and footwear trades, such as buttonholing. Machines were commonly purchased on the installment system, with machinists paying about 2s. 6d. per week.[83] Lavinia Casey, a shirt machinist, obtained a machine through this installment system. Unfortunately, during slack periods she was unable to meet her payments. When she fell into arrears, the Singer company took the machine back and she lost her investment. When she got new work, she began the cycle again.[84] As Schmiechen notes, "The hire system of Singer and others insured that the sewing machine became the most widely used invention of the second industrial revolution."[85]

Needlewomen more likely sewed by hand, and were mostly employed in the clothing trades. This trade was more prevalent in Somers Town and Lisson Grove than in Globe Town, perhaps reflecting its link to West End shops. Some needlewomen may have worked directly for middle-class families, as a form of day service. These women performed a variety of sewing tasks, probably on a casual basis.

Trimming makers. The manufacture of trimmings for dresses constituted an important Globe Town trade, as Bethnal Green was the center of trimming manufacture, but was not significant in either Lisson Grove or Somers Town. Dressmaking shops in the West End passed orders through City firms that functioned as middlemen to employers in the Bethnal Green area.[86] Trimmings were manufactured either in these employers' factories or in workers' homes.

The general term "trimmings" includes a variety of decorative additions to dresses, including braids, tassels, beadwork, and fringes. Each of these types of work involved a different process. Some work involved the use of machines, but it appears that most women in the trade worked by hand. Though a portion of trimming work required some skill, for the most part the trade was organized along sweated, unskilled lines. Often home workers would hire younger women or children to help with the easiest processes, such as simple beadwork.[87]

Milliners. Ladies' hat manufacture was located principally in the West End, as reflected in a higher concentration of milliners in Somers Town and Lisson Grove than in Globe Town. Traditionally this trade demanded expertise, and milliners ranked among the most skilled women workers in the London economy. The manufacture of a hat began with the shaping of the foundation on a wooden block. The milliner then covered this frame with the material of the hat, and pleated and stitched this covering. Finally, the material was cut into its exact size, the pleats were pressed, and the trimmings were applied. These trimmings varied greatly depending on fashion, but might include ribbons, artificial flowers, or other decorations. Some milliners performed all these processes, constructing the hat from start to finish, while in other cases, the production process was subdivided, and milliners specialized in particular steps.[88]

The established organization of millinery shops involved apprentices who lived on the premises. However, late in the nineteenth century, this system gave way to three modes of organizing millinery work. Some milliners worked in small shops on a daily basis and lived at home. These women often worked in both the retail portion of the shop and in manufacture. In other cases, milliners worked at home.[89] Gradually, factories developed in which many milliners produced hats on a wholesale basis. Jerry White describes one such factory early in the twentieth century that employed fifty milliners.[90] These trends replaced the previous pattern of apprenticeship and high skill levels in millinery with subdivided, less-skilled work, and probably resulted in a deterioration of wage rates.

Mantle makers. The manufacture of mantles (cloaks) was not sharply distinct from female portions of the general tailoring trade. However, a number of women were described specifically as mantle makers, especially in Somers Town and Lisson Grove. The major mantle-making processes done by women included sewing seams and finishing garments already cut out at a factory or warehouse. Finishing might include stitching on a collar, attaching buttons, and sewing buttonholes.[91] The women's portions of the trade were, typically, viewed as unskilled and paid poorly.

Box makers. Many women in Globe Town made cardboard and paper boxes, though surprisingly the trade was absent from Lisson Grove. These workers manufactured products ranging from fancy boxes (such as those used for chocolate) to plainer boxes (in which footwear or clothing was packaged), to the cheapest boxes (those used for matches). The skill level necessary for box making varied as well. The manufacture of fancy boxes required some training, and women in this branch of the trade might work as learners for up to three years. On the other hand, matchbox making could be learned quickly. This branch of the trade was common in Globe Town.[92]

Often, the materials used for making boxes would be cut in a workshop or factory. A woman folded the cardboard into the shape of the box. She then dipped a paper wrapping into glue that had been spread on a glueboard and wrapped it around the folded box, "laying it [the paper] on the glue-board herself and then putting it on the box, the gluey finger being raised and carefully kept away from the box." The paper wrapper held the box in place, and often provided decoration or a printed label.[93] Matchboxes required a slightly different process, as they included two different parts, the container and the case. Clementina Black described matchbox making as follows:

[O]ne motion of the hands bends into shape the notched frame of the case, another surrounds it with the ready-pasted strip of printed wrapper ... then the sandpaper or the phosphorus paper, pasted ready beforehand, is applied . . . the long narrow strip which is to form the frame of the drawer is laid upon the bright strip of ready-pasted paper, then bent together and joined by an overlapping bit of the paper; the edges of paper below are bent flat, the ready-cut bottom is dropped in and pressed down, and before the fingers are withdrawn they fold over the upper edges of the paper inside the top.[94]

Artificial-flower makers. Artificial-flower manufacture constituted an important women's occupation in Somers Town and in Lisson Grove. Unusual for a manufacturing occupation, this trade was less prevalent in Globe Town (table 3-3). The concentration of this work in the two northern districts reflects its link to fashionable West End millinery shops.

The manufacture of artificial flowers included a number of distinct processes. First the components of the flower were prepared. This included drawing wire to the proper length for the stem, cutting out the leaves and petals on power presses, and shading these parts by dipping them in dye. The various parts of the flower were then assembled, or "mounted," using glue and wire to hold them together.[95] Generally, workers in the trade specialized in cutting, shading, or mounting.

Summary: Women's work in female manufacturing trades. Opportunities for employment in female-dominated manufacturing trades reinforce the patterns found in mixed trades and domestic work. Women worked under difficult conditions. Their employment was irregular, and thus their earnings were unsteady. Women earned low wages, as they generally found employment in jobs viewed as unskilled, or their skilled positions faced dilution due to mechanization and the division of labor in the sweated system. Whether they did domestic jobs, worked in particular portions of mixed trades, or in specifically female manufactures, employed women in these neighborhoods supplied a flexible, poorly paid, easily exploited labor pool for the London economy.

Explaining the Division of Labor

The sexual division of labor that restricted women to these jobs did not rest on physical differences between men and women. Women worked under difficult conditions as cooks and laundresses. Women's jobs required strength and exertion (such as carrying milk or lifting heavy laundry and coppers filled with hot water). Working conditions cannot explain why some jobs became women's jobs, while men monopolized others.

The gendered division of labor reflects a complex interaction of cultural, economic, and legal factors in the context of changing work processes during industrialization. Preindustrial household economies already reveal defined roles for men and women, and these divisions persisted through industrialization. Many common women's jobs had links to domestic work or the manufacture of textiles and clothing. Craft and proto-industrial production established traditional divisions of labor in mixed trades before the Victorian period.[96] These established patterns supported powerful cultural notions about what was proper "women's work" that applied to exclusively women's trades and to women's jobs within mixed trades.

These ideas about gender roles persisted in a dynamic economic situation that made gendered divisions of labor in mixed trades the objects of contention. Changing technological and market conditions through the nineteenth century drove employers to disrupt traditional patterns of production in the name of more efficient and cheaper methods. In London, provincial competition often drove this process. Changes in the production process upset skill boundaries and sexual divisions of labor. More complex divisions of labor also allowed employers to introduce piece rates, which helped drive down costs and encouraged small-scale and home production.[97] Employers divided jobs that had been the preserve of skilled men into smaller, simpler processes. Often some portions of the task would remain men's work, defined as at least semiskilled. Other parts of the job became unskilled women's work.

Though the boundaries between men's and women's work shifted in this process, clearly defined sexual divisions of labor were reestablished. Thus the Royal Commission on the Poor Laws noted: "The excessive subdivision of labour and specialisation of machinery favours the intrusion of women into many trades hitherto occupied by men," but then observed that women were "not, in any considerable trade or process . . . being more largely employed to do work identical with that formerly done by men."[98] Male workers tried to defend their skills or at least their wages against this onslaught, with mixed success. Women workers also faced attacks on their skills and wages, but women in skilled positions were rarely effective at organizing and preserving their positions.

In tailoring, skilled and organized master tailors in the bespoke trade excluded women from the production process in the early nineteenth century. With the expansion of the ready-made clothing business, the position of skilled and organized male workers came under attack. Growing competition undercut these men's ability to preserve their wages and control the production process, as the tailors' defeat in the strike of 1834 illustrates.[99] Manufacturers in the cheaper branches of the trade subdivided the production process, and the sewing machine allowed even greater savings by eroding skills and reducing costs. These employers directed a larger share of the work to poorly paid women. The result, described above, was that women played significant roles, especially in the growing lower-quality branches of tailoring. Women over age twenty made up 32.1% of the tailoring trade in 1871, compared with 21.5% in 1851.[100] However, women continued to be excluded from some processes, such as the cutting out of garments, and these were defined as higher-skilled and better-paid jobs.

Bookbinding, too, had an established division of labor before the nineteenth century. Women performed the preparatory phases of the job, folding pages and sewing them together, while men did the actual binding. Due to mechanization, both men and women faced dilution of their skills. Women bookfolders and sewers faced the pernicious practice of employing large numbers of "learners" as traditional controls over apprenticeship broke down. Their wages deteriorated, and their skills became less valuable with the spread of machines. Male bookbinders faced many of these pressures, but their strong union helped them preserve high wage jobs despite changing technological conditions.[101] Whether men maintained their monopoly on skilled tasks or failed to prevent women from taking over parts of their trade, rigorous divisions of labor survived upheavals during the nineteenth century. The results restricted women to the poorest segments of the trades in work defined as unskilled.[102]

A broadly held assumption underpinned this process: that women should be paid less than men. As the Royal Commission on the Poor Laws reported, women's earnings were "regarded for the most part both by employers and employed as merely supplementary to those of the head of the family and the rate of wages is fixed on this assumption."[103] For employers, women offered a cheap source of labor, making feminization a viable strategy for reducing wages. In addition, low female wages enforced women's dependence within households and increased the prestige of the male breadwinner. Thus, the gendered division of labor, with its corresponding low pay for women, was a fundamental aspect of the organization of capitalist production in late-nineteenth-century London and formed a key feature reinforcing expectations of male privilege and power in poor London households.

The Culture of Female Employment

RHYTHMS OF WORK: SEASONAL AND CASUAL IRREGULARITY

Nearly all the manufacturing trades employing women in these neighborhoods produced finished consumer goods.[104] These trades were subject to seasonal fluctuations typical of London patterns, involving busy periods in early fall and again in spring, with severe slack periods in January and February. For example, the spring busy season for tailors lasted from around March to June, and the fall season peaked in October and November. Similarly, the spring season in dressmaking extended from April to July, with another busy period in October and November.[105]

For those workers employed in workshops or factories, "normal" hours generally ranged from 8 A.M. to 8 P.M. Monday through Friday, and from 8 A.M. to 4 P.M. Saturday. During busy periods, the workday extended, and workers often took work home to finish at night. On the other hand, during slack months, hours were shortened. Other workers, particularly home workers, simply had no work during these slow periods. Estimates of the overall quantity of work available in the tailoring industry suggested that some workers averaged two days' employment per week, while others might get up to three and a quarter days' work in the "average" week.[106]

In some trades, other rhythms added to seasonal variation of demand to create irregular work. For example, the customary weekly schedule of laundry work created demand for different workers on different days. Londoners in the late nineteenth century clung to the practice of beginning the wash on Mondays or Tuesdays, so the clean laundry could be used at the end of the week. The customary schedule meant that workers in different parts of the trade were busy for only parts of each week.[107] Black estimated that most washers worked only two days in the week, while ironers might find employment four or four and a half days.[108] In bookfolding, the monthly press required workers for a few days each month "to meet the emergency." Many of these women did not work in the trade outside these rush jobs.[109] Trimming makers suffered irregular work due to rapid changes in fashion. For example, Booth's survey found that "fringe is out of fashion, and the fringe makers suffer accordingly."[110]

One other source of irregular work affected women in these neighborhoods. Some trades, particularly the silk industry, suffered from a chronic shortage of work, linked to a permanent oversupply of workers. This condition kept wages depressed and made work unsteady.[111] Booth's survey estimated that one-quarter of a weaver's time would be lost due to inadequate demand.[112] Live-in domestic servants form the exception to this pattern of intermittent work; maids-of-all-work faced continuous toil, but charwomen and day servants were often employed casually.[113]

WAGES

Irregular work patterns explain the system of payment common in women's trades. For the most part, women in manufacturing earned piece rates and were not paid according to the hours they worked. Payment by the piece formed a central feature of the sweated system of production. In the clothing trades, the introduction of payment in this manner was a result of the defeat of tailoring workers in an 1834 strike.[114] In laundry work, methods of payment varied. Ironers were generally paid by the piece, while washers in commercial laundries earned time rates, generally including beer, when in relatively steady employment.[115] Most domestic work, such as charring and live-in service, paid time wages, as piece rates could not apply. Live-in servants earned small salaries, generally calculated on an annual rate, beyond their room and board.[116] But outside domestic work, most women workers in these areas earned piece rates.[117]

Paying workers by the piece rather than for their time offered employers significant advantages. The biggest boon to employers whose workers earned piece rates was that they only paid when work was available. In workshops, employees earned nothing while they waited for new orders. In addition, homework was made possible by piece rates. Workers paid by the hour must be supervised to ensure that they keep at their work. However, when workers earned piece rates, employers did not need to watch over them, thus permitting the sweated system of decentralized production to spread. In this system, employers eliminated the cost of the workshop and supervision; giving work out to home workers could reduce expenses significantly.[118]

Though calculating average figures for women's earnings would be useful, developing accurate wage figures is impossible. Even within a particular occupation, piece rates varied tremendously. These pay rates adjusted quickly to fluctuations in the demand for work or for labor. They were higher in busy seasons and dropped significantly during slack periods. Piece rates might also vary according to the location of the work. In artificial-flower manufacture, for example, higher rates were paid to those working in workshops than to home workers.[119] Finally, piece rates differed from employer to employer in the same district at the same time. One observer of the brush-drawing trade noted: "There is no uniformity of payment; it all depends, they tell you, on the shop you work for."[120] These variations in piece rates, combined with irregularity of employment, make "normal" or average wages impossible to determine.

Nonetheless, some broad estimates of female earnings can be made. Schmiechen estimates that an average wage for "a woman regularly employed full-time in the clothing trades in the middle and late 1880's" was 11s. per week.[121] In laundry work, washers might earn 2s. to 2s. 6d. for a full day's work, while ironers could earn 3s. to 3s. 6d. on a good day. But weekly and seasonal irregularity in the trade meant that these wages would not be consistent throughout the year.[122] In bookfolding and sewing, the particularly complete information from one firm presented by MacDonald offered annual weekly wages from 8s. 10d. to 10s. 11d. for the years 1885–99.[123] Women machinists and fitters in the footwear trades also earned approximately 10s. to 13s. for a full week's work.[124] Thus, an acceptable estimate of average earnings for full-time work in common female trades was 10s. to 14s. per week. However full-time employment was rare for women in these neighborhoods. Part-time or casual workers probably earned around 3s. or 4s. per week in sweated trades.[125] Overall, weekly women's earnings in these neighborhoods generally ranged from about 3s. to perhaps 14s., though most women probably earned closer to the lower figure due to the inconsistency of employment opportunities.

LOCATION OF WORK

London women worked in a variety of settings—in their own homes, in their employers' homes, in workshops and factories, and in the streets. The location of work depended both on the particular occupation and on a woman worker's age and marital status. Laundry and most common forms of manufacture in these three areas could be done at home. The most comprehensive information available on work locations comes from the 1901 census reports, which list information for all of England and Wales. The national figures underestimate the prevalence of homework in the metropolis, because factory production was more common outside London, while home and small workshop manufacture typified the London economy.[126] In some trades, such as boot and shoe manufacture or silk manufacture, factory production in the provinces skews the figures away from homework, though the London segments of the trades likely had a far higher proportion of home workers. Nonetheless, the figures offer useful comparisons among trades (table 3-4).

Homework offered the advantages to employers described above, but the 1901 figures also show a marked preference for homework on the part of married and widowed women. For many women with families, working at home offered the only viable way to integrate employment with domestic duties. Workers employed in workshops often moved into homework upon marriage.[127] But balancing homework with the domestic duties of a wife and mother was far from convenient. Home workers often faced longer hours than those who worked in shops or factories. Already overcrowded dwellings became more cramped with the materials needed for work, some of which could be dangerous to the workers and their families. One woman described the experience of living in a room used for drying laundry: "No-one who has not experienced it can imagine the misery of living with a firmament of drying clothes on lines overhead."[128] A final disadvantage of homework was the time spent bringing materials and finished products to and from the shop and waiting for payment or new orders. James Munro of Bethnal Green told the Select Committee on Sweating: "A home worker generally loses one-and-one-half days per week in taking and receiving work from the sweater."[129]

Workshops offered the opportunity for employers to supervise and control workers, and provided space for larger or more expensive machines. Another potential advantage to production in a workshop was secrecy. In trimming manufacture, for example, work on new patterns and samples was not given out to home workers, but was concentrated in the workshops.[130]

Despite the census's statistics, the distinction between these types of settings cannot be rigidly drawn. In busy seasons it was common for those employed in workshops or factories to take work home after hours for completion.[131] In many London sweated trades, small domestic workshops were common. Here small-scale "masters" worked in their own homes, but employed a couple of workers as well. Silk weavers' homes also belie the distinction between home and workshop, as the typical design involved a separate floor for the looms where weaving would take place above the family's dwelling. Thus, only blurred lines divided work at home, in the employer's home, and in a factory or workshop.

AGES AND MARITAL STATUS OF WOMEN WORKERS

Single women living in their parents' homes comprised the largest group of employed women. Overall, 40% of wage-earning women in the areas were under age twenty-five (table 3-5, fig. 3-1). Nearly half of employed women had never been married (48%), 30% were married at the time of the census, and 22% were widows. The census lists 34% of employed women as the daughters of their household heads. The next largest categories were household heads themselves, and wives of household heads, each of which accounted for one-quarter of employed women.[132]

In some trades, the breakdown of workers resembled this general pattern. However, other occupations employed demographically distinctive populations. Some employed many older women. In other cases, mostly young women worked in a trade. These patterns suggest that women changed

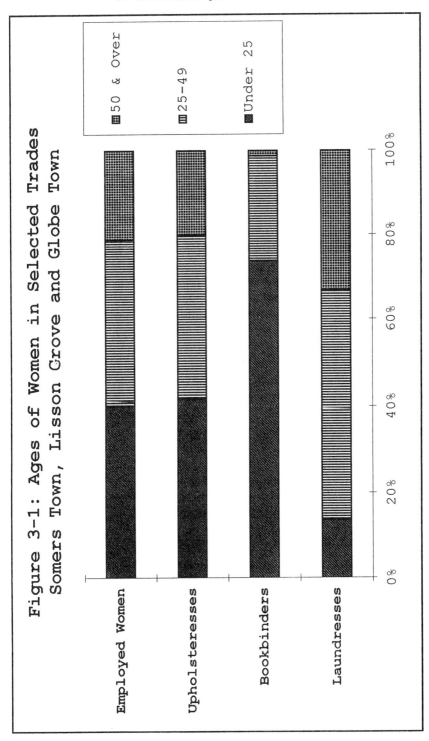

Figure 3-1: Ages of Women in Selected Trades Somers Town, Lisson Grove and Globe Town

jobs during their lives, and a pattern of life-course-specific occupations appears to have existed.[133]

Upholstery and mantle making exemplify trades in which the ages of women workers approximate the general population of employed women. Around four out of ten upholsteresses were between the ages fifteen and twenty-four, and a similar proportion of mantle makers fit this age group. Among all employed women in the three neighborhoods, 40% were between fifteen and twenty-four (table 3-6, fig. 3-1). Around half the women in each of these trades, and in the employed female population at large, were under age thirty.[134] These trades exemplify the "normal" demographic pattern in the female labor force.

In contrast, 70% of women in boot and shoe manufacture were between ages fifteen and twenty-four.[135] Similarly, three out of four female workers in the bookbinding trades, and 63% in trimming manufacture, were under age twenty-five (table 3-6, fig. 3-1). The tendency, discussed above, of bookbinding employers to hire many learners and dismiss experienced full-wage earners helps explain the youth of this workforce. Box making (65% under twenty-five) and general domestic service (76% under twenty-five) were also trades with unusually young female workforces.

On the other hand, some trades attracted an older workforce. Among laundresses, few were under age twenty-five and only 5% were between fifteen and nineteen (table 3-6, fig. 3-1). But over half the laundresses were between twenty-five and forty-nine, and a third were fifty or over. Female silk workers were also older on average than the general population of employed women.[136]

Often, particular characteristics of the trades account for unusual age distributions. For example, the situation of live-in domestic servants made it nearly impossible to continue in this occupation if a woman wanted to marry or have a family. Jobs such as laundry work, more suited to working at home, employed older, married women. The age of the silk-working population likely reflects the long decline of this trade in Globe Town. Few young women entered the trade, but those who had woven silk for decades continued to do so. These factors led to the development of women's mobility between trades over the course of their lives, as they responded to changing responsibilities and opportunities for employment. Young single women living at home often worked in workshops, for example in the boot and shoe trade. Married women were more likely to work at home, perhaps in the same occupation, or turn to laundry work or day domestic service, depending on local opportunities. As they grew older, women became even more likely to take up laundry work at home, though some manufacturing trades also had older female workforces.

Conclusion

Despite local variations, female labor markets in these three neighbor-hoods reflect the shared conditions of London capitalism and sexual in-equality prevalent in the nineteenth century. A persistent division of labor directed women into the least attractive portions of mixed trades. Predomi-nantly female trades shared these poor working conditions and low wages. The organization of these trades offered inconsistent work and thus inter-mittent wages. During peak seasons, women worked extended hours, tak-ing work home if they were employed in a factory or workshop. Yet out-side the busy season, women's wages declined or disappeared. These women formed a convenient surplus of labor on which the sweated system of pro-duction depended; middle-class families took advantage of it to have their domestic work done for them. The rewards paid to these impoverished working women were limited and irregular.

The long hours, low wages, and exploitative conditions suffered by female workers were exacerbated by government policies. Attempts to in-tervene in workplaces having fewer than fifty employees began with the Workshop Act of 1867. This legislation, pertaining to women and children employed outside the home in workshops, principally regulated hours of work. Despite lax enforcement, this act helped drive production out of work-shops and into workers' homes. Amendments enacted four years later did not solve the problems. Ironically, new regulations enacted in 1878 ex-empted workshops employing only female labor. Effective inspection and regulation of workshops in these areas did not commence until around the turn of the century.[137]

Thus, female labor in the sweated trades operated in a regulatory shadow. Large factories were subject to more effective state intervention, and the sweated system expanded to take advantage of the lack of over-sight. The conditions of home and domestic workers were unaffected by government action. The complicity of male workers seeking to protect their positions, employers enforcing perceptions of women's abilities, and an economic and political system that encouraged sweating confined women to the bottom rungs of the labor market. This division of labor left women dependent on male wage earners and weakened their positions in house-holds and domestic relationships.

4

Relentless Labor:
Women's Employment and the Life Course

In April 1881, the census enumerator recorded Emma Knight, living in Lisson Cottages, behind Great James Street, in Lisson Grove. She was forty-five, as was her husband, a carpenter named Joseph. The couple lived with two of their children—Emma, who was nineteen, and Ellen, aged thirteen. Emma and her daughters were among 193 Lisson Grove women employed as dressmakers, earning low wages, and suffering from the irregularity of employment characteristic of female manufacturing work in London. Her experience in the labor market appears fairly typical of women's employment in London poor neighborhoods.

When we consider Emma Knight's position in her household, however, questions arise. As a married woman in a household with three other wage earners, Emma Knight's employment strikes a discordant note with the prevalent view of married women's roles in the late nineteenth century. The withdrawal of married women from paid employment has been advanced as an essential feature of late-Victorian Britain. While the assumption that middle-class wives should shun employment for the joys of domesticity was well established by the last years of the century, some scholars have argued that even among the lower ranks of British society, wives withdrew from paid work.[1] Others have recognized the significance of married women's employment to family economies, but argued that these women sought wages only in times of severe distress. Wage earning formed a stop-gap measure to "tide a family over a period of great poverty."[2] According to this view, poor women accepted the male-breadwinner ideal and felt that the proper role for married women did not involve waged work. It was only "in response to crises" that they violated the separate-spheres ideology and engaged in paid employment.[3]

But the behavior of women like Emma Knight reveals a different pattern of paid employment. Despite the division of labor that confined them to poorly paid, unattractive jobs, wage earning formed a regular and accepted part of the experience of poor women in London throughout their lives. They could not realistically expect employment to be a mere interlude, fitting neatly into a few years between childhood and marriage. Women entered the labor force when they were single or widowed. But they also earned wages as married women when their domestic duties were least heavy as well as in cases of extreme poverty. Rather than embrace the separate-spheres ideology and the male-breadwinner ideal, many married women earned wages when their household economies were relatively stable. During these periods of reduced economic strain, these women also faced lighter burdens of household work that allowed such employment.[4] The complementary responsibilities of married women—domestic work and paid employment—dovetailed through their life courses, forming a constant heavy burden of labor.

The widespread assumption that married women were driven to earn wages only by economic emergencies must be replaced with an explanation stressing the life course. As an analytical tool, the life-course approach views transitions in people's lives (including decisions to enter or leave paid employment) in the context of their changing family situations.[5] When applied to women's employment, it suggests that factors including age, marital status, relation to other household members, and the type of family in which they lived formed key determinants shaping women's lives. In most cases, the domestic responsibilities faced by women in different life-course positions shaped their wage earning.[6] The periods in married women's lives in which domestic work made the greatest claim on time and energy were also the moments of most severe financial hardship. Yet wives were least likely to seek paid employment in these years. The accepted responsibilities of married women included both unpaid domestic work and wage earning. The balance between them was determined to a great extent by women's life-course positions, not simply by the demands of economic crises.

Were Married Women Employed?

The manuscript census, with information on each individual and household, offers the most exhaustive and richest source on employment and household structures. But this source presents certain problems related to the likely underrepresentation of women's employment.[7] Absolute figures derived from the census do not provide reliable information on the total participation of women in wage earning. But the schedules do allow us to compare the participation rates of women in different household situations and at various points in their life courses.

Even using the census's deflated figures, it is clear that a significant portion of London women did not give up wage earning upon marriage. Overall, 22.8% of married women in Somers Town, Lisson Grove, and Globe Town were engaged in employment regular enough to be listed by the census enumerators.[8] It is impossible to determine accurately how many more were engaged in informal wage-earning activities, were temporarily not employed on census night, earned wages only in winter or summer (and thus were not employed on census night in April), or simply had their employment denied by their husbands or the enumerators. Wage earning by married women, then, was neither extraordinary nor unusual. Married women were most commonly employed before they turned twenty or after age forty (table 4-1, figure 4-1), so those who were between twenty and forty in 1881 were probably employed at other times during their married lives. Indeed, one historian has estimated that the percentage of married women listed in the census as employed reflects about half the total of women who were employed full-time at some point during their marriages.[9] When we include the casual and part-time wage earning so prevalent in these neighborhoods, it is clear that employment was common among married women.

The Determinants of Women's Employment

Women's labor-force participation reflects complex decisions of individuals. Perhaps the most important set of issues shaping women's decisions to earn wages involved the composition of their households. As the fundamental economic units in poor neighborhoods, households shaped strategies of earning and spending, within culturally defined norms and expectations. Individual interests did not disappear within households, and conflict among household members over resources and privilege were common, but every individual's economic role can best be understood by considering his or her position in a household economy. The understanding of women's employment patterns through their life courses must remain sensitive to the significance of household structures and economies.

SINGLE AND WIDOWED WOMEN

Even historians who deny married women's participation in waged work recognize the prevalence of employment among single and widowed women.

This pattern offers a useful starting point for the explanation of women's employment stressing their life-course positions. Among single adult women, employment was common regardless of age. Overall, three-quarters of single adult women in the three neighborhoods were employed.[10] Of course, most single women were young; about half of all adult single women were between ages fifteen and nineteen, and 73.6% of these were employed on census night in 1881. In every adult age group up to sixty to sixty-four, better than seven of ten single women were employed. The highest proportion of employed single women was among forty- to forty-four-year-olds, 88.2% of whom were employed.

As young adults, single women generally lived with their parents; 82.3% of unmarried fifteen- to nineteen-year-old women were daughters of their household heads, and nearly three-quarters of them were employed. For example, at no. 60 Aldenham Street in Somers Town, seventeen-year-old Lucy Godden lived with her parents, James and Lucy. Her forty-nine-year-old father was employed as a carpenter, and her mother, who was aged forty-five, worked as a dressmaker. Lucy, who like both her parents was born in the parish of St. Pancras, was also employed as a dressmaker.

As she grew older, the single woman might move out on her own, becoming the head of a household, in which case she was very likely to be employed. Overall, 7.3% of adult single women were household heads, and 85.0% of them were employed. Two-thirds of the single female household heads lived by themselves. Mary Mullins was born in St. Marylebone, thirty-five years before the census of 1881 counted her. She was unmarried, and lived on her own in Highworth Street, Lisson Grove. Mary also worked as a dressmaker.

At times, single women lived with siblings who headed households. These sisters of household heads accounted for 3.7% of adult single women. They were slightly less likely than most single women to be employed, but still, 69.6% of them earned wages. For example, Ellen Hopton lived with two of her brothers in North Street, Globe Town. None of the siblings was married. Her older brother, John Hopton, listed by the census as the household head, worked as a foreman at the docks. John was fifty-five years old. Ellen, who was fifty-three at the time of the census, was employed as a tailoress, and her forty-eight-year-old brother, Abney, served as a commercial clerk. All three were born in Mile End. Overall, a high proportion of adult single women were employed, regardless of their age or position in the household.

The same was true of widowed women, who also commonly earned wages in all age groups. Overall, 69.8% of widows were employed, including nearly three-quarters of those widows under age sixty. It is only later in life, above age sixty, that the proportion of widowed women who were employed drops, to 64.6% among sixty- to sixty-four-year-olds, and 47.7% among widows aged sixty-five and over.

Most widows (80.0%) were the heads of their own households. Nearly three-quarters of these widowed household heads (73.4%) were employed, which is not surprising, given the severe financial difficulties facing female-headed households in these neighborhoods. At no. 32 Pleasant Place, Globe Town, the widow Mary Ann Manis, who was thirty years old, lived with her three children. She had two sons: William, aged thirteen, and John, aged eleven. Her daughter, Mary Elizabeth, was nine. None of the children was employed, and Mary Ann worked as a needlewoman. Maria Smith, a widow born in St. Marylebone, lived in Hereford Street, Lisson Grove, with her three children. The two oldest—John, who was eleven, and nine-year-old Ada—attended school. Her youngest daughter was a year old. Maria struggled to keep her household economically solvent by working as a charwoman.

Widows sometimes lived with their married children. Among widows aged sixty-five or older, 16.9% were either the mother or mother-in-law of their household head. These older widows who lived with adult children were less likely to earn wages. Only about a quarter of them (26.0%) were listed as employed by the census. Jane Wells, a seventy-four-year-old widow born in Hampshire, lived in Bridgewater Street, Somers Town, with her daughter and son-in-law, Sarah and Charles Harris, and their children. Charles worked as a costermonger, and thirty-three-year-old Sarah was employed as a laundress. The five children, all born in St. Pancras, included fifteen-year-old Sarah, who was employed as a shell worker. The four younger children, a girl and three boys, ranged in age from thirteen to five. Jane Wells was not employed, but probably managed the household while her daughter did laundry work.

MARRIED WOMEN

While most historians have agreed that life-course factors such as age and marital status shaped single or widowed women's employment, the influence of these factors has not been recognized as the major determinant of married women's wage earning. As noted above, historians who acknowledge wage earning by working-class wives have stressed that such employment was exceptional, a temporary measure to maintain the family during an economic emergency. This argument misses the key influence of changing domestic responsibilities facing married women in different life-course positions. These burdens shaped wives' employment even when their families were not in economic crises.

The Life Course

The pattern of married women's employment in different age groups reveals that these women were employed most frequently when they were under age twenty or aged forty and above (table 4-1, fig. 4-1). In all three neighborhoods, the age group with the highest proportion of employed married women was the youngest (ages fifteen to nineteen). This figure declined in the age groups covering the twenties and thirties, particularly in the thirty- to thirty-four-year-old age group, and rose again above age forty.

The life-course explanation that married women's employment was shaped to a considerable extent by family structure contradicts the view that married women only sought paid work in times of severe economic crisis. Those stages of the life course during which domestic responsibilities placed the greatest burdens on women corresponded to the most difficult periods economically. Conversely, when domestic work was lightest, the household was also likely to be in the strongest economic position. Thus, married couples without children had limited financial needs, and the requirements of domestic work were relatively low. However, when a couple had young children who did not contribute to the household economy but consumed resources, the family's financial burdens rose. Wally Seccombe describes this as the "phase of peak drain in the family cycle."[11] At the same time, the amount of domestic work necessary to care for these children added to the responsibilities of the working-class wife and mother. When children joined the labor force and contributed to the household economy, the family's economic position improved. Older children, particularly girls, helped their mothers with the housework, thus reducing their domestic labor.[12] When economic need was most severe, domestic responsibilities were likewise heaviest. Conversely, when domestic work was relatively light, the household was in a comparatively strong economic position (see table 2-11).[13]

The argument that wives earned money only in times of "crisis" in the family economy suggests that wives were employed most often when their families' economic need was greatest. If her husband was employed, even if his wages were low and somewhat irregular, a wife with no dependent children would be more likely to be able to balance the household budget without entering the labor force than would her neighbor with young children

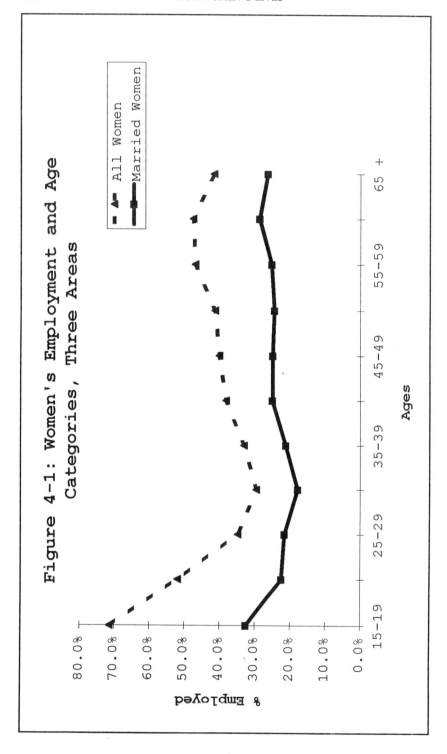

Figure 4-1: Women's Employment and Age Categories, Three Areas

at home. Thus the theory that extraordinary economic straits motivated married women's employment would predict that such employment should be rarest among married women with no dependent children, and most common among those with dependent children at home (when the families' economic status was most precarious).[14]

Data from the three areas, however, reveal that wives were least likely to be employed when they had children living with them and their household responsibilities were heaviest, though the economic position of their household was weakest. Conversely, at those moments when households were most solvent without their income, married women were most likely to earn wages. These findings are illustrated by the inverse relationship between employment of married women and the number of coresident offspring (table 4-2). While 28.5% of wives with no children at home were employed, this portion declines with additional children, reaching a low of 15.4% of those with four or more coresident offspring. The more children she had living at home, the less likely a married woman would be employed.

Another measure of a household economy's viability involves the percentage of household members who earned wages, reflecting the ratio of wage earners to the number of household members. A low percentage indicates few contributors to the domestic economy, but many mouths to feed, while a high ratio indicates a more stable relationship between the numbers of earners and consumers in a household. Married women in households with relatively high percentages of other earners, and thus more promising economic situations, were most likely to earn wages themselves (table 4-3).[15] In households with low percentages of other earners, married women were unlikely to earn wages, even though these households would appear to face more severe economic conditions.

A more sophisticated breakdown of family types reinforces this view, and suggests that family structure and life-course factors exerted a major influence on married women's employment. If we divide family life into seven stages, taking into account the age of the wife, the number of coresident offspring, and the employment of those offspring, we again find that wives were employed most commonly when the ratio of earners to expenses was highest (table 4-4, fig. 4-2).[16] Women with no children (type 1 or 6), with a single son or daughter over age twenty (also type 6), or with more wage-earning children than nonearning offspring living at home (type 5) were most likely to be employed. Older wives were also frequently employed, though less often in Somers Town. In all three areas, when the household economy should have been most stable, and economic emergencies rarest, many wives were employed. On the other hand, those with a single very young child (type 2) or with only nonearning children (type

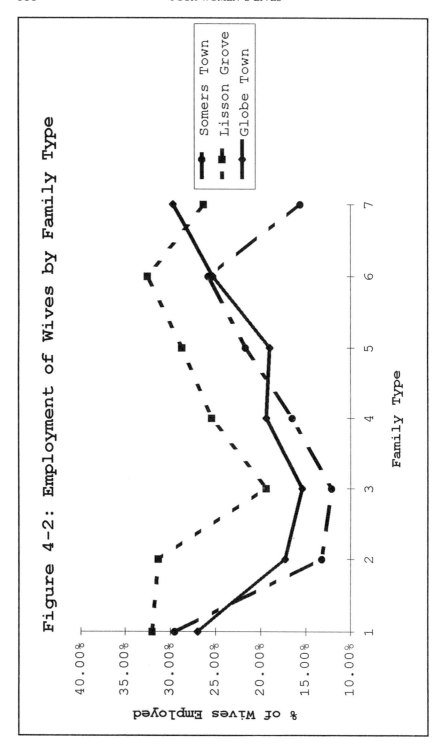

Figure 4-2: Employment of Wives by Family Type

3) were least likely to be employed. Those moments at which the household economy was most likely to suffer economic crises (types 2 and 3) correspond to the times at which wives were *least* likely to be employed.[17]

Some examples illustrate these patterns. William and Ellen Shorting lived at no. 8 Devonshire Place in Lisson Grove. William, aged twenty-two, worked as a carman. His wife, Ellen, also twenty-two, earned wages as a milk carrier. The two lived by themselves and exemplify a type 1 family. About three blocks away in Burne Street lived the Deans, a type 3 family. Thomas Dean, a thirty-year-old carman, and his wife Fanny Dean, twenty-eight, lived with their three children. The oldest, six-year-old William, attended school, as did four-year-old Thomas. The baby, Lucy, was a year old. The census reports that none of these children was employed, nor was Fanny. William and Hannah Crow lived by themselves at no. 41 Stafford Street, about four blocks west of the Deans. William, aged forty-eight, also worked as a carman, while forty-seven-year-old Hannah did needlework. The Crows fit family type 6.

Though it is impossible to determine the exact wages earned by these residents of Lisson Grove, William Shorting, Thomas Dean, and William Crow all worked as carmen, and probably earned comparable wages. The Deans had to support a family of five on Thomas's earnings alone. In contrast, the Shortings and Crows had to support only the two adults. Yet of the three wives, Ellen Shorting and Hannah Crow were employed, while Fanny Dean was not. Of course, the burden of domestic work fell harder on Fanny Dean, caring for her husband and three young children, including baby Lucy, compared with Ellen Shorting and Hannah Crow, who managed households of two adults. The Crow and Shorting families appear less likely to have faced economic crises than the Deans, yet the Crow and Shorting women entered the labor market.

In Somers Town, three families headed by cabinetmakers also exemplify this pattern. John and Sarah Gentry, who lived at no. 26 Drummond Crescent, fit into family type 1. Thirty-one-year-old John worked as a cabinetmaker, while his wife, two years older than he, earned wages as a needlewoman. About a block north of the Gentry household, John and Elizabeth Hodge lived in Clarendon Square with their two daughters, Elizabeth, aged three, and Maria, only two months old. John also worked as a cabinetmaker, while Elizabeth was not employed, according to the census. This family exemplifies family type 3. John and Clara Munro lived in Charles Street, around the corner from both the other families. John was a cabinetmaker who also worked as a house decorator. Clara was fifty-two, six years older than her husband, and worked as an upholsteress. The couple lived by themselves, falling into family type 6.

In West Street, Globe Town, we find John and Sarah Ann Selwood. John, a boot maker, was born in Bethnal Green, and was twenty-eight. His wife was an eighteen-year-old trimming maker, working with beads. A couple of blocks north, in Pleasant Place, Henry and Rosa Purchase lived with their three sons—Henry, aged eight; William, aged five; and Albert, a two-year-old. Henry also worked as a boot maker, while Rosa was not employed. South of Green Street, in Tuscan Street (Charles Street), lived Robert and Mary Ann Lyons, who both worked as boot makers, as did their fifteen-year-old son, Albert. They also lived with their daughter Frances, a twenty-one-year-old tailoress, and her youngest brother, Joseph, aged eleven. The Selwoods fit family type 1, the Purchases type 3, and the Lyons family type 5.

Regardless of whether the household head worked in road transport, furniture manufacture, or the footwear industry, or whether the families lived in Lisson Grove, Somers Town, or Globe Town, economic strain alone cannot explain these patterns. In each neighborhood, those with young children at home (type 3 families) were likely to face the greatest financial difficulties. The Deans in Lisson Grove and Purchases in Globe Town lived off the earnings of the husbands and fathers, lone breadwinners in families with two adults and three small children. The Hodges in Somers Town faced a situation only slightly less precarious, with two adults and two children supported by John's earnings as a cabinetmaker. Yet the wives in these families were not employed. In contrast, wives were employed in families with lighter domestic burdens, or with grown, employed children who could be expected to help out around the house and contribute to the household budget. All these examples, reflective of the figures shown in table 4-4, cast doubt on the accuracy of an explanation of married women's employment based on economic emergencies and provide evidence for the importance of household structure in shaping married women's employment.

The decision to seek waged work appears to have been shaped principally by the demands of domestic work in the household. But the impact of domestic responsibilities was not utterly devoid of economic considerations. The decision to withdraw from employment likely reflects a sensitivity to the benefits to the household economy of domestic work as compared to those of waged work. In all types of families, wives who concentrated on domestic work could save money by shopping for bargains, negotiating more effectively with merchants, and spending more time preparing meals from cheaper foods.[18] When the household included young children, the relative value of this "domestic ingenuity" rose. As the domestic work necessary to sustain their families increased, the relative advantages of full-time domestic work as opposed to waged work grew, and many women withdrew from the labor force temporarily. As their children grew older and began to help with the domestic work, these women again earned wages. Thus, life-course factors formed a key determinant of married women's employment.

Other Factors

Though household structure played an important and underestimated role in shaping married women's labor-force participation, other influences also helped determine whether or not married women sought paid work. A woman's employment decision was formulated in the context of her personal situation, conditions in her household, and within her particular neighborhood economy. These factors might have included severe poverty, as previous observers have noted, but they also included local economic conditions, women's access to employment and to services, conditions in specific trades, and cultural influences.

The Globe Town silk industry illustrates the influence of local economic conditions on wives' labor-force participation. Wives of silk weavers were employed more often than the wives of household heads in any other common occupation in these neighborhoods. Of 199 silk weavers' wives, 82 were employed (41.2%). Weavers and their wives often both worked looms, and 88% of employed silk weavers' wives worked in the silk trade (70 weavers, 1 silk picker, 1 silk winder). This reflects the particular structure of silk weaving, which maintained some semblance to traditional family production despite changes in the trade. For example, at no. 17 Ames Street, in the heart of what remained of the silk district in Globe Town, Thomas Johns and his wife, Eliza Johns, both wove silk. Thomas was sixty-two, and Eliza was fifty-five. Their children, however, worked in other trades, their son Thomas as a furniture polisher, and young Joseph as an office boy. Life-course factors also partially explain the high rate of employment among wives of weavers. Silk weavers were older than most workers in the neighborhoods, and 68.8% of weavers' wives fit into family types 5, 6, and 7 (compared to 26.2% of all wives).[19] Thus life-course influences would lead us to expect a high level of wives' employment in silk weavers' families.

Wives' decisions to seek paid employment were shaped by their job opportunities and by possibilities for employment of others in their households. For example, in Lisson Grove, 25.0% of wives were employed, while in Somers Town 18.1% of wives earned wages and in Globe Town, 18.9%. The difference between rates of employment was greatest among middle-aged wives. In Lisson Grove, 31.5% of married women between ages forty and fifty-four were employed, compared to 24.5% in Somers Town and 20.9% in Globe Town. In the local labor market around Lisson Grove jobs ordinarily filled by these married or widowed women were widely available. Examples of these jobs include charring and laundry work, important in Lisson Grove, and to a lesser extent in Somers Town, but not so important in Globe Town. In Lisson Grove, these women might have earned wages while their daughters remained at home because of the more common opportunities for older women's employment in the neighborhood. Daughters ages ten to nineteen were least likely to be employed in Lisson Grove. In Globe Town, 37.4% of daughters in this age group were employed, and in Somers Town 33.8% , but in Lisson Grove only 30.3% of these daughters earned wages. The Cates family in William Street illustrates this pattern. Charles Cates was a sixty-year-old cabdriver. His wife, Eliza Cates, also sixty, worked as a laundress. Their daughter, Sarah Cates, aged fifteen, had no occupation according to the census. Local employment opportunities in Lisson Grove appear to have attracted some mothers into the labor market while their teenaged daughters performed unpaid domestic work at home.

Another factor that appears to have exerted influence over married women's labor-force participation was place of birth. A large majority of the populations of these neighborhoods were born in and around London, and 72.2% of wives in the areas were born in the London region.[20] Overall, 21.0% of London-born wives were employed, while 18.2% of those wives born outside the London area were listed as employed by the census. But this small difference underestimates the influence of this factor, as a larger percentage of London-born wives was in type 3 families, in which employment was least likely.[21] In every family type, those wives born in London were more likely to have been employed than wives born outside London. This difference was most pronounced among the younger wives in type 2 and 3 families, when the households included young children (16.7% of these London-born wives were employed, compared to only 12.7% of those born elsewhere).

This disparity may reflect two aspects of London-born women's better integration into their neighborhoods. These women might have had better access to job opportunities through more extensive knowledge of local labor markets and integration into networks of information about these possibilities. Because of the preponderance of casual, temporary, and irregular employment in the areas, these contacts could make it easier to find employment opportunities that could be juggled with domestic work. A new arrival might have fewer opportunities and fewer choices in employment, making her less likely to earn wages.

Also, wives who grew up in the area more likely benefited from established kin or neighborhood relationships through which they could receive help with domestic work such as child-minding. These sources of alternative arrangements for domestic work could free London-born wives to earn wages, even in type 2 and 3 families when they had small children. If, as has been argued above, domestic responsibilities formed a key determinant of wives' wage earning, the impact of domestic help from a mother, mother-in-law, or sister can explain London-born wives' greater labor-force participation.

A small number of households in these neighborhoods can be categorized as lower middle class, by virtue of the household head's occupation as a shopkeeper, civil servant, etc. Those households with pretenses to middle-class respectability were more likely to enforce notions of the impropriety of married women's employment. Every effort might be made to avoid the entrance of wives into the labor market, and if wives in these households were employed, their wage earning would generally have been hidden from the census enumerators. An example of this lower-middle-class respectability is found among policemen. There were forty-three married household heads who worked as policemen in the three neighborhoods. Only one of their wives was employed. Grocers also exemplify the small lower-middle-class presence in the neighborhoods. Of the wives of thirty-four married heads of households who were grocers in the areas, only one was listed as employed. In these cases, wives probably did work in the shop alongside their husbands, but this work was probably not paid, and not admitted to the enumerators. Another way to locate households that can be categorized as middle class is through servant holding. Among wives in servant-holding households, only 8.0% were employed. The elevated standards of middle-class respectability also increased the domestic work of lower-middle-class women if they did not employ servants.[22] It is likely that ideas of middle-class respectability helped shape attitudes in these households and led wives to remain outside the labor force, or deny their work to enumerators.

Economic Influences

Though life-course factors, local labor market conditions, and other considerations influenced married women's employment, it would be inaccurate to discount severe economic need entirely in accounting for these patterns. Though it is impossible to estimate the income and expenses of each household with any accuracy, the occupation of the household head played a great role in determining the financial position of the household.

In some cases, the economic contribution of husbands appears to have influenced the employment patterns of their wives. Overall, 20.1% of wives of employed household heads were themselves employed.[23] Wives of some of the lowest-paid and most casual workers were more likely to seek employment than were wives of other men. For example, among wives of general laborers, who worked in the worst-paid and least regular of occupations (and a quite common one), 27.2% were employed. Similarly, 28% of wives of general porters worked for wages. Though direct comparisons of skill and wage levels among occupations is often difficult, the example of bricklayers and bricklayers' laborers offers a clear contrast. Bricklayers had higher status, were better paid, and probably were more consistently employed than were their laborers.[24] Among the wives of bricklayers' laborers, 34.7% earned wages, compared to 21.7% of wives of bricklayers. These examples show that, in some cases, wives of workers in low-status, poorly paid jobs were more likely to work for wages.

However, this pattern is not consistent across common men's occupations. An 1887 inquiry surveyed wages of workers in St. George's-in-the-East. Though the absolute wage figures must be questioned due to the unreliability of self-reported wages and the casual and seasonal nature of these trades, comparison is possible. Twelve of the occupations were important occupations in the three neighborhoods studied here (table 4-5). Some of the poorly paid husbands' occupations (such as general labor) had a high percentage of employed wives, but husband's wages do not offer a reliable guide to the likelihood of wives' employment. Though railway porters earned the second lowest wages in the survey, only 15.4% of their wives were employed, compared to 20.1% of wives of all employed men.[25] Conversely, bricklayers earned the highest wage among the trades listed, yet slightly more of their wives were employed than the average of all wives of employed husbands. Thus, though we cannot entirely discount the impact of husbands' poor wages on wives' employment, the relation between this factor and married women's employment, essential to the explanation of wives' employment based on economic crises, appears inconsistent.

Even in those trades that seem to enforce the link between poor pay of husbands and wives' employment, family structure shaped these patterns. For example, among wives of general laborers, the pattern of differential rates of employment in various family types holds true (table 4-6). In general laborers' type 3 families, relatively few wives were employed. Conversely, in type 1, 5, and 6 families the highest percentages of wives were employed. F. Petty, who worked with Somers Town women at the St. Pancras

School for Mothers, described the experience of one neighborhood woman: "She knew her husband was only a casual labourer, but as she kept on work[ing] after her marriage, she did not feel his having no regular wage. With an increasing family she had to give up work, and finds it very hard at times."[26] This woman's domestic responsibilities forced her out of the labor force, despite the financial struggles that ensued.

The weakness of the link between husbands' occupations and wives' tendencies to enter the labor force does not, however, eliminate economic need as an influence on women's employment. In the very poorest households, those headed by women, the number of children and the burden of domestic responsibilities become less important than the need to earn some income, and women were likely to seek employment in all types of families. Because of the low pay offered in women's jobs, these households generally suffered from extreme poverty. Their heads were generally widows (75.5% of female household heads were widows), and were often employed despite the domestic burdens they faced. Even in type 3 families, where their domestic responsibilities were greatest, 83.6% of female household heads were employed. Maria Smith, the widowed mother of three young children in Lisson Grove, exemplifies this pattern. She worked at charring in addition to caring for her family. Under the most extreme conditions, when women faced the nearly insurmountable challenge of supporting families without the contribution of an adult male earner, life-course factors played a reduced role in shaping patterns of women's employment. But the employment of wives in these neighborhoods was primarily shaped by their life course and household structure. Other influences included local conditions, employment opportunities in particular occupations, and involvement in local employment and mutual-aid networks.

Conclusion

Employment played an important role in the lives of poor women in London. Nearly all young single women were employed, particularly after leaving school. In some cases, the extent of this employment depended on factors such as their mothers' wage-earning opportunities. If a woman remained single, wage earning would likely be a constant throughout her life, whether she lived on her own, with siblings, or in another household arrangement.

After marriage, women faced constant work. When the effort and time necessary to complete housework were limited, married women often earned wages in the labor force. During these periods women combined unpaid domestic work with wage earning. When domestic responsibilities became too great they were likely to replace wage earning temporarily, despite the rising financial needs of their families.

In leaving the labor force, women did not withdraw from work, or even enjoy a reduced burden of labor. Though it was little appreciated except perhaps by their children, their unpaid domestic work was difficult, and the effective management of a poor household's budget required skill, expertise, and effort. Ross has outlined the "relentless physical labor" expended by poor London mothers in the care of their young children, as well as the benefits to their families of these women's domestic ingenuity.[27] Yet the census enumerators left the "occupation" category blank for these women. This undervaluation of domestic labor as less than real work has persisted. Whether they earned wages as well as managed the household, or concentrated their efforts in domestic work, "relentless" appears to be an appropriate description of the toil facing these women throughout their lives.

These patterns raise the important question of the women's motivation. Why did they seek employment when their financial position was least desperate? Of course, these women worked for the money. But this point does not go far enough, as their need for money was greater when they had young children, but were less likely to be employed. Though it is impossible to know exactly what these women thought, their behavior reflects a culture of female work in these neighborhoods. Women simply expected to work hard throughout their lives.[28] When it was possible, given their domestic responsibilities, this work would be in paid employment, and their wages certainly formed a welcome addition to the household budget. A member of the Select Committee on Sweating, surprised at this attitude, asked Isabella Killick, the East End trouser finisher, "Your husband earned good wages, and you took to tailoring and got something extra?" Killick responded, "I always did do the tailoring; I never liked to sit idle."[29] Another woman gave evidence of this view before a separate parliamentary commission: "[A] woman is looked upon as lazy unless she takes her share in contributing to the family income."[30]

The evidence from Somers Town, Lisson Grove, and Globe Town indicates that women in stable working-class London neighborhoods applied this approach. But London was not England, and London's economic conditions differed from those elsewhere in many respects. Though few other detailed studies of household economies and women's employment exist, there appears to be considerable regional variation. Karl Ittman found that in Bradford, "women worked in large numbers before marriage; once they married, however, their involvement in wage labor began to decline." Married women in older age groups were less likely to be employed than were their younger married neighbors. Even once the children grew up, "the mother's monetary contribution continued to decline."[31] In contrast, Richard Whipp argues that "women pottery workers remained at work not only beyond adolescence but more especially beyond their twenties."[32] These women, like poor London women, expected to earn wages whenever it was possible throughout their lives. Only further research will show how typical women in London and the Potteries were.

This culture of work, including paid employment, contrasts sharply with the norms of middle-class culture in this period, dominated by the domestic ideal in which respectable wives did as little work as possible, and certainly did not earn wages.[33] It also challenges the idea that working-class women accepted a notion of a female sphere that did not include paid work. Rather than try to avoid paid employment, these women expected to earn wages whenever their other responsibilities allowed it. Such employment did not violate principles of domesticity or working-class gender roles, because it was consistent with the general expectations of women's behavior—that they would work hard throughout their lives. Work, paid and unpaid, was an accepted and expected, though not always recognized or appreciated, component of poor women's lives.

5

"The Ills I Had to Bear":
Gender, Power, and Well-Being

In a manner typical of the autobiographies of her working-class contemporaries, Grace Foakes emphasized her mother's importance to her Wapping childhood: "My whole life centred around my mother."[1] While her mother's hard work and Foakes's affection for her are manifest, she also observed the relationship between her parents: "Father worked when there was work available and was the head of the household. He controlled the running of it and the conduct and behavior of the children . . . I write much about my mother, as it was she who was always there, but she had little say in anything."[2]

The nature of family relationships and the positions of men and women in households form key issues in the study of women's lives through history. Scholars have debated the impact of capitalism and industrialization on women's positions, coming to widely varying conclusions.[3] One view, conveniently described as the "pessimist" position, claims that industrialization disrupted a family economy in which men and women had both performed productive, valued labor. By disconnecting home and work and depriving women of their significant role in resource production, capitalist industrialization doomed women to powerless domesticity. The male-breadwinner ideal became the norm, and, as a result, women's positions in households deteriorated.[4]

The "optimists" argue, in contrast, that industrialization brought expanded opportunities for women's wage earning. Access to independent earnings caused a significant improvement in the status of both single and married women. Edward Shorter argues: "The weekly wage packet turned into a weapon in the struggle for domestic power. . . . And this new economic strength would help serve married women to lever themselves into a higher social status *vis-à-vis* the men around them."[5] Both the optimists and pessimists agree that productive labor brings status in the household. Those who earn wages (for the optimists) or who are integral parts of the family economy (for the pessimists) can claim power in households. The major disagreement concerns whether the advent of industrial capitalism increased women's access to such economic opportunities or decreased it, thus improving women's positions or causing them to deteriorate.

The experience of poor women in late-Victorian London appears potentially consistent with the view of the optimists. These women earned wages in their local labor markets much of their lives. The optimist position suggests that they should have been in strong positions in their domestic relationships, as their wages would provide the weapons to undercut male domestic power. But despite their wage earning, women among the London poor suffered under conditions of severe gender inequality.[6] Their employment did not undercut patriarchy, and their husbands enjoyed power and privilege.

The vast majority of women lived in families, as daughters, sisters, mothers, and wives, while few lived on their own. In Somers Town, Lisson Grove, and Globe Town, only 2.8% of women between the ages of fifteen and fifty-nine lived alone.[7] Unsteady employment and low pay enforced by the division of labor caused almost certain impoverishment for those outside a family structure. Women among the London poor were thus more anxious to get married than were men.[8] Ironically, this lack of alternatives also weakened women's positions within their households, making them dependent upon men and enforcing unequal domestic relationships.[9]

Rarely did jobs open to women pay wages adequate for even single women without dependent children to make ends meet on their own. Earning and expense data presented above allowed for a broad estimate of 6s. per week for work in common women's jobs. The household budgets described above indicate that rental of one room might cost about 3s. 6d. per week, while an estimated 2s. 6d. would be devoted to the food and other needs of an adult woman. Thus, in theory, a single woman could just balance her domestic budget and potentially live outside the family structure.

However, this ignores cultural expectations and the material benefits of family life. Most commonly, single women lived with their parents before marriage, turning their wages over to their mothers as contributions to the household budget. Elizabeth Roberts attributes this to the moral authority of parents, and clearly this factor affected young women's willingness to contribute to their parental households.[10] The precariousness of their financial positions also influenced this pattern. Parental families offered essential support for young single women.

The ability to stretch 2s. or 3s. per week into an adequate food budget for an adult woman depended upon savvy shopping and bargaining with merchants and time-consuming food preparation. An "independent" young woman would lose the advantages of sharing domestic work with her mother and sisters and no longer benefit from the savings produced by her mother's domestic ingenuity. As Ellen Ross notes: "Mother's aptitude for bargaining with the pawnshop assistant, the shopkeepers and the school board visitors; her domestic arts; her friendship with the landlady—all were worth solid cash."[11]

In addition, though a steady wage of 6s. might prove adequate, it was unlikely that young women could count on regular earnings at this level. Within her parental household, the irregularity of her wages might be offset by other earners in the family. On her own, the erratic wages paid in female occupations presented a more serious problem. Thus, only 1.4% of single women between the ages fifteen and twenty-nine in these areas lived by themselves. Single men in this age group were more than twice as likely to live on their own, but this still means only 3.1% of them.[12]

Mothers of dependent children in poor neighborhoods were even less able to support themselves. The meager and irregular wages paid to women made mothers and their young children dependent on husbands and fathers. Without a portion of the higher wages paid to men, families relying on women wage earners were almost certain to fall into poverty. Booth's survey found that 74% of those living in female-headed households in East London were in poverty, compared with 35% of the total population.[13] The gendered division of labor enforced women's need to live with male earners, making marriage nearly essential.[14]

For both men and women among the urban poor, setting up a household as a married couple offered practical and emotional advantages over the alternatives. For men, though, access to better jobs than those open to women made life outside these domestic relationships economically feasible. Even considering irregularity of work and wages, men's earnings usually exceeded the 6s. estimated as the minimum for an individual to survive on his or her own. Though men could live outside families, most of them chose to marry, and they enjoyed privileged positions in these relationships. Because of their different positions in the local labor markets, men and women entered domestic relationships in unequal positions. This inequality in households compromised women's welfare.[15]

Cultural imperatives reinforced these patterns within households. The attitudes and expectations of neighbors and family members exerted a powerful influence over men and women. Women were expected to marry and to place the highest priority on the welfare of their husbands and children. Carl Chinn argues: "Nearly all mothers of the urban poor were united by an adherence to an ideal of motherhood in which self-sacrifice was the dominant notion."[16] Entrenched ideas and economic realities made the health and potential earnings of husbands protected resources in the family economy. Even when men were out of work, and despite the value of women's work to the survival of their families, men's potential contributions were seen to be more important than those of women.[17] This idea gave men a privileged status in households at women's expense.

But this gender inequality is multifaceted and difficult to measure or document.[18] One way to evaluate women's status is in terms of their "well-being." By examining the conditions of women's lives, we gain insight into both their power and the oppression they suffered.[19] Women's access to and control over resources and their share in leisure and work form essential components of well-being. The physical welfare of women must be considered, as well as the authority they enjoyed and the respect given them. Such an analysis reveals the nature of gender relations in poor London households.

Access to and Control over Resources

Men and women living together in domestic relationships were expected to fulfill certain responsibilities. Women managed the domestic sphere, while men were expected to provide a financial contribution to the household budget. The husband generally turned over part of his weekly earnings to his wife for familial expenses. William Harding, a laborer living in Christ Church Residences, Lisson Grove, left work on Saturday, "came home and gave her [his wife] some money with which she paid the rent, stocked the house with food, purchased some things for the children, and took clothes of her husband out of pawn."[20] George Acorn reports that his father turned over 18s. per week to his mother, whenever he earned enough. Acorn's mother was then expected to provide food for the family and manage the household budget to supply its needs.[21] In Somers Town, Charles Samuel Thomas, a forty-six-year-old pianoforte maker of Clarendon Street, when charged with assaulting his wife, Catherine, testified that he came home from work and gave her 14s. 6d. to keep house for the week. Charles William Hambling, a cabman, claimed that he gave his wife 2s. or 2s. 6d. per day. Clara Kane of Johnson Street reported that her husband, an upholsterer, gave her 14s. per week.[22]

The contribution to family finances constituted the principal responsibility of husbands. The centrality of this contribution to the definition of a good husband is illustrated by William Harding. After he gave his wife a portion of his earnings, the two began to quarrel, and Harding attacked his wife with a fire poker. But in court he stressed that he had turned over money to his wife directly upon being paid on Saturday. Despite the violence, the court determined that his wife was to blame, and she agreed.[23] Hester Lee, living in Devonshire Street, Lisson Grove, exemplifies the flip side of this perception. When she finally sought a separation from her husband, James, she claimed that he was often out of work and when he did earn money, "he spent it on himself."[24]

Frequently, the husband's contribution would be inadequate to supply the needs of the household, and the wife faced the responsibility for balancing the household budget through the contribution of employed children, her own earnings, or other means. Women controlled their own earnings and at least part of those brought in by employed children living at home.[25] With these resources, she managed the financial life of the household. Karen Oppenheim Mason has argued that such control over resources forms a key factor in evaluating gender inequality.[26]

Yet significant limitations reduced the efficacy of women's control over these funds in improving their position. While women determined how money would be spent, the reality of poverty in these neighborhoods made this responsibility a burden more than a source of power. Because she was in charge of family finances, shortfalls became her problem. John Blake recalled his father's approach: "When he handed over his quota to Mum, and he had kept a small amount for pocket money, he considered his duty had been carried out, but Mum['s] only started from then, with all the worry of making ends meet."[27] Ross expresses the paradox of women's financial management in poor households: "The arrangement gave wives considerable domestic power, but it also made them solely responsible for sustaining life under very unpromising conditions."[28] Meanwhile, their husbands "carried on in the accepted manner, blithely unaware of their wives' sufferings."[29] The obstacles facing these women because of their responsibility for the family budget were particularly severe at those stages in the family cycle when they had only young children at home. As discussed above, at these stages family finances were most precarious, yet women's additional domestic responsibilities made it difficult for them to seek their own wages to boost their families' incomes.

In these situations, husbands' regulation of the size of their contributions to the family economy exacerbated the difficulties facing their wives. The amount of money he provided to his wife depended upon a husband's particular tastes, the couple's relationship, and neighborhood norms and customs. The tendency for husbands' domestic contributions to remain stable over the course of married life illustrates wives' lack of independent claims to their husbands' wages. Despite increasing demands on household finances accompanying the presence of young children, husbands often maintained a maximum level of support established early in their marriages. George Acorn's father's contribution remained at 18s. per week despite a growing family and increased expenses.[30] Pember Reeves describes the frustrations of a wife whose husband did not understand the additional difficulties she faced when the couple had a second young child:

> He makes his wife the same allowance, and expects the same amount of food. She has more mouths to fill, and grows impatient because he does not understand that, though their first baby did not seem to make much difference, a boy of three, plus a baby, make the old problem into quite a new one.[31]

While unstable earnings meant that this contribution was reduced in times of slack work or unemployment, increases in wages often did not result in augmented family budgets.[32] Thus wives faced higher expenses without their husbands' contributing more to the household. The husband's ultimate control over his wages leads Wally Seccombe to conclude that, despite their management of the domestic budget, "women did not 'control the purse strings' in any meaningful sense."[33]

These patterns operated in the context of cultural conditions that limited women's share of resources. This phenomenon is most apparent in the allocation of food among family members. Inequalities in diet between men and women in poor families have been well documented.[34] Fathers and husbands received larger quantities of food and more regular meat than did mothers and daughters. In Alice Linton's poor London household, the father had butter on his bread, while the rest of the family made do with margarine.[35] Joseph Williamson recalled of his mother: "She would sit at table watching us eat, and she would make little balls of dry bread and put them in her mouth. . . . I cannot remember her having a proper meal with us when we were children." Observers in St. Pancras noted "the extraordinary tendency of women to starve themselves."[36]

One might argue that this merely reflected the greater caloric needs of men, but the often large differences in food consumption persisted when wives were pregnant and breast-feeding. At these times, women's nutritional needs were comparable to those of men, but their food consumption remained less than that of their husbands.[37] The impact of this differential nutrition can be seen in the death of an infant child of the Bath family, described in chapter 2. Eight children had been born to the couple, but only two survived. The coroner's report attributed the infant's death to his mother's weak condition due to a lack of nourishment.[38]

Ironically, women's nominal control over domestic finances did not lead to improved access to resources, as women themselves enforced this unequal distribution. Women diverted large shares of food, clothing, etc., to their husbands and tried to hide their sacrifice.[39] Pember Reeves described the response of the working-class wife with inadequate household resources: "She decides to feed him sufficiently and to make what is over do for herself and the children."[40] Though women managed household budgets, the inadequacy of these budgets and women's own approaches to distributing resources left them shortchanged, giving men a disproportionate share of household resources while women practiced what one observer called "the art of doing without."[41]

Share of Work and Leisure

Besides distributing goods, households allocated responsibilities for work and access to leisure. In these neighborhoods, an unequal share of the work fell upon women. Within families, a division of labor as strong as that in paid employment defined men's and women's responsibilities. This division of obligations required the husband to turn over a reasonable portion of his wages to his wife for application to the household's needs and wives to maintain the household as best they could.

These complementary domestic roles were far from equitable. The more elastic definition of women's duties required domestic work, financial management, and often wage earning as well. This combination of wage earning and domestic responsibilities led Richard Church to describe his mother as "having to live two lives in one."[42] Women's ultimate responsibility for the welfare of their families led them to do whatever was necessary to keep the household afloat. The varied and ingenious strategies women adopted to stave off the effects of poverty on their families were discussed in the second chapter above. The previous chapter showed that women shouldered a double burden of wage earning and domestic work for much of their lives, giving up their earning only when domestic responsibilities grew heaviest. A popular London music hall song recognized, "But when once a girl's wed, / she's a drudge and a slave."[43] One woman quoted by Elizabeth Roberts noted: "The women, they worked and worked. They had their babies and worked like idiots. They died, they were old at forty."[44] John Blake recalled the amazing quantity of work his mother faced: "How it was all done by one pair of hands goodness knows."[45]

Though some men occasionally helped with domestic tasks, the demands of housework fell almost exclusively on women. This gendered division of labor within the household applied to children as well as to parents. It was determined "by authority structures and rules of conduct that dictated that certain tasks could not be asked of men or boys."[46] Housekeeping was women's work, even when the women in the household were employed for many hours during the week. Both men and women in these neighborhoods often worked long hours under difficult conditions in their paid employment. However, paid work was only the beginning of the labor required of women. The arduous tasks required of women at home made their work endless, and their share of the households' labor far greater than that of their husbands.

Despite tremendous obligations placed upon them by the household division of labor, women found time to participate in the vibrant cultures of leisure in poor neighborhoods. In part due to the crowded conditions in their homes, the urban poor sought relaxation outside their homes.[47] Drinking was an important part of life, to the distress of middle-class observers. Though pubs are often considered a male environment, and men did drink with their mates, women also frequented public houses. Those interviewed by Booth's investigators described the situation as "hopeless," and one of the informants complained that Globe Town women were "shameless about going into Public Houses." In Lisson Grove, the Phoenix pub appears to have been particularly popular among women.[48]

In poor London neighborhoods, couples visited pubs together. Ellen Grace, who lived in Aldenham Street, Somers Town, went with her neighbor to a pub in Phoenix Street on a Saturday night in March 1879. There they met their husbands, Joseph Grace, a zinc worker, and John Hopkins, a van driver for the Midland Railway Company.[49] On a Tuesday night in 1879, Ellen Fogg of Devonshire Street went to the Sun in Lisson Street with her husband.[50] In November 1882, Joseph Sutton, a carver and gilder, and his wife, Alice Sutton, who lived in Ely Place, visited the Nelson beer house in Globe Road. There Joseph enjoyed a game of dominoes until a fight broke out.[51] These incidents catch women in Somers Town, Lisson Grove, and Globe Town in their free time, drinking in pubs with their husbands and friends.

Music halls played a growing role in the leisure of working-class Londoners.[52] Lewis Abraham Dyer, living in Tuscan Street, and his new wife, Lydia, went out on a Thursday evening. After going for a walk in the neighborhood and shopping for some furniture, the couple stopped in at the Foresters' Music Hall, in Cambridge Road.[53] While pubs and music halls were important sites for leisure, the streets themselves were also filled with life.

Neighborhood streets were the sites of vibrant activity, sometimes serious, sometimes joyous, sometimes violent. Men and women walked the streets, visited, gossiped, played, shopped, and fought in the streets. Houses were often open to the streets, and women would participate in street life even when in their homes. Observers interviewed by Booth's team complained about the lively street scenes in Lisson Grove. In Manning Place, women stood in their doorways while children played around a fire in the street. In Devonshire Place, doors were open to the street, and women stood at the windows.[54]

Just walking in the streets was a common leisure activity. In John Blake's Poplar neighborhood, residents enjoyed promenading in the East India Dock Road: "Thousands of people congregated there on the 'Weekend Walk.'"[55] Young people made particularly good use of these occasions, dressing in their best clothes and seeking opportunities for romance.[56] Blake recalled: "All the teenagers walked up and down here, and it was known as 'Monkey's Parade.' More romance went on here than in any other part of Poplar."[57] Married adults also found excitement in strolling the streets. James Knowles, a thirty-year-old carman living in Sidney Street, Somers Town, went out walking with his wife. Somehow the two were separated, and she ended up walking with Edward Edwards. When Knowles caught up to his wife and Edwards, he assaulted them both.[58]

Women were integral parts of the lively pub and street culture in these neighborhoods. They stole a few moments in the pub, at their doorways, or in the streets for enjoyment and relaxation. However, women's claims to such leisure were weaker than those of their husbands. Women's access to time and money for their own leisure depended on conditions in the family economy. Expenditure on women's leisure was a luxury. Men reserved their pocket money before their wages were contributed to the household budget. This gave male drinking or other leisure a protected status, despite the financial difficulties facing the family.[59] Even within the cramped confines of the home itself, men's leisure was privileged, as seen in the protection of the father's chair and in wives' attempts to quiet children so they would not disturb their father's rest.[60] When it was necessary, wives sacrificed their leisure to maintain their families; men were not expected to do so. Sometimes, women's leisure would be limited to snatches of conversation and gossip with other women that was integrated into domestic work such as getting water or washing clothes.[61]

The Physical Well-Being of Women

The analysis of the status and position of women must take into account their physical well-being, including health and subjection to physical and sexual domination. The unhealthy conditions in these neighborhoods were highlighted in chapter 2 above. Women in the areas suffered significant and nearly constant health problems. In the years before World War I, investigators found working-class women to be undersized due to poor health and nutrition.[62] Though all residents of these neighborhoods were subject to unhealthy conditions, outside of childbirth women were less likely than their menfolk to receive health care. Poor women suffered persistent ills, ranging from the uncomfortable to the fatal.[63]

Poor nutrition, a major contributor to the ill health of these women, has already been discussed. In environments of poor sanitation and poor health that led to widespread infectious disease, nutrition was crucial in determining who remained healthy and who suffered illness. Tuberculosis, the greatest threat among these illnesses, reflected environmental factors such as diet and sanitation, and may have been exacerbated by repeated pregnancies. Besides increasing susceptibility to bacterial and viral infection, deficient diets led to widespread rickets, which added to complications in pregnancy and childbirth.[64]

These complications occurred in a broader context of reproductive practices in which women had limited access to health care. Orcn argues: "The care that the wives of laborers received during pregnancy and child-birth was seriously deficient."[65] One obstacle preventing these women from receiving decent treatment was the cost. Maternal health expenditures came out of the general domestic budget over which women had control. We have seen mothers' tendencies to ignore their own needs in providing for other family members. These women disregarded their own dietary and other requirements in allocating household resources, and they also ignored medical problems they suffered, particularly during pregnancy. Catherine Pryer, a thirty-nine-year-old resident of Drummond Crescent in Somers Town, died due to hemorrhaging following a miscarriage. She did not see a doctor for nine days after her miscarriage.[66] One working-class woman described her attitude to difficult and painful pregnancies: "I took for granted that women had to suffer at these times, and it was best to be brave and not make a fuss."[67] Another counted this as "one of the ills I *had* to bear."[68] Pregnant women seldom received medical care, even when their pregnancies were difficult and complicated.

Though the care poor London women received during delivery exceeded that of poor women in other cities due to the many medical institutions prepared to serve them, this health care still left much to be desired. Medical students who cared for many poor women during childbirth were notoriously poorly trained in obstetrics before 1896. Some well-trained midwives served poor populations in London, but many births were attended by informally trained "granny" midwives.[69]

These factors made pregnancy and childbirth damaging to women's physical well-being.[70] All observers of poor women in this period agree that "confinements remained, for many women, dangerous, painful and unpleasant."[71] Jane Lewis argues: "Each pregnancy further exacerbated poverty and sickness."[72] Margaret Llewelyn Davies, in her introduction to a collection of letters from working-class women relating to childbirth, noted: "[T]he mere physical strain of pregnancy and childbirth succeeding each other with scarcely an interval for ten or twenty years renders a healthy bodily and intellectual life impossible."[73]

As this passage indicates, the high birthrate in these areas multiplied the physical costs of pregnancy and childbirth. Though fertility rates across the country declined in the last decades of the nineteenth century, among the urban poor fertility remained high.[74] Women had little access to safe and effective birth control and probably could not count on cooperation from their husbands in limiting their fertility.

In the face of the physical and economic cost of repeated pregnancy and childbirth, some women resorted to abortion. It appears that women's attempts to end their pregnancies voluntarily were common.[75] Abortion offered working-class women advantages over other potential methods of family limitation. It did not require the participation of their husbands, which was important because fertility and its regulation were commonly considered women's responsibility.[76] Llewelyn Davies argued: "The habit of taking such [abortifacient] drugs has spread to an alarming extent in many places among working women."[77] Seeking the aid of an abortionist or "using a knitting needle themselves" may have been less common, but all these efforts to control reproduction could be dangerous or even fatal to the women involved.[78]

Recourse to abortion reflects the fact that sex among the urban poor in this period was rarely an arena for mutuality or cooperation. The privacy surrounding the sex lives of men and women in these areas shields this behavior from historians. However, married women clearly did not control their own bodies.[79] Chinn's oral histories reflect that "many men would beat their unwilling wives into agreeing to satisfy their urges."[80] Ross concurs: "Women who would fight furiously over a husband's sixpence spent on drink, would yield regretfully to an unwanted sexual advance."[81] One working-class woman noted that women's sufferings would continue "until he realises that the wife's body belongs to herself," and she complained of laws that enforced practices of "the woman belonging to the man, to have and to own, etc."[82] The lack of control over sexual contact, without safe and effective birth control, compounded the trials and dangers of pregnancy. This sexual domination, at times including the violent imposition of sex on wives, formed a significant component of gender inequality in these neighborhoods.[83]

Though most aspects of poor Londoners' sexual lives remain hidden, marital tension and conflict are more evident to the historian. The separate responsibilities of men and women often created tension within households. If men failed to contribute to the household budget, or if their wives did not keep up the home, quarrels often arose, and violence was a common occurrence in these families.[84] A. S. Jasper reports that his father would complain if his mother did not provide cress with Sunday tea. His mother did not take these complaints calmly, as his father contributed little to the household budget: "She would go berserk and clump the old man for all she was worth."[85] Edward Williams, whose sister was married to John Henry Bugg, a brush maker living in Somers Town, fought with his brother-in-law over Bugg's failure to bring home money to his wife. In the quarrel, Bugg stabbed Williams in the chest and elsewhere.[86]

In Lisson Grove one morning, Henry Parsley, a coachman, gave his wife, Ann, 3d. "to keep her and the children for two days." Ann challenged her husband, pointing out the inadequacy of this paltry sum. The conflict grew and later, in Stafford Street, the two came to blows, and Henry kicked and punched his wife.[87] It is not surprising that Ann Parsley would confront her husband over his contribution to the budget. It appears that the norm for financial contribution when possible was about 14s. 6d. per week, while Parsley's allowance would total less than one shilling over the week.[88] Ann Parsley's case exemplifies what Ross has described as the "sheer despair" facing wives whose husbands failed to provide a decent contribution to the household budget.[89]

In the violence that often accompanied marital conflict, women were not simply passive victims. Often, they defended themselves and their interests aggressively.[90] When Richard Bayes, living in Stephen Street, Lisson Grove, came home drunk and renewed a quarrel with his wife, she fought back. Aided by a friend, Catherine Scanlan, she responded to his threats and beatings violently, and the two women injured Richard "badly."[91] Thomas Morgan, who grew up in South London, reports that his father would strike his mother "like he'd hit a man," but "she'd punch him back and they'd finish up on the floor both of them, punching at one another."[92]

George Acorn's mother also did not suffer abuse or irresponsibility by her husband passively. In a passage cited prominently by Ross, Acorn reports that his mother faced his father with "fierce questions and taunts" when he returned home drunk.[93] In a Somers Town battle over family finances, Mary Ann Winton, of Bridgewater Street, stabbed her husband, who she claimed had beaten her repeatedly over the course of eleven years.[94] In another case, Maria Hold, a forty-five-year-old woman living in Clarendon Square, hit her husband, William, on the head with a fire shovel—under great provocation, she claimed. These women struggled to defend themselves and to attain what was believed to be their right: the man's contribution to the household budget.

Though they sometimes fought back and were occasionally helped by friends or relatives, women were often injured severely by their husbands' beatings. Emma McNally, who lived with George Smith, a shoemaker, in Great James Street, Lisson Grove, was brought into court to testify against him. Her entrance caused a stir among observers in the court, as "her face was one mass of bruises and discolouration, and her eyes almost entirely closed." Smith and McNally had quarreled over a small amount of money, and he locked her in and began beating her with a stick. When she hid under the bed, he continued poking her and striking her with the stick.[95] Mary Ann Catlin, of Devonshire Place, was so badly beaten that she had to be helped into the courtroom by her children, and could not stand to give evidence of her husband's violence.[96]

William Sherman, a milk seller in Drummond Street, Somers Town, was charged with assaulting his wife, loosening some teeth and blackening her eye. Though this was the third black eye that Elizabeth Sherman had suffered from her husband's fists in the past nine months, William was released.[97] Eliza Rayment, the wife of a laborer living in Clarendon Place, was the victim of repeated beatings by her husband. After serving some months in prison for ill-treating her, he continued the abuse, which eventually caused her death in June 1879.[98]

This persistent violence against women was exacerbated by two factors. Without men's financial contribution it was extremely difficult for women to manage their household budgets. Thus, even badly beaten wives were reluctant to give evidence that might lead to prison for their husbands. Even Mary Ann Catlin, mentioned above, who had been sent to the hospital by her husband's violence, said in court that she "had nine children to support, and she did not wish to prosecute her husband."[99] Emily Nixon, living in Hereford Street, Lisson Grove, was reluctant to testify against her husband, who had beaten her, "as she had a family of children."[100] After Bernard Krell, a general dealer living in Seymour Court,

Churchway, in Somers Town, tried to slit his wife's throat with a kitchen knife, he went free. She refused "'to go against her husband'" and did not appear in court.[101] Even when men were less than generous with their contributions to the household budgets, their wives knew that they faced severe economic difficulties without this contribution, and thus they often had to live with the violence.

In addition, marital violence was an accepted part of married life.[102] William Harding, whose contribution to his wife's budget was described above, was cleared of blame, though he assaulted his wife with a poker. In court, she argued that she had been at fault, aggravating him after he gave her money. Harding defended himself by noting that he came home and turned over the money shortly after finishing work on Saturday. Upon ordering his release, Mr. Cooke, who was presiding, observed that "it was clear that the prisoner took her home the money directly." The crowd at court approved of the decision.[103] Harding, his wife, the officer presiding over the court, and the crowd all viewed his contribution to the family budget to be more salient than the fact that he had struck his wife with a dangerous implement.

Though neighbors frequently interfered in each others' lives and affairs, they were reluctant to interfere in domestic quarrels. Ross has argued that working-class communities respected the "'right' of husbands to beat up wives," and neighbors usually stayed out of such conflicts.[104] Upon the death of Sophia Cooper, of Christ Church Residences in Charles Street, Lisson Grove, neighbors suggested that abuse by her husband caused her death. Emma Pascoe commented, however, that "there were so many rows in the house that she [i.e., Pascoe] rarely took notice of these husband and wife quarrels."[105] On the night that Eliza Rayment was beaten to death by her husband, their neighbors in Somers Town heard the noise and came out of their houses. Yet they did not interfere or call the police. This case illustrates Ross's argument: "The sound of shouting and blows would cause them to collect on stairs, landings, and at windows, but fights would normally be allowed to continue."[106] Fights between husbands and wives were not subject to the intervention of neighbors, unlike other aspects of life in these neighborhoods. Widespread acceptance of violence between spouses permitted the pervasive ill-treatment of married women in poor London neighborhoods.

Power and Authority

Carl Chinn has argued that poor women enjoyed great power and authority in their households and neighborhoods. He compares the role of mothers to a "generalship," claiming that their responsibility for household management allowed women to "escape from a subordinate role."[107] It is his view that women made family decisions, shaped the behavior of other family members, and allocated the household budget. Children's devotion to their mothers and women's authority in households and neighborhoods made women the "arbiters of their own and their families' lives." In his view, a "hidden matriarchy, then, both balanced and superseded the open patriarchy" among the urban poor.[108]

Chinn argues that the vibrant street and neighborhood culture in poor neighborhoods was dominated by women. Elizabeth Roberts partially agrees, noting that their moral stature allowed women to wield significant power.[109] Women controlled local networks of mutual aid. The streets formed the central play areas for children, and mothers supervised their own children and others in the neighborhood.[110] Chinn cites women's enforcement of community moral and behavioral standards. These arenas of authority suggest to Chinn that women, and particularly mothers, controlled poor communities.[111]

In evaluating women's power, it is useful to distinguish between household dynamics and patterns of interaction in communities.[112] The picture of female authority in households must be qualified by a significant degree of male oversight.[113] Although women exerted nominal control over household expenditures, men reserved "the license to blame and abuse those wives who proved less than financial wizards."[114] Women decided where and how to allocate resources within the economic and cultural constraints described above, and if husbands disapproved of this management they made their unhappiness clear, often violently. Alfred Young, a laborer in Burne Street, Lisson Grove, was dissatisfied with the food his wife served him for tea. He pressed his complaint by striking her three times with a shovel.[115]

Day-to-day control over children was the province of their mothers, who would often resort to boxing ears or throwing objects at recalcitrant children. Yet the ultimate threat of the father's more stern discipline made him the higher authority over the children.[116] Mothers reprimanded children, but "the fact that fathers were presumed to be the ultimate authority in the household underpinned the daily demands mother made for obedient service from her children."[117] Samuel Govier, of Drummond Street, Somers Town, illustrates this male oversight. He found his son to be unacceptably dirty and beat both his wife and the boy.[118] Grace Foakes reported: "In our household his [her father's] word was law and nobody dared dispute it."[119]

In poor communities, women operated powerful networks of mutual aid and used gossip as a weapon to enforce moral and behavioral standards. But the authority of neighborhood women chiefly operated in a network of women and children. Men were marginal to the channels of gossip that regulated neighborhood hierarchies among women. While men's behavior might come in for abuse or criticism from neighborhood "matriarchs," the dense hierarchies of reputation in these communities chiefly concerned the behavior of women.[120] The cultural imperatives that women enforced often bolstered patriarchal authority. Llewelyn Davies observed: "Both in law and in popular morality, the wife is still the inferior in the family to the husband."[121] Even Chinn acknowledges the complexity of these patterns of authority. While arguing for a "hidden matriarchy," he notes that women were "usually assenting to overt male supremacy."[122] If women were the "generals" in their households and neighborhoods, perhaps their husbands should be compared to commanders in chief.

Affection and Respect

Women's responsibility for care of the household and children and the self-sacrifice described above helped win for mothers among the urban poor the devotion and affection of family members. Many children, particularly daughters, contributed to household tasks and developed insight into the burdens carried by their mothers. Jane Lewis observes: "Most daughters . . . understood and appreciated the constraints experienced by their mothers."[123] Carl Chinn argues that this recognition was shared even by "hooligans" who otherwise rejected standards of acceptable behavior.[124] This sensitivity to mothers' hardships bred powerful feelings among poor children, many of whom were devoted to their mothers. As they grew older, they aided their mothers by helping around the house and contributing to the household economy. Through the self-denial and sacrifice described above, mothers earned the devotion, respect, and love of their children.[125]

Some observers have argued that self-sacrifice and unending toil for their families gave women's lives "purpose."[126] One woman interviewed by Elizabeth Roberts viewed her mother's position this way: "It must have been a terrible life. It was all work. . . . But they enjoyed it."[127] Other children of the urban poor took a different view, noting that their mothers had been denied happiness in the struggle to keep their families going.[128] Obtaining any accurate picture of the happiness of these women is not possible, as even oral histories and autobiographies generally reflect children's recollections and perceptions of their mothers' experiences in this period. Their children's affection must have been a source of some cheer to poor mothers, amidst their effort and self-sacrifice. It may have led children to share their earnings more willingly with their mothers. Yet this devotion did not subvert the patterns of gender inequality in poor households.

Conclusion

The complex factors shaping these marital power relations reflected a mixture of mutual interests, affection, and bargaining over authority and resources. Amartya Sen has described this process as "cooperative conflict," to reflect the interaction of individual and shared interests among family members. While family members shared areas of mutuality and affection, they also distributed resources, power, and privilege. By limiting the viability of women's financial position outside marriage, the sexual division of labor impaired women's positions in these "cooperative conflicts," leading to "asymmetrical" domestic relationships.[129]

Within households, women had limited access to material resources, took on greater burdens of work, and enjoyed less leisure than did men. Their physical condition was compromised by poor health conditions, widespread physical abuse, the dangers of repeated pregnancy and childbirth without access to effective birth control, and sexual subjugation to their husbands. Though women did manage household resources, economic and cultural restrictions demanded that they channel them to the benefit of their husbands and children, not to their own well-being. The patterns described in this study show that, among the urban poor, patriarchy had not been superseded.[130]

Rather than break down the system of domestic patriarchy, women's wage earning formed an integral part of this pattern of male dominance. Women's wage earning contributed to the excess burden of work falling on married and unmarried women. It made it more difficult for women to find time for leisure and enjoyment. The fact that their wages were devoted to the household budget meant that the resources they brought to the domestic economy were unequally directed to the well-being of the male household head.

The sexual division of labor in local labor markets offers a partial explanation for this phenomenon. Women's jobs paid poorly, and it was unlikely that even a woman without children could avoid poverty without a male breadwinner. Thus, wage earning did not break women's economic dependence on men. Instead, their limited earning capacity reinforced their subordination to men.[131] Only when jobs open to women pay decent wages can such earning provide the option of independence. The feasibility of independence from a male breadwinner would likely improve women's position within households and could help undercut the gender inequality evident in poor London households.

Yet economic dependence caused by the sexual division of labor provides only a partial explanation for the domestic relationships described in this chapter. Powerful cultural patterns also enforced gender inequality in poor London households. Men and women assumed that certain behaviors were appropriate in domestic relationships. Women were expected, and expected themselves, to accept self-sacrifice, devoting themselves to the well-being of their husbands and children before their own. Rather than cultivate personal interests, perhaps in conflict with those of their husbands and even children, women were expected to adopt attitudes of mutuality, sacrificing their individual well-being.[132]

Conclusion:
"The Aim of Every Girl"

G. R. Sims, investigating the terrible conditions in poor London neighborhoods, observed a dying woman doing her family's laundry: "It is a glorious lot in life, these people's—is it not?—to toil on and struggle . . . giving their youth and age to the hardest labour for a wage that barely staves off starvation."[1] Poor London women confronted an extraordinary range of pressures imposed on them by the economic system that condemned their families to suffer in miserable poverty and cultural forces that defined women's subordinate places in labor markets and households. Yet these women were not cowed into passive submission by the burdens they faced. Instead, they confronted the challenges of their lives with energy, initiative, and often creativity.

The thousands of residents in poor neighborhoods supplied the London economy with an essential supply of cheap labor. The men and women who made clothes, built houses, carried goods and people, and cleaned homes, offices, and clothes provided the foundation for the glittering wealth of the metropolis. But their own lives were plagued by daunting poverty. They lived in neighborhoods on the margins of the urban fabric, far removed from the impressive squares of the affluent West End, even if only a few blocks away. Most residents of these forlorn districts lived beneath Booth's poverty line, and the vast majority of the rest clung to positions just beyond poverty until a lost job or another mouth to feed disrupted their household economies.

The demands of local labor markets and legacies of decades of development amidst nearly nonexistent government regulation created miserably crowded and unhealthy conditions in these neighborhoods. Families packed into single rooms and sometimes took in lodgers to share the space. Woeful sanitary provisions left smelly, unhealthy pools and piles of waste festering in alleys and streets. Communicable diseases exacted a heavy toll

138

on populations weakened by poor nutrition, resulting in inflated death and disease rates.

Women's share of these burdens was significantly greater than that of men. Both men and women faced the difficulties of exploitative labor conditions, but women earned less. The gendered division of labor restricted them to the least attractive jobs. Yet they sought wage-earning opportunities whenever their other responsibilities allowed, even at those times when their household economies were relatively strong due to the contributions of wage-earning children. These women expected to work hard throughout their lives, balancing wage earning with domestic work at various stages in their life courses.

Though the London labor market presented significant challenges to unskilled men trying to find relatively stable employment, women faced even more daunting tasks in maintaining their households amidst such poverty. In addition to their wage earning, domestic work required hours of effort and creativity. One survey estimated that laundry alone for a family of five took ten hours per week.[2] Shopping on such tight budgets demanded a practiced eye, well-honed bargaining skills, and the cultivation of relationships with local merchants who might provide credit. Women developed relationships with neighbors on whom they could rely for aid in times of need. Domestic management also required the ability to deal with landlords or rent collectors, and pawnbrokers.

These women exerted extraordinary efforts on behalf of their families. They sought to maximize their husbands' contributions to the household budget, arranged for their children to contribute to it when possible, and earned cash themselves when they did not have too much domestic work. They manipulated spending through the use of credit, buying adulterated goods, or even stealing. Women also managed consumption, by creatively turning meager provisions into meals and by denying themselves food, even when they were ill or pregnant.

Cultural prescriptions enforced many of the burdens facing poor women. Keeping their families together in the face of such tremendous challenges was simply expected of women. They accepted the self-sacrifice this required as part of being women. Their priorities included the protection of their children, the care of their husbands, and the preservation of their households. They placed little emphasis on their own well-being and personal position. Rather, they pursued a single-minded struggle to keep their families afloat, whatever this took.[3] This outlook, described as "familist" or "mutualist," was central to women's behavior and their values in poor neighborhoods.[4] Women held their households together, even when it required them to sacrifice their own well-being.

Through their embrace of mutuality and self-sacrifice and their tireless efforts, women preserved and enforced a system of gender inequality that subjected them to exploitation beyond that suffered by their husbands and sons. Yet poor women enjoyed few alternatives. They lived in crowded, close-knit neighborhoods in which residents kept a close watch on one another's activities. Women were particularly active in enforcing standards of behavior, observing and judging the actions of other wives and mothers. Those who defied accepted practices would become the subject of ostracization and bitter gossip.[5] As linchpins in these neighborhood networks of information-sharing and reputation, women helped force each other to behave. In order to live in her neighborhood and in relatively peaceful coexistence with her husband, a woman had no choice but to adhere to the established mores.

However, perhaps women could have escaped from these constraints in other ways. Married women could, potentially, have left the husbands who demanded such sacrifice, abandoned their children, and fled the neighborhood in which they would be stigmatized and criticized. Alternatively, single women might have avoided marriage and children, and thus the relationships that required them to compromise their well-being. Aside from the emotional costs involved in these alternatives, the economic position of women made them impractical.

Significant benefits accrued to those who remained resident in particular neighborhoods over time. Relationships with neighbors, kin, and local merchants could be essential in making ends meet. Established residents could count on aid from their neighbors in difficult times. Reputations requiring time to develop offered the possibility of credit from neighborhood shops and vendors. Social networks and kinship ties also facilitated the location of work opportunities in casual and unstable local labor markets. Thus, moving out of a neighborhood was economically costly. This is evidenced by the stable populations of late-Victorian poor districts, in which people moved often, but seldom moved far.[6]

The most significant constraints on women grow out of their economic insecurity. If women earn living wages, they can remain single or leave their husbands without subjecting themselves and their children to severe hardship. But the division of labor in local labor markets made this impossible, tying women to male earners and enforcing their lack of alternatives.[7] Within these households, poverty, lack of access to birth control, and cultural mores compelled women to sacrifice personal well-being for the benefit of their families. Grace Foakes describes this phenomenon, appearing mystified by women's apparent choice: "It was the women . . . who had the hardest time. For what with child-bearing, poor housing, unemployment and the constant struggle to make both ends meet, their lot wasn't an enviable one. Yet surprisingly enough it was the aim of every girl to get married."[8] Given conditions in local labor markets and communities, these women's embrace of marriage with all its struggles and self-sacrifice is less surprising.

One would think that the severe constraints placed on their lives would give rise to paralyzing despair. Indeed, historians have detected a fatalistic acceptance of their fate on the part of some working-class women.[9] But most women in poor London neighborhoods struggled actively, energetically and often successfully to maintain their families. They schemed, labored, cooperated, and fought to keep their homes and families afloat. Our understanding of the economic deprivation and patriarchal subjection under which they lived should not blind us to the active, even heroic struggles of these women to defend their households, their neighbors, and their dignity.[10]

Female solidarity formed an important weapon in the battle for survival in these neighborhoods.[11] Women were available and willing to help their neighbors in times of crisis. These relationships of mutual support and aid were vital to the maintenance of families in poor neighborhoods. Ironically, these efforts preserved households in which men received the lion's share of benefits. But they should not be confused with passive victimization.[12] Ross's portrait of poor London mothers battling their children's illnesses reveals their determination and energy.[13]

Though this solidarity was not conceived in terms of national politics or working-class consciousness, it was often confrontational. Women fought, at times violently, against the authorities who contributed to their poverty. Police, landlords, and parish officials were the objects of hostility and contention. When an off-duty police sergeant took a six-year-old Somers Town boy into custody, the neighborhood women challenged him. When the boy tried to get away, "a gang of women surrounded him [the sergeant] and attempted to mob him" and rescue the boy.[14] Though they were not interested in suffrage or involved in unions or high politics, struggles over power and authority in their neighborhoods and households formed a significant part of women's experience. In this broader sense, these women were active politically, rescuing suspects from police custody, defying landlords, and challenging parish officials.[15]

The early chapters of this book analyzed poor London households in the contexts of stable working-class communities. Local labor markets drove the development of these neighborhoods and determined their character and their poverty. Residents shared dependence on casual and seasonal work and competed for jobs, but also provided essential networks of information about work opportunities. Also economically valuable were relationships of mutual aid among neighbors and stable relationships with local merchants. In these various ways, poor communities operated as economic units, in which men and women filled distinct and well-defined economic roles.

But in examining the dynamics of women's life courses and domestic relationships, the poor neighborhood's cultural importance also becomes clear. Communities upheld standards that bound their members to acceptable behaviors. These cultural boundaries, drawn and enforced by women, affected women and children most directly. They included powerful gender roles that required self-sacrifice and mutuality on the part of poor women. In combination with local economic conditions, these cultural forces created the arenas in which poor women played out their lives.

One of the most common and influential approaches to women's history in the nineteenth century applies the concept of "separate spheres," identifying the division of men's and women's activities as the key defining feature in Victorian gender relations. This concept has proved useful, particularly in analyses of middle-class women's lives, yet critics have recently pointed out significant problems in the use of separate spheres as an analytical approach.[16] The study of poor and working-class women reinforces this skepticism by pointing out ways in which the "spheres" of working-class women were far different from those open to respectable middle-class women.

Despite recent criticisms of the concept of separate spheres, it is clear that widespread and deeply held ideas of proper gender roles restricted middle-class women's public activities and offered them the domestic realm as their own.[17] While the home was characterized as the appropriate sphere for these women, their presence in public, particularly in cities, was limited. In the last decades of the century, some middle-class women began to challenge these restrictions, moving into previously male-dominated public spaces. Pursuing philanthropy, employment, political activism, and new patterns of shopping, middle-class women headed into the streets of the metropolis in the 1880s. Simply walking the streets constituted a rebellious act for these women. By asserting their claim to these urban spaces, some middle-class women "transgressed the acceptable boundaries of gender and sexual decorum."[18] These women were subject to harassment and criticism in staking out a place in the "contested terrain" of city streets. But many more middle-class women remained safely ensconced in domesticity.

While these middle-class women struggled to overcome the limitations imposed by middle-class notions about gender, women in poorer neighborhoods encountered very different limitations and struggles. They faced the exploitation of an economic system dependent on casual labor and cheap women's wages, a system whose profits helped support their middle-class "sisters." A very different set of gender expectations demanded unending labor, paid and unpaid, and self-sacrifice to maintain their households. Poor women had little in common with the ladies who ventured into their neighborhoods as philanthropists and struggled to break down middle-class gender barriers; they did not share a common female "sphere." Yet ideas about the proper roles of men and women restricted both middle-class and poor women's actions and privileged their husbands and fathers. As wage earners and household managers, as wives, mothers, and neighbors, gender ideology formed a key determinant of these poor women's lives.

Table 1-1. Population of St. Pancras and the Somers Town Subdistrict

Year	St. Pancras		Somers Town Subdistrict	
	Population	Growth Rate	Population	Growth Rate
1801	31,779	------	------	------
1811	46,333	45.8%	------	------
1821	71,838	55.0%	------	------
1831	103,548	44.1%	------	------
1841	129,763	25.3%	28,910	------
1851	166,956	28.7%	35,641	23.3%
1861	198,788	19.1%	39,099	9.7%
1871	221,465	11.4%	38,533	-1.4%
1881	236,258	6.7%	34,369	-10.8%
1891	234,379	-0.8%	33,829	-1.6%
1901	235,317[a]	0.4%	30,132	-10.9%
1911	218,387	-7.2%	------	------

Note: Population figures for the following tables come from the census general reports, *Census of Great Britain, 1851*, Parliamentary Papers 1852-3, vol. 85; *Census of England and Wales for the Year 1861*, Parliamentary Papers 1863, vol. 53; *Census of England and Wales, 1881*, Parliamentary Papers 1883, vol. 79; *Census of England and Wales, 1891*, Parliamentary Papers 1893-4, vol. 105; *Census Returns of England and Wales, 1901*, Parliamentary Papers 1902, vol. 120; *Census Returns of England and Wales, 1911*, Parliamentary Papers 1912-3, vol. 111.

[a] Indicates that the boundaries of this district were changed in 1899.

Table 1-2. Population of Marylebone and the Christchurch Subdistrict

Year	Marylebone		Christchurch Subdistrict	
	Population	Growth Rate	Population	Growth Rate
1801	63,982	------	------	------
1811	75,624	18.2%	------	------
1821	96,040	27.0%	------	------
1831	122,206	27.2%	------	------
1841	138,164	13.1%	28,911	------
1851	157,696	14.1%	33,895	17.2%
1861	161,680	2.5%	34,913	3.0%
1871	159,254	-1.5%	33,944	-2.8%
1881	154,910	-2.7%	33,700	-0.7%
1891	142,404	-8.1%	33,827	0.4%
1901	133,301[a]	-6.4%[a]	39,536[a]	16.9[a]
1911	118,160	-11.4%	36,509	-7.7%

[a] Indicates that the boundaries of this district were changed in 1899.

Table 1-3. Population of Bethnal Green and the Green Subdistrict

Year	Bethnal Green		Green Subdistrict	
	Population	Growth Rate	Population	Growth Rate
1801	22,310	------	------	------
1811	33,610	50.6%	------	------
1821	45,676	35.9%	9,655	------
1831	62,018	35.8%	------	------
1841	74,088	19.5%	16,766	73.7%[a]
1851	90,193	21.7%	23,555	40.5%
1861	105,101	16.5%	31,789	35.0%
1871	120,104	14.3%	42,433	33.5%
1881	126,961	5.7%	47,932	13.0%
1891	129,132	1.7%	------	------
1901	129,680[b]	0.4%[b]	------	------
1911	128,183	-1.2%	------	------

[a] Growth rate over twenty years.
[b] Indicates that the boundaries of this district were changed in 1899.

Table 1-4. Places of Birth

Region of Birth	Percentage of the 1881 Population of			
	Somers Town	Lisson Grove	Globe Town	London
London Region	78.6	77.0	88.0	69.7
Southeast	1.6	2.0	0.9	3.4
South Midlands	3.2	3.5	1.5	4.0
East	2.6	2.9	4.0	5.1
Southwest	2.6	2.8	0.9	4.4
West Midlands	2.0	2.1	0.9	2.5
North Midlands	0.7	0.6	0.3	1.1
Northwest	0.7	0.3	0.4	0.9
Yorkshire	0.4	0.3	0.3	0.8
Northern	0.3	0.2	0.1	0.5
England (unspec.)	0.1	0.2	0.0	0.7
Wales	0.4	0.6	0.1	0.5
Scotland	0.8	0.7	0.2	1.3
Ireland	2.9	4.7	0.6	2.1
Other U.K. Islands	0.1	0.1	0.0	0.1
Non-U.K.	1.1	0.6	0.8	2.8

Table 1-5. Fertility Ratios in 1881 (Per 100 Married Women)

Married Women Ages	Somers Town	Lisson Grove	Globe Town
15-19	59	64	86
20-24	112	88	117
25-29	126	113	145
30-34	117	116	138
35-39	87	84	112
40-44	53	60	73
45-49	23	15	28

Table 1-6. Percentages of Adults Ever Married, 1881

	Somers Town	Lisson Grove	Globe Town
Men	63.8%	61.4%[a]	63.9%
Women	73.7%	76.4%	72.1%
Total	68.9%	64.6%	68.0%

[a] The low proportion of adult men ever married in Lisson Grove reflects the population of the large lodging houses, filled with single adult males, in the neighborhood.

Table 1-7. Streets with Servant-Holding Households

Neighborhoods and Streets	Total Hholds	% of Hholds	# Servant Hholds	% of Servant Hholds
Somers Town:				
Chalton St.	412	10.1%	14	17.3%
Ossulston St.	254	6.2%	10	12.3%
Clarendon St.	268	6.6%	9	11.1%
Chapel St.	22	0.5%	9	11.1%
Clarendon Sq.	248	6.1%	7	8.6%
Total	1204	29.5%	49	60.5%
Lisson Grove:				
Devonshire St.	353	11.5%	8	17.0%
Bell St.	110	3.6%	6	12.8%
Hereford St.	215	7.0%	5	10.6%
Great James St.	167	5.5%	5	10.6%
Total	845	27.6%	24	51.0%
Globe Town:				
Green St.	290	7.0%	60	44.8%
Globe Road	287	6.9%	20	14.9%
Victoria Park Sq.	40	1.0%	15	11.2%
Total	517	12.5%	95	70.9%

149

Table 1-8. Occupation of Heads of Servant-Holding Households

	Number of Household Heads		
Occupation	Somers Town	Lisson Grove	Globe Town
Publicans, etc.	12	10	25
Bakers	5	5	8
Butchers	4	2	8
Other Food	18	10	15
Boot & Shoemakers	1	0	16
Other	41	18	61

Table 1-9. Common Relationships of Kin to Household Heads

Relationship	N	% of kin
Grandchild	437	27.7%
Sibling	331	21.3%
Niece/Nephew	308	19.5%
Parent	138	8.7%

150

Table 1-10. Family Types, 1881

Family Type	Somers Town		Lisson Grove		Globe Town	
	N	%	N	%	N	%
Individual Living Alone	492	12.1%	368	12.0%	300	7.2%
Only Unrelated People	125	3.1%	112	3.7%	76	1.8%
Couple, No Other Relations	627	15.4%	480	15.7%	504	15.7%
Parent(s) and Children, No Kin	2377	58.5%	1833	59.9%	2809	67.8%
Extended, Other Kin Present	442	10.9%	268	8.8%	452	10.9%

Table 1-11. Household Sizes, 1881

Number in Household	Somers Town		Lisson Grove		Globe Town	
	N	%	N	%	N	%
1	493	12.1%	368	12.0%	300	7.2%
2	869	21.4%	682	22.3%	670	16.2%
3	670	16.5%	567	18.5%	635	15.3%
4	566	13.9%	433	14.1%	659	15.9%
5	524	12.9%	372	12.1%	509	12.3%
6	394	9.7%	288	9.4%	438	10.6%
7	244	6.0%	171	5.6%	355	8.6%
8	149	3.7%	89	2.9%	274	6.6%
9	80	2.0%	54	1.8%	160	3.9%
10 or more	81	2.0%	40	1.3%	146	3.5%
Total Households	4070	100%	3064	100%	4146	100%
Mean Size	3.95		3.86		4.60	

Table 2-1. Booth's Classification of the Populations, 1887-1889

	Somers Town		Lisson Grove		Globe Town	
Classification	N	%	N	%	N	%
A & B (very poor)	582	3.8%	5151	23.5%	3772	20.8%
C & D (poor)	7466	49.3%	4407	20.1%	6221	34.3%
E & F (comfortable)	6528	43.1%	11,413	52.0%	7559	41.6%
G & H (well-to-do)	556	3.7%	972	4.4%	602	3.3%

Note: Booth, Life and Labour vol. 2, app., table 1, sheets 10, 12, 25. The areas in Booth's data do not conform exactly to those examined in this study. In each case, Booth's definition of areas underestimates the proportions of the poor in the neighborhoods. The part of Somers Town included in these figures excludes the northern part of the neighborhood, in which those streets classified by Booth as the poorest lay. This explains the relatively low proportion of "very poor" in the Somers Town statistics. The Lisson Grove figures include more comfortable areas to the south and northwest of the neighborhood. The numbers for Globe Town include the populations of streets along the edges of the neighborhood that were more comfortable than those in Globe Town proper. The areas in this table correspond to those Booth called 23a and 23b (Somers Town), 26b and 27c (Lisson Grove), and 58a and 58b (Globe Town).

Table 2-2. Men Occupied in Building and General Work, 1881

% of Employed Men in Building and General Work			
Somers Town	Lisson Grove	Globe Town	London
24.0%	32.4%	18.2%	19.5%

Table 2-3. Common Occupations of Somers Town Men, 1881

Occupation	% of Employed Men		Rank in London	Location Quotient[a]
	Somers Town	London		
Building Trades	14.6%	10.9%	1	1.35
Road Transport	10.5%	5.8%[b]	5	1.82[b]
General Workers	9.4%	8.7%	2	1.08
Food Processing & Selling	5.6%	6.9%	4	0.82
Furniture	5.2%	2.2%	15	2.33
Iron, Steel, etc.	4.3%	3.0%	8	1.45
Railroads	4.1%	2.0%	17	2.07
Printing	4.1%	2.6%	12	1.59
Musical Instrument Making	3.5%	0.5%	40	6.71
Other	38.8%	57.6%	-----	-----

[a] The location quotient is determined by dividing the number of men in a trade in one particular area by the total in that trade throughout London, and dividing this quotient by the proportion of all occupied men in the neighborhood to the total occupied male population of London. This gives a figure reflecting the over- or underrepresentation of the trade in the particular area. A location quotient of 1.00 would indicate that a trade is as common in the locality as throughout the metropolis. Stedman Jones, Outcast London, app. 2, table 7.

[b] The occupational categories in this study are slightly modified from those in the census general report. These occupational categories are estimated for London figures.

Table 2-4. Common Occupations of Lisson Grove Men 1881

Occupation	% of Employed Men		Rank in London	Location Quotient
	Lisson Grove	London		
General Workers	16.6%	8.7%	2	1.91
Building Trades	15.9%	10.9%	1	1.46
Road Transport	12.5%	5.8%[a]	5	2.18[a]
Food Processing & Selling	6.8%	6.9%	4	0.99
Animal Care, etc.	4.3%	1.1%	27	3.81
Communications	4.2%	1.6%[a]	20	2.72[a]
Boot & Shoemaking	4.0%	2.8%	9	1.45
General Dealers	3.9%	1.5%	22	2.60
Iron, Steel, etc.	3.3%	3.0%	8	1.11
Other	28.5%	58.0%	-----	-----

[a]Occupational categories estimated for London figures.

Table 2-5. Common Occupations of Globe Town Men, 1881

Occupation	% of Employed Men		Rank in London	Location Quotient
	Globe Town	London		
Boot & Shoemaking	11.7%	2.8%	9	4.24
General Workers	10.9%	8.7%	2	1.25
Textiles	8.1%	2.0%	16	4.00
Building	7.3%	10.9%	1	0.68
Food Processing & Selling	7.2%	6.8%	4	1.05
Furniture	6.6%	2.2%	15	2.95
Road Transport	6.1%	5.8%[a]	5	1.05[a]
Wood	4.1%	1.4%	23	3.01
Communications	2.7%	1.6%[a]	20	1.72[a]
Printing	2.2%	2.6%	12	0.86
Others	33.1%	55.3%	-----	-----

[a] Occupational category estimated for London figures.

Table 2-6. Distribution of Women in Domestic Work, 1881

	Somers Town		Lisson Grove		Globe Town		London	
	N	%	N	%	N	%	N	%
Laundry	381	43.6%	455	48.1%	180	34.9%	48,559	15.8%
General Service	261	29.9%	261	27.6%	219	42.4%	240,133	77.9%
Charring	192	22.0%	197	20.8%	77	14.9%	19,334	6.3%
Others	39	4.5%	32	3.4%	40	7.8%	47	0.0%
Total	873		945		516		308,073	
% of Employed Women		38.0%		53.6%		20.5%		51.9%

Table 2-7. Common Women's Occupations in Somers Town

Occupation	% of Employed Women		Rank in London	Location Quotient
	Somers Town	London		
Domestic Work	38.0%	51.9%	1	0.73
Clothing	22.4%	20.4%	2	1.09
General Workers	4.6%	1.3%	12	3.63
Other Professionals	3.3%	1.8%	6	1.84
Paper	3.1%	1.5%	8	2.04
Textiles	2.8%	2.8%	4	0.99
Home Fittings	2.6%	0.8%	15	3.45
General Dealers	2.1%	1.4%	9	1.58
Furniture	2.0%	0.6%	16	3.25
Food Processing & Selling	1.9%	1.6%	7	1.16
Books	1.9%	1.3%	11	1.46
Others	15.5%	14.6%	-----	-----

Table 2-8: Common Women's Occupations in Lisson Grove

Occupation	% of Employed Women		Rank in London	Location Quotient
	Lisson Grove	London		
Domestic Work	53.6%	51.9%	1	1.03
Clothing	22.1%	20.4%	2	1.08
Food Processing & Selling	3.2%	1.6%	7	1.98
Other Professionals	2.2%	1.8%	6	1.23
General Workers	2.2%	1.3%	12	1.75
Home Fittings	2.2%	0.8%	15	2.85
General Dealers	1.9%	1.4%	9	1.38
Institutional Service	1.8%	2.2%	5	0.84
Other	10.8%	18.7%	-----	-----

Table 2-9. Common Female Sweated Manufactures in Somers Town and Lisson Grove

Occupation	Percentage of Employed Women	
	Somers Town	Lisson Grove
Clothing	22.4%	22.1%
General Work [a]	4.6%	2.2%
Home Fittings[b]	2.6%	2.2%

[a] Among general workers, the majority were machinists (59% in Somers Town and 87% in Lisson Grove). These women probably worked in the clothing or boot and shoe trades.

[b] In both Somers Town and Lisson Grove, 95% of these workers made artificial flowers.

Table 2-10. Common Women's Occupations in Globe Town, 1881

Occupation	% of Employed Women		Rank in London	Location Quotient
	Globe Town	London		
Domestic Work	20.5%	51.9%	1	0.40
Clothing	18.1%	20.4%	2	0.89
Textiles	15.3%	2.8%	4	5.41
Boot & Shoemaking	9.5%	1.1%	14	8.43
Paper	7.9%	1.5%	8	5.31
General Workers[a]	7.2%	1.3%	12	5.71
Animal Hair Products	2.7%	0.4%	21	7.74
Other	18.8%	20.6%	-----	-----

[a] Among Globe Town women listed as general workers, 90% were described as machinists, many of whom were likely employed in the boot and shoe industry. Stedman Jones, Outcast London, 27 n. 42a.

Table 2-11. Model Family Budgets and the Family Structure

Weekly Family Budget Characteristics		Family Structure:			
		Early in Marriage, No Children	Two Children at Home, None Employed	Three Children at Home, All Employed	Later in Life, No Children at Home
Expenses					
Rent	One Room	3s. 6d.	3s. 6d.	3s. 6d.	3s. 6d.
	Two Rooms	6s. 6d.	6s. 6d.	6s. 6d.	6s. 6d.
Food	Male Head	3s. 6d.	3s. 6d.	3s. 6d.	3s. 6d.
	Wife	1s. 9d.	1s. 9d.	1s. 9d.	1s. 9d.
	Children	0	3s. 6d.	5s. 3d.	0
Other Expenses	Family	1s. 6d.	3s.	3s. 9d.	1s. 6d.
Total Expenses	One Room	10s. 3d.	15s. 3d.	17s. 9d.	10s. 3d.
	Two Rooms	13s. 3d.	18s. 3d.	20s. 9d.	13s. 3d.
Income	Husband	14s. 6d.	14s. 6d.	14s. 6d.	14s. 6d.
	Wife	6s.	6s.	6s.	6s.
	Children	0	0	18s.	0
Bottom Line — Wife not Employed					
	One Room	4s. 3d.	*-9d.*	14s. 9d.	4s. 3d.
	Two Rooms	1s. 3d.	*-3s. 9d.*	11s. 9d.	1s. 3d.
Bottom Line — Wife Employed					
	One Room	10s. 3d.	5s. 3d.	20s. 9d.	10s. 3d.
	Two Rooms	7s. 3d.	2s. 3d.	17s. 9d.	7s. 3d.

Note: The estimates for rent are based on a combination of the three neighborhoods. The cost of food for the husband is taken from Pember Reeves, and the cost of food for the wife and children is estimated at 1s. 9d. per person per week, based on information from Booth and Pember Reeves. The extremely conservative figure of 9d. per week for other expenses is derived from Booth and intended to represent minimal expenditure. Booth, Life and Labour, 1:134–40; Pember Reeves, Round About a Pound a Week, 133.

Table 3-1. Women in Common Mixed Trades

Occupation	Percentage of Employed Women			
	All Three Areas	Somers Town	Lisson Grove	Globe Town
Boot and Shoemakers	4.3%	1.0%	1.2%	9.4%
Silk Workers	3.8%	0.0%	0.1%	9.7%
Tailoresses	3.3%	1.5%	2.6%	5.6%
Brush Makers	1.6%	1.5%	0.1%	2.7%
Bookbinders	1.2%	1.8%	0.1%	1.3%
Upholsteresses	0.9%	1.6%	0.7%	0.4%
Milk Sellers	0.7%	0.3%	2.0%	0.2%
Total	15.8%	7.7%	7.0%	29.3%

Table 3-2. Common Domestic and Related Occupations

Occupation	Percentage of Employed Women			
	All Three Areas	Somers Town	Lisson Grove	Globe Town
Laundresses	15.5%	16.6%	25.8%	7.1%
General Servants	11.1%	11.2%	14.5%	8.7%
Charwomen	7.1%	8.4%	11.2%	3.1%
Nurses	2.6%	3.1%	2.1%	2.3%
Cooks	1.0%	1.0%	1.9%	0.4%
Total	37.2%	40.3%	55.4%	21.7%

Table 3-3. Common Predominantly Female Manufacturing Trades

Occupation	Percentage of Employed Women			
	All Three Areas	Somers Town	Lisson Grove	Globe Town
Dressmakers	8.1%	10.9%	11.0%	3.5%
Machinists	3.9%	2.7%	1.9%	6.4%
Needlewomen	3.0%	3.8%	4.0%	1.5%
Box Makers	2.9%	1.4%	0.0%	6.4%
Artificial-Flower Makers	1.7%	2.5%	2.0%	0.6%
Trimming Makers	1.6%	0.2%	0.4%	3.9%
Milliners	1.0%	1.4%	1.1%	0.7%
Mantle Makers	1.0%	1.4%	1.2%	0.6%
Total	23.3%	24.1%	21.7%	23.6%

Table 3-4. Home Work in Selected Trades, England and Wales, 1901

Occupation	Percentage of Home Workers		
	Single Women	Married & Widowed Women	All Women
Dressmakers	43.4%	77.7%	49.6%
Laundresses	25.9%	46.2%	37.2%
Needlewomen	22.9%	60.3%	35.1%
Brush Makers	12.6%	49.0%	26.1%
Tailoresses	12.6%	45.0%	21.1%
Milliners	16.3%	61.0%	20.4%
Boot & Shoemakers	9.0%	48.1%	18.6%
Upholsteresses	7.8%	33.0%	14.6%
Silk Workers	3.9%	17.1%	7.2%
Bag & Box Makers	2.5%	27.4%	6.7%
Bookbinders	0.8%	5.9%	1.4%

Note: Census Returns of England and Wales, 1901, Parliamentary Papers 1903, vol. 84.

Table 3-5. Ages of Employed Women

Age Group	All Three Areas		Somers Town		Lisson Grove		Globe Town	
	N	%	N	%	N	%	N	%
5-14	278	4.2%	91	4.0%	55	3.1%	132	5.2%
15-24	2362	35.9%	749	32.7%	546	30.9%	1067	42.4%
25-34	1115	17.0%	380	16.6%	302	17.1%	433	17.2%
35-44	992	15.1%	348	15.2%	348	19.7%	296	11.8%
45-54	845	12.8%	336	14.6%	260	14.7%	249	9.9%
55-64	608	9.2%	229	10.0%	167	9.5%	212	8.4%
65 & over	377	5.7%	161	7.0%	88	5.0%	128	5.1%
Total[a]	6577	-----	2294	-----	1766	-----	2517	-----

[a] Totals exclude three women whose age was undetermined.

164

Table 3-6. Ages of Women in Particular Occupations, Three Neighborhoods

Occupation	Age Groups		
	Under 25	25-49	50 & Over
Laundresses	13.8%	53.1%	33.1%
Bookbinders	73.7%	25.0%	1.3%
Upholsteresses	41.7%	38.3%	20.0%
All Employed Women	40.1%	38.7%	21.1%

Table 4-1. Married Women's Employment by Age

Age	Percentage of Women Employed			
	Somers Town	Lisson Grove	Globe Town	All Three Areas
15-19	26.5%	50.0%[a]	22.7%	32.5%
20-24	19.4%	26.5%	23.0%	22.5%
25-29	18.0%	25.3%	22.4%	21.6%
30-34	16.3%	25.2%	14.8%	17.8%
35-39	21.5%	23.9%	18.9%	21.2%
40-44	24.1%	33.2%	20.8%	25.1%
45-49	24.3%	29.2%	22.7%	25.0%
50-54	25.4%	31.4%	18.8%	24.6%
55-59	22.8%	27.0%	27.3%	25.4%
60-64	29.2%	36.8%	24.8%	28.8%
65+	22.2%	28.1%	29.1%	26.5%
Total:	21.3%	28.0%	20.7%	22.8%

[a] This high percentage of married women who were aged fifteen to nineteen in Lisson Grove represents a total of only thirty-seven people, of whom nineteen were employed.

Table 4-2. Employment of Wives by Coresident Offspring

Number of Offspring[a] Living at Home	Percentage of Wives Employed			
	Somers Town	Lisson Grove	Globe Town	All Three Areas
0	27.9%	31.3%	26.6%	28.5%
1	17.2%	29.8%	21.2%	22.2%
2	14.6%	22.6%	17.6%	17.9%
3	15.3%	21.7%	15.4%	17.0%
4	12.8%	16.3%	17.1%	15.4%
5 or more	12.5%	20.2%	15.3%	15.4%

[a] Among "offspring" are included spouses of sons and daughters.

Table 4-3. Employment of Wives and Percentage of Other Earners

Percentage of Other Household Members Employed	Percentage of Wives Employed			
	Somers Town	Lisson Grove	Globe Town	All Three Areas
0-20%	11.9%	15.5%	13.5%	13.5%
21-40%	12.9%	19.9%	16.2%	16.0%
41-60%	16.3%	27.2%	18.9%	20.1%
61-80%	17.0%	26.8%	20.2%	20.4%
81-100%	27.6%	32.3%	25.9%	28.3%

Table 4-4. Employment of Wives by Family Type

Family Type	Percentage of Wives Employed			
	Somers Town	Lisson Grove	Globe Town	All Three Areas
1: Wife under 45, no offspring	29.5%	32.0%	27.0%	29.5%
2: Wife under 45, 1 child less than 1 year old	13.2%	31.3%	17.3%	19.9%
3: Offspring at home, none employed	12.1%	19.4%	15.4%	15.3%
4: Offspring at home, fewer than half employed	16.5%	25.4%	19.4%	19.7%
5: Offspring at home, half or more employed	21.7%	28.7%	19.0%	22.3%
6: Wife 45 or over, no offspring or only one over age 20 at home	25.8%	32.5%	25.3%	27.5%
7: Wife age 65 or over	15.6%	26.3%	29.7%	24.0%
Total	18.1%	25.0%	18.9%	20.2%

Table 4-5. Estimated Men's Wages and Percentage of Wives Employed

Occupation	Estimated Wage	% of Wives Employed
Dock Laborers	17s 0d	25.0%
Railway Porters	20s 4d	15.4%
Shoe Makers	21s 0d	23.8%
Carmen	21s 0d	20.5%
General Laborers	21s 2d	27.2%
Tailors	22s 7d	19.6%
Butchers	25s 2d	12.3%
Bakers	25s 10d	11.3%
Policemen	29s 3d	2.3%
Wheelwrights	30s 8d	3.3%
Carpenters	30s 10d	13.2%
Bricklayers	31s 1d	21.7%
All Employed Men	------	20.1%

Note: Wage estimates come from <u>Statements of Men in Selected Districts of London</u>, Parliamentary Papers 1887, vol. 71, and reflect survey data from St. George's-in-the-East in 1887. Rates of wives' employment come from the Somers Town, Lisson Grove, and Globe Town data used for this study.

Table 4-6. Employment of Wives of General Laborers by Family Type

Family Type	% of Wives Employed
1: Wife under 45, no offspring	34.9%
2: Wife under 45, 1 child less than 1 year old	27.3%
3: Offspring at home, none employed	22.8%
4: Offspring at home, fewer than half employed	26.1%
5: Offspring at home, half or more employed	30.2%
6: Wife 45 or over, no offspring or only one over age 20 at home	36.9%
7: Wife age 65 or over	13.6%
Total	27.2%

Appendix 1:

Methodological Appendix

Boundaries of the Neighborhoods

This study is built in part on a comparative case study of three neighborhoods. These areas have been chosen to include similar levels of poverty, following Booth's map of poverty in London in the 1880s.[1] The settings were selected to include one poor neighborhood in the heart of the East End and two others representing poor areas nestled into the rest of London. This design looked for variation in how labor markets and general conditions in East London compared with those in other parts of the metropolis and affected the men and particularly the women living there. A number of possible locations, some in East London, others scattered throughout the metropolis, were considered. Globe Town, of the East London areas, and Somers Town and Lisson Grove, among isolated poor neighborhoods, were chosen because of the quality of the census records preserved for them.

After choosing the general areas for study, the neighborhoods were defined more exactly. The three neighborhoods were marked by distinct boundaries, formed by topographic features or economic distinctions. Somers Town's borders included major streets and a change in the character of the area. On the southeast, the Midland Railway complex determined the edge of Somers Town by demolishing part of the neighborhood and constructing a goods depot. On the south and west, Euston Road and Seymour Street formed the borders of Somers Town. To the north and northeast, the neighborhood came to an end with the beginning of more affluent areas beyond the Somers Estate, the Oakley Square area belonging to the Bedford Estate, and part of the Aldenham School or Brewers Estate. The area within these boundaries, corresponding roughly to the Somers Estate, formed the neighborhood of Somers Town.[2]

Lisson Grove, as defined for this study, included a set of poor streets tucked among more comfortable housing. Its borders included major streets to the east and west (Lisson Grove Road and Edgware Road) and important crossroads on the north and south (Church Street, the Marylebone Road, and Chapel Street). However, a distinct area within these borders has been excluded from study, a corridor running east and west from Exeter Street to Edgware Road along Earl Street and

Little Exeter/Little Carlisle Street, and an area connected to this corridor running north and south between Church and Bell Streets and west of Manning/Carlisle Street. Because the inhabitants of these streets were markedly better off than those in Lisson Grove proper, the area under study here excludes them.[3]

Large streets and topographical boundaries distinguished the neighborhood of Globe Town. Major streets, Cambridge Road and Old Ford Road, marked its western and northern boundaries. On the east, the Regent's Canal ran along the edge of Globe Town, and the southern boundary was formed by the Great Eastern Railway tracks. The neighborhood lay almost entirely in the eastern section of Bethnal Green, though a few streets in the southwestern corner of the neighborhood were in Mile End Old Town.

Of the three neighborhoods, Lisson Grove encompassed the smallest area and housed the fewest inhabitants. It covered approximately 38 acres, housing just under twelve thousand men, women, and children in 1881. Somers Town was somewhat larger, including 54 acres where about sixteen thousand people resided. Globe Town contained the most land, 120 acres and the largest population, over 19,000. Just over 22 of these acres, however, were uninhabited, including the Victoria Park Cemetery and land in the western part of Globe Town that remained open space.

The Data

Data on the residents of these neighborhoods have been taken from the enumerators' books of the 1881 census, available at the Public Record Office on microfilm. After defining the neighborhoods, information on every resident, 46,957 individuals, was coded and entered into a computer statistical package. The enumerators' books include the name, address, relation to household head, age, sex, marital status, occupation, and place of birth for each individual.

In the preparation of the data set, the only significant methodological issue involved the coding of occupational data. Occupations have been categorized according to a scheme based on that used in the census general reports for 1881.[4] However, some subcategories in the general report have been combined for this study, and others have been broken down into more detailed categories. For example, the census category "Persons Engaged in Commercial Occupations" includes the subcategories "Merchants and Agents," "Dealers in Money," and "Persons Occupied in Insurance." For this study, these have all been combined into a single category, "Business." But the census combines printing, newspaper distribution, and book production and selling into a single subcategory, "Books." For this study, these occupations have been separated into the three categories "Printing," "Books," and "Newspapers."

The resulting data set offers detailed information on every person in these neighborhoods. Men, women, and children can be located in households and streets and in the local labor markets.

Appendix 2

"Possible Servants"

Three characteristics of "possible servants" in Higgs's sample led to his conclusion that these women were not employed outside their homes. First, many of the women (47%) were "additions to the normal nuclear family," that is, they were neither household heads, nor the wives or daughters of heads. Higgs argues: "These sisters, nieces, mothers-in-law and aunts showed many of the characteristics of being dependents of the households in which they lived."[1] But in the neighborhoods under study here, few of the possible servants were additions to the nuclear family. Only 15% represented relations other than head, wife, daughter, or stepdaughter.[2]

Second, Higgs argues that many of the "possible servants" in Rochdale lived in households that may have required extra household help. He notes that only 64% of the households with these servants had married heads in Rochdale in 1871.[3] But in Somers Town, of 170 households with possible servants living in them 71% had married male household heads, and another 24% had female household heads.[4] Only 9 of the 170 households (5%) had a male head without a wife, indicating the need for domestic help. Thus, it is difficult to argue that these possible servants lived in households that obviously needed extra hands around the house.

Finally, in Higgs's sample many of the possible servants lived in and were relatives of fairly well-off household heads, and the nature of many of the occupations of these people might mean that extra help around the household was required.[5] Once again, possible servants in Somers Town, Lisson Grove, and Globe Town do not fit this pattern. The heads of their households reflect the general distribution of occupations in the three neighborhoods, including many building workers, workers in road transport, boot and shoemakers, and clothing workers. The two most common occupations pursued by heads of households that included possible servants were charring and general labor.[6] Of the occupations representing over 1% of possible servant household heads, only the four greengrocers fit Higgs's description of relatively well-off retailing families that might require extra help from a family member around the home. Possible servants in these neighborhoods were generally not additions to the nuclear family, few of them lived in households without a female head or wife, and they did not live in households that would ordinarily keep servants. Thus, it is likely that the majority of these "possible servants" worked as day servants outside their homes.

Notes

INTRODUCTION

1. *East London Observer*, 14 June 1879.
2. M. Vicinus, *Independent Women: Work and Community for Single Women, 1850–1920* (London: Virago, 1985), chap. 7; J. R. Walkowitz, *City of Dreadful Delight: Narratives of Sexual Danger in Late-Victorian London* (Chicago: University of Chicago Press, 1992), chap. 2.
3. L. Davidoff and C. Hall, *Family Fortunes: Men and Women of the English Middle Class, 1780–1850* (Chicago: University of Chicago Press, 1987), 359.
4. Martin Daunton describes this as "a threshold between public and private which was ambiguous and permeable." M. J. Daunton, "Housing," in *The Cambridge Social History of Britain, 1750–1950*, ed. F. M. L. Thompson (Cambridge: Cambridge University Press, 1990), 2:202.
5. J. Blake, *Memories of Old Poplar* (London: Stepney Books, 1977), 12.
6. Charles Booth Collection, British Library of Political and Economic Science, London School of Economics, B 73:8, A 38:14.
7. C. Booth, *Life and Labour of the People in London* (London: Macmillan, 1904), 2:21. The numbers just above poverty (i.e., in Booth's class "E") ranged from 42% of the population of East London to 38% in Central London; see 1:35, 308–9. On the insecurity experienced by those in class "E," see A. Davin, *Growing Up Poor: Home, School and Street in London, 1870–1914* (London: Rivers Oram Press, 1996), 22–27.
8. The 1889 dock strike and burst of union organization formed a short-lived exception. See G. Stedman Jones, "Working-Class Culture and Working-Class Politics in London, 1870–1900: Notes on the Remaking of a Working Class," in *Languages of Class: Studies in English Working Class History, 1832–1982* (Cambridge: Cambridge University Press, 1983), 212.
9. For notable exceptions, see G. Stedman Jones, *Outcast London: A Study in the Relationship between Classes in Victorian Society* (New York: Pantheon Books, 1984) and Davin, *Growing Up Poor*.
10. This includes those found by Booth to be poor at the moment of his survey and those just above poverty, who likely suffered in poverty at other times. The impact of changing life-course positions on poverty is discussed below.
11. For examples, see E. Ross, *Love and Toil: Motherhood in Outcast London, 1870–1918* (Oxford: Oxford University Press, 1993); idem, "Survival Networks: Women's Neighbourhood Sharing in London before World War I," *History Workshop Journal* 15 (1983); and idem, "'Fierce Questions and Taunts': Married Life in Working-Class London," *Feminist Studies* 3 (1982).

12. P. J. Waller, *Town, City and Nation: England, 1850–1914* (Oxford: Oxford University Press, 1983), 25, 51–52.

13. E. Ezard, *Battersea Boy* (London: William Kimber, 1979), 18.

14. G. Foakes, *Between High Walls: A London Childhood* (London: Shepheard-Walwyn, 1972), 22.

15. Ezard, *Battersea Boy*, 30–31. See also Ross, "Survival Networks," 5, appendix.

16. Ross, "Survival Networks," 8–10, 14; D. R. Green and A. G. Parton, "Slums and Slum Life in Victorian England: London and Birmingham at Mid-Century," in *Slums*, ed. M. Gaskell (Leicester, U.K.: Leicester University Press, 1990), 81.

17. Blake, *Memories of Old Poplar*, 8, 45–46.

18. Green and Parton, "Slums," 80.

19. G. Foakes, *My Part of the River* (London: Shepheard-Walwyn, 1974), 56.

20. G. Acorn, *One of the Multitude* (London: William Heinemann, 1911), 104–5.

21. Booth Collection, B 216:75.

22. Of the 36,776 men who furnished information on the duration of their local residence, 34,056 had lived in their neighborhood over a year. *Tabulation of the Statements of Men Living in Certain Selected Districts of London in March 1887*, Parliamentary Papers 1887, vol. 71, 4.

23. St. Pancras Health Department, "Housing of the Working Classes Act, 1890, Minutes of Evidence" (1893): 140. As chapter 1 will show, this exaggerates the length of time these stable working-class communities existed.

24. A key exception to this pattern was the husband's prerogative of reserving a portion of his wages for his own use, independent of the household budget.

25. In a brief but nuanced discussion of the concept, Louise Tilly enumerates "such decisions as when and where to migrate, when and whom to marry, which family members should do wage work, which have access to education, and so on" as typical manifestations of family strategies. L. Tilly, "Beyond Family Strategies, What?" *Historical Methods* 20 (1987): 124. See also T. K. Hareven, "The History of the Family and the Complexity of Social Change," *American Historical Review* 96 (1991): 95–124.

26. Ross, *Love and Toil*, 133–35.

27. Acorn, *One of the Multitude*, 85.

28. C. Dyhouse, *Girls Growing Up in Late Victorian and Edwardian England* (London: Routledge and Kegan Paul, 1981), 11.

29. Acorn, *One of the Multitude*, 123.

30. For critical comments on this approach, see E. P. Hennock, "The Measurement of Urban Poverty: From the Metropolis to the Nation, 1880–1920," *Economic History Review*, 2d ser., 40 (1987): 208–9. An alternative reading more sympathetic to Booth's methods can be found in K. Bales, "Charles Booth's Survey of *Life and Labour of the People in London* 1889–1903," in *The Social Survey in Historical Perspective, 1880–1940*, ed. M. Bulmer, K. Bales, and K. Kish Sklar (Cambridge: Cambridge University Press, 1991), 90–91.

31. Booth, *Life and Labour*, 1:159. See also Bales, "Booth's Survey," 91.

32. J. Gillis, *For Better, For Worse: British Marriages, 1600 to the Present* (Oxford: Oxford University Press, 1985), 249.

33. See, for example, F. M. L. Thompson, *The Rise of Respectable Society: A Social History of Victorian Britain, 1830–1900* (Cambridge: Harvard University Press, 1988), 181.

34. Thus we see the biggest difficulty in Booth's classification scheme.

35. D. R. Green, *From Artisans to Paupers: Economic Change and Poverty in London, 1790–1870* (Aldershot, Hants, U.K.: Scolar Press, 1995), 181–82.

36. The best overview of these issues is found in E. Higgs, "Women, Occupations and Work in the Nineteenth Century Censuses," *History Workshop Journal* 23 (1987): 59–80.

37. E. Ross, "Survival Networks," 11. A related source of income, the taking in of lodgers, also generally escaped enumeration in the census. However, it is possible to determine the prevalence of this activity.

38. S. Rose, *Limited Livelihoods: Gender and Class in Nineteenth-Century England* (Berkeley: University of California Press, 1992), 81.

39. Elizabeth Roberts notes that, despite these complications, "such data will be used in this . . . and obviously will continue to be used in similar historical work." E. Roberts, *Women's Work, 1840–1940* (London: Macmillan, 1988), 19.

CHAPTER 1. LITTLE COMMUNITIES: NEIGHBORHOODS AND HOUSEHOLDS

1. Foakes, *Between High Walls*, 2.

2. Foakes, *My Part of the River*, 107.

3. G. R. Sims, *How the Poor Live and Horrible London* (New York: Garland, 1984), 46.

4. G. Weightman and S. Humphries, *The Making of Modern London, 1815–1914* (London: Sidgwick & Jackson, 1983), 134; A. Wohl, *The Eternal Slum: Housing and Social Policy in Victorian London* (London: Edward Arnold, 1977), 31.

5. L. Clarke, *Building Capitalism: Historical Change and the Labour Process in the Production of the Built Environment* (London: Routledge, 1992), 188–89.

6. Ibid., 259.

7. N. Pevsner, *The Buildings of England: London, Except the Cities of London and Westminster* (Harmondsworth, U.K.: Penguin, 1952), 356.

8. Booth Collection, B 216:75.

9. The Somers Town subdistrict includes areas to the east, north, and west of Somers Town proper, but is the smallest unit for which the census general report lists population figures.

10. T. C. Barker and M. Robbins, *A History of London Transport* (London: George Allen and Unwin, 1963), 1:5.

11. Ibid., 1:115; G. Clinch, *Marylebone and St. Pancras* (London: Truslove and Shirley, 1890), 59; G. Mackenzie, *Marylebone: Great City North of Oxford Street* (London: Macmillan), 140.

12. A. J. D. Stonebridge, *St. Marylebone: A Sketch of its Historical Development* (London: n.p., 1952), 12–13.

13. J. Whitehead, *The Growth of St. Marylebone and Paddington: From Hyde Park to Queen's Park* (London: Jack Whitehead, 1989), 11.

14. T. Smith, *A Topographical and Historical Account of the Parish of St. Mary-le-bone* (London: John Smith, 1833), 218.

15. Though this registration district included an area larger than Lisson Grove, it forms the smallest unit for which population figures are available in census general reports. This area included a large zone to the east of Lisson Grove extending to the parish boundary. The total acreage of this district was slightly more than five hundred acres, but it included much uninhabited land, while Lisson Grove itself included only about thirty-eight densely inhabited acres.

16. *Census of Great Britain, 1851*, Parliamentary Papers 1852–53, vol. 85; *Census of*

England and Wales for the Year 1861, Parliamentary Papers 1863, vol. 53; *Census of England and Wales, 1881,* Parliamentary Papers 1883, vol. 79.

17. M. D. George, *London Life in the Eighteenth Century*, 2d ed. (Chicago: Academy Chicago, 1966), 188; A. K. Sabin, *The Silk Weavers of Spitalfields and Bethnal Green: With a Catalogue and Illustrations of Spitalfields Silks* (London: South Kensington Museum, 1931), 13; Booth, *Life and Labour*, 4:240. J. Argyle, who wrote the analysis of the silk industry in Booth's survey, estimates that these looms employed fifty thousand people.

18. Booth, *Life and Labour*, 4:240–41; Green, *Artisans to Paupers*, 159; L. D. Schwarz, *London in the Age of Industrialisation: Entrepreneurs, Labour Force, and Living Conditions, 1700–1850* (Cambridge: Cambridge University Press, 1992), 37–38; S. Snaith, *Bethnal Green, 1851–1951* (London: Bethnal Green Public Libraries, 1951), 9.

19. The silk trade suffered further decline following the 1860 agreement with France allowing the free import of French silk. See A. Wilson, *London's Industrial Heritage* (Newton Abbot, Devon, U.K.: David and Charles, 1967), 86.

20. W. J. Fishman, *East End, 1888: Life in a London Borough among the Labouring Poor* (Philadelphia: Temple University Press, 1988), 61; Stedman Jones, *Outcast London*, 107; P. G. Hall, *The Industries of London since 1861* (London: Hutchinson, 1962), 56, 82–83.

21. Hall, *Industries of London*, 42–43, 48, 75–77; Booth, *Life and Labour*, 4:69; Stedman Jones, *Outcast London*, 102, 106. Stedman Jones also cites the expansion of the docks through the nineteenth century as an important source of employment for surplus labor left by the declining silk industry.

22. It is likely that much of the growth between 1821 and 1841 occurred in the first years of the 1820s, before the crisis in silk production.

23. The population of Greater London increased by 10.2% between 1901 and 1911, including 33.5% growth in the "outer ring." Waller, *Town City and Nation*, 25. See also D. R. Green, "The Metropolitan Economy: Continuity and Change, 1800–1939," in *London: A New Metropolitan Geography*, ed. K. Hoggart and D. R. Green (London: Edward Arnold, 1991), 12.

24. Stedman Jones, *Outcast London*, 138ff.; Green, *Artisans to Paupers*, 152–53.

25. Stedman Jones, *Outcast London*, 81–88.

26. Ross, "Survival Networks."

27. Stedman Jones, *Outcast London*, 87–88.

28. Ellen Ross describes this as "the consolidation . . . of socially relatively uniform working-class neighborhoods." Ross, *Love and Toil*, 23.

29. I am grateful to Charles Tilly for his guidance on this issue.

30. It is difficult to determine the exact location of birth for those who are listed as born simply in Middlesex, Surrey, or Kent. Though some of these people were surely born in metropolitan portions of these counties, it is impossible to know exactly how many were London-born. If we include the three bordering counties, 78.6% in Somers Town, 77.0% in Lisson Grove, and 88.0% of the population in Globe Town was born in the London region, compared to 69.7% of the whole London population.

31. The London-wide figures include those listed as born in "Intra-metropolitan" Surrey, Kent, and Middlesex. The percentages for London exclude those born at sea. London figures come from *Census of England and Wales, 1881*, Parliamentary Papers 1883, vol. 80.

32. This includes those whose place of birth is listed simply as "Mile End." In addition, 9.2% of the Somers Town population, 12.1% in Lisson Grove, and 6.9% in Globe

Town listed merely "Middlesex" or "London" as their birthplaces. Many of these people were probably born in the neighborhoods themselves.

33. Of those born outside the metropolitan counties whose place of birth was identified, 36.5% originated in this region.

34. Nearly a third of the migrants from these counties in Globe Town were between the ages thirty-five and forty-nine, compared with less than 15% of the rest of the Globe Town population.

35. This region includes the counties of Hertfordshire, Buckinghamshire, Oxfordshire, Northamptonshire, Huntingdonshire, Bedfordshire, and Cambridgeshire.

36. For analyses of the context of migration and the common links between areas of origin and particular destinations, see L. Page Moch, *Moving Europeans: Migration in Western Europe since 1650* (Bloomington: Indiana University Press, 1992), 13–18, 126–43, and C. Tilly, "Transplanted Networks," Working Paper no. 35, Center for Studies of Social Change, New School for Social Research, 1986.

37. Charles Booth found that 85% of a sample of English migrants to London came between these ages. See E. Lampard, "The Urbanizing World," in *The Victorian City: Images and Realities*, ed. H. J. Dyos and M. Wolff (London: Routledge and Kegan Paul, 1973), 16–17.

38. Even after 1881, when foreign immigrants flowed into the East End, Globe Town was not a common destination. These immigrants generally settled to the south and west, particularly in Whitechapel.

39. The total population of the three areas was 46,957—23,601 men and 23,353 women, with 3 individuals of undetermined sex.

40. In the few houses with live-in servants in the areas, the ratio was almost identical to the London figures: 88 men to 100 women. However, in Lisson Grove many of those described as "servants" worked as warehousemen or barmen and were male. Lisson Grove servant-holding households had a surprising 146 men per 100 women.

41. Lampard, "Urbanizing World," 16. This theory is supported by the fact that the ratio of adult men to women is lower than the overall ratio in the neighborhood. Among those over fifteen, the Globe Town population included nearly equal numbers of men and women (5,569 men and 5,570 women).

42. In another slight anomaly, the Lisson Grove male population declines only slightly between ages fifteen to nineteen (621) and twenty to twenty-four (593). This trend reflects the population of the large lodging houses. In these houses, 20.0% of the men were aged twenty to twenty-four, compared with 9.8% of the male population in Lisson Grove as a whole.

43. See L. Tilly and J. W. Scott, *Women, Work and Family* (New York: Holt, Rinehart and Winston, 1978), 169. I am grateful to Louise Tilly for her advice in calculating this ratio.

44. This figure was calculated according to the formula presented by J. Hanjal, "Age at Marriage and Proportions Marrying," *Population Studies* 7 (1953): 111–36.

45. The age structure of married women was similar across the three neighborhoods. For example, 70.3% of wives were under age forty-five in Somers Town, 72.6% in Lisson Grove, and 70.3% in Globe Town.

46. A. McLaren, *Birth Control in Nineteenth-Century England* (New York: Holmes and Meier, 1978), 220. See also Ross, *Love and Toil*, 102.

47. The Annual Report of the Registrar General listed these figures for registration subdistricts, but not for these specific areas.

48. Registrar General, *Quarterly Return of Marriages, Births and Deaths*, 1881.

49. Only related people were included in 87.3% of Somers Town households, 88.7% of those in Lisson Grove, and 87.1% of households in Globe Town

50. Of all nonrelatives 64.6% were lodgers, while another 16.2% were servants. The figures for lodgers include those classed in the census as "boarders."

51. M. Anderson, *Family Structure in Nineteenth Century Lancashire* (Cambridge: Cambridge University Press, 1979), 53, 101–2; J. Modell and T. K. Hareven, "Urbanization and the Malleable Household: An Examination of Boarding and Lodging in American Families," in *Family and Kin in Urban Communities, 1700–1930*, ed. T. K. Hareven (New York: New Viewpoints, 1977), 164–86.

52. M. Anderson, "Household Structure and the Industrial Revolution: Mid-Nineteenth-Century Preston in Comparative Perspective," in *Household and Family in Past Time*, ed. P. Laslett with R. Wall (Cambridge: Cambridge University Press, 1972), 220; K. Ittman, *Work, Gender and Family in Victorian England* (New York: New York University Press, 1995), 203.

53. In Somers Town, 63.2% of households with lodgers included only one, while the figure for Lisson Grove is 71.4%, and for Globe Town, 71.0%. Anderson also found that small-scale lodging was common, as 69% of the households having lodgers that he found in 1851 Preston had only one or two lodgers. Anderson, *Nineteenth Century Lancashire*, 47.

54. Of lodgers in the three neighborhoods, 68.7% were born in the London region, compared to 82.0% of all residents.

55. This difference is less striking than that discovered for Bradford by Ittman. He found that women headed 20.5% of all Bradford households in 1881, but over 36% of those that included lodgers. Ittman, *Work, Gender and Family*, 203 n. 98.

56. Servant-holding households made up 2.0% of Somers Town, 1.5% of Lisson Grove, and 3.2% of Globe Town households.

57. Booth classified four of these five streets as purple, indicating a mixed population, while Chapel Street fell into the pink or "comfortable" category. C. Booth, *Charles Booth's Descriptive Map of London Poverty* (1889; reprint, London: London Topographical Society, 1984).

58. Green Street and Victoria Park Square were classified as pink mixed with red (comfortable and well-to-do), while Globe Road was mostly purple (mixed population) and pink (comfortable). Ibid. In the major servant-holding Globe Town streets, 18.4% of the households included servants, and in Somers Town 24.0% of households in the key streets included servants.

59. Though Bell, Great James, and Hereford Streets were classified as purple (mixed population) by Booth, Devonshire Street fell into the dark blue category, indicating a very poor street. Ibid.

60. In Lisson Grove, 44% of servants were employed in domestic work; in Somers Town, 56%; and in Globe Town, 62%. Others were commonly occupied processing, storing, or serving food and beverages. In this analysis, "servant" describes a relationship to the household head (listed in the census), as opposed to an occupation, though in many cases the census listed "servant" as an individual's occupation as well.

61. Overall, 47% of heads of servant-holding households worked in food service or food processing and selling. Eighteen percent ran pubs, coffeehouses, or beer houses, and another 12% were bakers or butchers. In Globe Town, 12% of servant-holding households were involved in boot and shoe production.

62. D. Chaplin, "The Structure of London Households in 1851," cited by L. Lees,

Exiles of Erin: Irish Migrants in Victorian London (Ithaca: Cornell University Press, 1979), 134.

63. Individuals who lived alone comprised 3.1% of the population of Somers Town and the same proportion of Lisson Grove residents. But only 1.6% of Globe Town residents lived alone.

64. Only 18.1% of people living alone in the three areas were under age thirty (64.4% of the entire population was under thirty). But 55% of those living alone were aged fifty or over (compared with 12.5% of the population). Of these older people living alone, 71.2% were women.

65. Of households 77.3% included more than one individual and only related people.

66. These figures count spouses of children as extended kin. Elsewhere in this study sons and daughters-in-law are considered as "offspring."

67. Ittman, *Work, Gender and Family*, 202; Anderson, "Household Structure," 220.

68. Of kin 26.3% were aged fifteen to twenty-four, compared with 18.8% of the entire population. Of kin 10.3% were sixty-five or older, of whom 79.6% were women. For a discussion of the impact of kin on household economies in Bradford, see Ittman, *Work, Gender and Family*, 202–3.

69. This pattern is also clear from the generational structure of households in the areas. The vast majority of households included only one or two generations (96.4% in Somers Town, 96.9% in Lisson Grove, and 95.7% in Globe Town).

70. Men married, on average, at age 26.1 in Somers Town, 25.2 in Lisson Grove, and 25.1 in Globe Town.

71. The lower Lisson Grove figure reflects the large lodging houses in that neighborhood. When these households are excluded, 75.5% of these young single men lived with their parents.

72. See Ross, *Love and Toil*, 158–61.

73. Foakes, *Between High Walls*, 72.

74. Acorn, *One of the Multitude*, 79.

75. In contrast, 96.2% of these married men were heads of their own households, and 96.1% of married women under age forty-five were either household heads or wives of heads of households.

76. On the contributions of children to the family economy, see Davin, *Growing Up Poor*, chaps. 9 and 10.

77. But when Catherine and the boy were forced by poverty into the workhouse, the authorities found John and prosecuted him for failure to maintain them. He was sentenced to one month's imprisonment with hard labor. *Marylebone Mercury*, 20 March 1880.

78. *Marylebone Mercury*, 1 October 1881 and 8 October 1881.

79. In this case, the new couple did get officially married, upon which her first father-in-law prosecuted her for bigamy and she was convicted. *East London Observer*, 29 November 1879.

80. P. Laslett, "Mean Household Size in England since the Sixteenth Century," in *Household and Family in Past Time*, ed. Laslett with Wall, 138.

81. W. A. Armstrong, "A Note on the Household Structure of Mid-Nineteenth-Century York in Comparative Perspective," in *Household and Family in Past Time*, ed. Laslett with Wall, 206; Anderson, "Household Structure," 219.

82. Lees, *Exiles of Erin*, 136.

83. Stedman Jones, "Working-Class Culture,"182.

CHAPTER 2. "I OFTEN WANT BREAD": THE CAUSES OF POVERTY

1. Booth, *Life and Labour*, 1:5 n.
2. Ibid., 2:21.
3. Hennock, "Measurement of Urban Poverty," 210.
4. Green, *Artisans to Paupers*, 181–82.
5. Booth Collection, B73:3, 3A:41. The survey included 1,623 children, while the data used in this study count 3,082 children these ages in Lisson Grove.
6. This Booth survey also did not count every household included in Somers Town, though it did count those in the northern section excluded from table 1. Among the children surveyed here, 585 or 18.3% were "very poor." Booth Collection, B73:6–14.
7. Ibid.
8. Booth, *Life and Labour*, 1:146–55.
9. This level was estimated by Booth to be necessary to keep a family out of poverty, and those households earning below this fell into class "D," among the poor. J. H. Treble, *Urban Poverty in Britain* (New York: St. Martin's Press), 16–50; D. Reeder, introduction to *Charles Booth's Descriptive Map of London Poverty* (1889; reprint, London: London Topographical Society, 1984).
10. Booth, *Life and Labour*, 1:147.
11. One scholar has called this "probably the major insight of recent scholarship on industrial capitalism." P. Joyce, "Work," in *Cambridge Social History of Britain, 1750–1950*, ed. Thompson, 2:131.
12. R. Samuel, "Workshop of the World: Steam Power and Hand Technology in Mid-Victorian Britain," *History Workshop Journal* 3 (1977): 6–72.
13. Green, *Artisans to Paupers*, 73ff.; J. Schmiechen, "State Reform and the Local Economy: An Aspect of Industrialization in Late Victorian and Edwardian London," *Economic History Review*, 2d ser., 28:3 (1975): 413–28.
14. Green, *Artisans to Paupers*, 82.
15. Stedman Jones, *Outcast London*, 26.
16. *Census of 1881*. The occupational categories used in this study generally conform to those in the general report, though some adjustments have been made. The category "road transport" has been estimated for the London population.
17. Booth, *Life and Labour*, 1:147.
18. *Report of the Royal Commission on the Poor Laws and the Relief of Distress*, Parliamentary Papers 1909, vol. 37, 1151.
19. E. Hobsbawm, "The Nineteenth-Century London Labor Market" (1964), in *Workers: Worlds of Labor* (New York: Pantheon, 1984), 137.
20. P. L. Garside, "London and the Home Counties," in *Cambridge Social History of Britain 1750–1950*, ed. Thompson, 1:503.
21. Figures for the occupational, demographic, and household structure of the three neighborhoods come from the census enumerators' books of 1881, while those for London as a whole come from the census general report, *Census of 1881*.
22. Hall, *Industries of London*, 72–73.
23. Ibid., 83–85; *Report of the Select Committee of the House of Lords on the Sweating System*, Parliamentary Papers 1888, vol. 20, 5787, 6160, 6188–96, 7243–44, 7757–58, 7705.

24. Hall, *Industries of London*, 85.

25. Wilson, *Industrial Heritage*, 30. In 1904, the Brinsmead factory employed three hundred men, and the Collard and Collard factory had five stories, with a circular well through which pianos were hoisted between floors. L. T. Newman, "It All Began with J. C. Bach: A History of Piano Making in Camden," *Camden History Review* 1 (1973): 30.

26. F. Kelly, *The Post-Office London Directory for 1881* (London: Kelly & Co., 1881).

27. The location quotient for carriage and coach building was 2.81.

28. Barker and Robbins, *London Transport*, 1:105, 241, 261.

29. F. M. L. Thompson, "Nineteenth-Century Horse Sense," *Economic History Review*, 2d ser., 29 (1976): 65. Of those engaged with animals, 83.4% were occupied with horses. In addition, 58.4% of those in the iron and steel category (ranking ninth among Lisson Grove occupations) were various sorts of smiths, many of whom served the horse population.

30. Stedman Jones, *Outcast London*, 109–11.

31. Booth, *Life and Labour*, 4:69, 161–64, 168–69; Hall, *Industries of London*, 75, 85–86; *Report on the Sweating System*, 5029. One such sawmill lay along the Regents Canal at the eastern edge of Globe Town.

32. Silk workers form the majority of those listed in the category "textiles."

33. The area around Cranbrook and Alma Roads was the site of the last silk weavers in East London, who remained there into the 1930s. G. F. Vale, *Old Bethnal Green* (London: Blythendale Press, 1934), 38; A. K. Sabin, *Silk Weavers*, 16–18; Booth, *Life and Labour*, 4:245, 255.

34. General dealers were another overrepresented occupation among Lisson Grove men, with a location quotient of 2.61.

35. Of those Lisson Grove women who were either general domestic servants or domestic indoor servants and whose relationship to the household head could be determined, 58% were daughters of the head, and only 11% were described as "servant." In Somers Town, 47% were daughters and 25% were "servants."

36. In Somers Town, other common manufacturing processes employing females included upholstery, carpets, draperies, embroidery, and paper box and bag making.

37. The category "nurse" is ambiguous, referring to a person caring for children, assisting in a medical facility, working as a sick nurse in someone's home, or assisting new mothers.

38. Hospitals in the vicinity of Lisson Grove included the Medical and Surgical Home in St. John's Wood, St. Agnes Hospital, the Samaritan Free Hospital, and Queen Charlotte's Lying-In Hospital. Near Somers Town, hospitals included the Foundling Hospital, the hospital at University College, and the Royal Free Hospital.

39. In Lisson Grove, milk sellers and dairy women were particularly numerous among those in the food processing and selling trades.

40. The limitations of the census as a source for information on women's employment must be kept in mind and have been discussed in the introduction.

41. Of twenty-three examples of Somers Town residents, nineteen worked in Somers Town, or within a half mile of the neighborhood. Three others worked in North London, within a mile and a half of the area, and only one worked a long distance from his home. *Camden and Kentish Towns, Hampstead, Highgate, Holloway and St. Pancras Gazette*, 1879–89 (hereafter cited as *CKTSP Gazette*). Of thirteen Lisson Grove residents for which this information is available, ten worked in the neighborhood, and two more worked in southern St. Marylebone. Again, only one worked far from the neighborhood. *Marylebone Mercury*, Booth Collection, B73:161–74.

42. Booth Collection, B73:174.

43. Booth Collection B182:55; *East London Observer*, 17 April 1880, 2 December 1882; F. Warner, *The Silk Industry of the United Kingdom: Its Origin and Development* (London: Drane's, 1921), 61.

44. Boot and shoe, silk, furniture, clothing, matchbox, and brush making were all concentrated in the vicinity of Globe Town.

45. Stedman Jones, *Outcast London*, 108; Hall, *Industries of London*, 87; Booth, *Life and Labour*, 4:299.

46. London County Council, *Minutes of Proceedings*, 1913, 1:653–54. Among casual workers, residence near potential employment opportunities was even more essential.

47. Stedman Jones offers the best discussion of casual labor in London. Stedman Jones, *Outcast London*, pt. 1. See also Treble, *Urban Poverty*, 55–71.

48. J. White, *The Worst Street in North London: Campbell Bunk, Islington between the Wars* (London: Routledge and Kegan Paul, 1986), 31–44.

49. Acorn, *One of the Multitude*, 234–40.

50. Stedman Jones, *Outcast London*, 33–51; Treble, *Urban Poverty*, 71–80.

51. W. Swan, "The Journal of William Swan," in *The Journals of Two Poor Dissenters 1786–1880* (London: Routledge and Kegan Paul, 1970), 86–90.

52. The census recorded a single occupation for each individual, and thus was not sensitive to dovetailing by individual workers.

53. Stedman Jones, *Outcast London*, 39–40.

54. P. Malcolmson, *English Laundresses: A Social History, 1850–1930* (Urbana: University of Illinois Press, 1986), 12.

55. Stedman Jones, *Outcast London*, 41.

56. Ibid., app. 2, table 11.

57. Though this improvement was due to declining prices, casual and seasonal underemployment undercut these benefits. E. Hobsbawm, *Industry and Empire: From 1750 to the Present Day* (Harmondsworth, U.K.: Penguin, 1969), 162–64.

58. Some female-headed households included adult males who contributed significantly to the household budget, as might be the case with a widow supported by her sons.

59. When George Acorn left school and went to work, he earned 6s. a week as a shop boy in a furniture manufacturing shop. He gave his mother 5s. 6d. of his wages. Acorn, *One of the Multitude*, 116–17.

60. E. Roberts, "Working-Class Standards of Living in Barrow and Lancaster, 1880–1914," *Economic History Review*, 2d ser., 30 (1977): 319.

61. Booth, *Life and Labour*, 1:134–40.

62. Booth calculated this total by counting each man aged twenty or above as one full adult, women fifteen or older as three-quarters of a full adult, and younger children as their age, divided by twenty. Thus, a family consisting of a husband, wife, and four children aged twelve, nine, six, and three, would total the equivalent of 3.25 full adults.

63. These figures represent averages, as Booth calculated income and expenditure over a five-week period.

64. M. Pember Reeves, *Round About a Pound a Week* (1913; reprint, London: Virago, 1979).

65. Expenditure on food, particularly for women and children, was probably lower in the early 1910s than in the early 1880s, as the price of bread declined by over 15% between these periods. P. Mathias, *The First Industrial Nation*, 2d ed. (London: Methuen, 1983), 441–42.

66. Booth, *Life and Labour*, 1:136–39.
67. Ross, *Love and Toil*, 108–9.
68. Wohl, *Eternal Slum*, 42.
69. Booth, *Life and Labour*, 1:143.
70. Rents in Somers Town for one room were generally 2s. 6d. to 5s. weekly; for two rooms, 5s. to 7s. 6d. In Globe Town, one room might cost 2s. 6d. to 3s. 6d. weekly, while two rooms ranged from about 4s. 6d. to 5s. 6d. Lisson Grove rents for one room ran about 2s. 6d. to 5s., and for two rooms residents paid 8s. to 9s. 6d. See A. August, "The Other Side of 'Outcast London': Women in Three Poor Neighborhoods" (Ph.D. diss., Columbia University, 1993), 68.
71. This general figure is between the amounts reported by Booth in the poor and very poor household averages.
72. This figure is significantly lower than those cited in the average households in Booth's survey, but part of this difference derives from the fact that his figures include the husband's spending money. The figure discussed here refers to the household money turned over by the husband after he deducted his spending money. See *CKTSP Gazette*, 23 August 1884, 4 October 1884, 8 September 1888.
73. These wage estimates are based on a variety of sources and are broad enough to cover the majority of cases.
74. Ross, "Fierce Questions," 585–86.
75. Booth Collection, B215:95–96.
76. *Marylebone Mercury*, 5 July 1879.
77. Booth Collection, B182:99.
78. Acorn, *One of the Multitude*, 123.
79. *Marylebone Mercury*, 22 November 1879.
80. St. Pancras, "Annual Report of the Medical Officer of Health" (1890): 75; (1891): 75–76, Camden Local History Library.
81. St. Pancras, Health Department, "Housing of the Working Classes," 57. This quote is from a document dated February 1891 that was read at the enquiry.
82. *Marylebone Mercury*, 11 September 1880.
83. Foakes, *Between High Walls*, 67.
84. R. S. Roberts, "Rereadings: Gavin, H., *Sanitary Ramblings*," *East London Papers* 8 (1965): 110.
85. D. Owen, *The Government of Victorian London, 1855–1889: The Metropolitan Board of Works, the Vestries and the City Corporation* (Cambridge: Harvard University Press, 1982), 272–73, 302–3; St. Marylebone, "Annual Reports of Medical Officer of Health" (1883): 124, Marylebone Local History Library.
86. Wohl, *Eternal Slum*, 7.
87. H. Gavin, *Sanitary Ramblings: Being Sketches and Illustrations of Bethnal Green, a Type of the Condition of the Metropolis and other Large Towns* (London: Churchill, 1848), 10–11. Though every street in the district did not suffer such conditions, these examples are typical of many Globe Town streets.
88. Owen, *Government of Victorian London*, 134–37.
89. *Marylebone Mercury*, 29 October 1881.
90. Booth Collection, B225:33.
91. Booth Collection, B183:95.
92. White, *Worst Street*, 95–101.
93. *East London Observer*, 17 April 1880.

94. *Eastern Argus*, 31 March 1883.

95. Registrar General, *Quarterly Return of Marriages, Births and Deaths*, 1881.

96. Marylebone, "Medical Officer of Health Reports" (1883): 24, (1890): 30.

97. Ross, "Survival Networks," 11–12, 16.

98. Acorn, *One of the Multitude*, 76.

99. Booth Collection B73:169.

100. *East London Observer*, 17 April 1880.

101. Ross, "Fierce Questions," 585–86.

102. Ibid., 576; F. Miller, *Saint Pancras Past and Present: Being Historical, Traditional, and General Notes of the Period* (London: F. Miller, 1874), 88; P. Johnson, *Saving and Spending: The Working-Class Economy in Britain, 1870–1939* (Oxford: Clarendon Press, 1985), 144–50, 165ff.; White, *Worst Street*, 74; Acorn, *One of the Multitude*, 69.

CHAPTER 3. "THE WORK IS QUITE DIFFERENT":
THE SEXUAL DIVISION OF LABOR AND WOMEN'S JOBS

1. *Report on the Sweating System*, 1542–48, 1853.

2. Problems with the census enumerators' books as a source for total numbers of employed women are discussed in the introduction.

3. *Census of 1881*.

4. S. Alexander, "Women's Work in Nineteenth-Century London: A Study of the Years 1820–1850," in *The Rights and Wrongs of Women*, ed. A. Oakley and J. Mitchell (Harmondsworth, U.K.: Penguin, 1976), 111.

5. The major exception to this pattern was live-in domestic service. These servants worked long hours throughout the year, earning steady but very low wages.

6. A. Phillips and B. Taylor, "Sex and Skill: Notes towards a Feminist Economics," *Feminist Review* 6 (1980): 79. See also Rose, *Limited Livelihoods*, 28–29; M. Barrett, *Women's Oppression Today: The Marxist/Feminist Encounter*, rev. ed. (London: Verso, 1988), 181–82.

7. An example of the latter process was in dressmaking. The different processes were gradually subcontracted out to less-skilled workers, undercutting the position of what had been an unusually highly paid and skilled female workforce.

8. Alexander, "Women's Work," 10.

9. The total number of men employed in boot and shoe manufacture in these neighborhoods was 943, while 282 women worked in the trade.

10. This does not include the many Globe Town women described on the census as machinists, many of whom worked in footwear manufacture.

11. *Report on the Sweating System*, 406.

12. J. Schmiechen, *Sweated Industries and Sweated Labor: The London Clothing Trades, 1860–1914* (Urbana: University of Illinois Press, 1984), 29ff.; H. Bradley, *Men's Work, Women's Work: A Sociological History of the Sexual Division of Labour in Employment* (Cambridge: Polity Press, 1989), 147; Booth, *Life and Labour*, 4:75.

13. Booth, *Life and Labour*, 4:75–78, 112; R. Mudie-Smith, *Sweated Industries: A Handbook of the "Daily News" Exhibition* (1913; reprint, New York: Garland, 1980), 82.

14. Booth, *Life and Labour*, 4:103–4; *Report on the Sweating System*, 4324–30.

15. *Report on the Sweating System*, 1108–13, 4223.

16. Booth, *Life and Labour*, 4:90–91.

17. Schloss's description also reveals the precarious economic position of these small employers, whose earnings were meager and inconsistent.

18. Bradley, *Men's Work, Women's Work*, 147–50; Green, *Artisans to Paupers*, 170–73; Schwarz, *London*, 194–99.

19. Only one woman worked in silk manufacture in Somers Town and Lisson Grove.

20. Vale, *Bethnal Green*, 38; Booth, *Life and Labour*, 4:240.

21. Warner, *Silk Industry*, 61; Booth, *Life and Labour*, 4:247.

22. Sabin, *Silk Weavers*, 16–17.

23. For an ordinary week's work, patterned weaving was estimated to pay 25s., compared to 15s. for plain weaving. Booth, *Life and Labour*, 4:247–50. Due to the shortage of employment in the silk trade, weavers seldom worked full weeks, so actual wages were significantly lower.

24. The tailoring of women's clothing (as distinct from dressmaking) was dominated by male workers, while the manufacture of men's outerwear involved men and women. J. Morris, "The Characteristics of Sweating: The Late Nineteenth-Century London and Leeds Tailoring Trade," in *Unequal Opportunities: Women's Employment in England, 1800–1918*, ed. A. V. John (New York: Basil Blackwell, 1986), 106.

25. C. Meyer and C. Black, *Makers of Our Clothes* (London: Duckworth, 1909), 45; Morris, "Sweating," 107; *Report on the Sweating System*, 1941–43.

26. In addition, the availability of employment in domestic work in the immediate vicinity of Somers Town and Lisson Grove made it less likely that women in these areas would take up tailoring.

27. Meyer and Black, *Makers of Our Clothes*, 27; Booth, *Life and Labour*, 4:44; D. Bythell, *The Sweated Trades: Outwork in Nineteenth-Century Britain* (New York: St. Martin's), 77.

28. Meyer and Black, *Makers of Our Clothes*, 30–31, 38.

29. Booth, *Life and Labour*, 4:258.

30. Ibid., 4:257; Meyer and Black, *Makers of Our Clothes*, 59. In contrast, boot and shoe finishing included the cutting of the sole, a job reserved for men.

31. An exception to this pattern is provided by female waistcoat makers, who were involved in the high-quality portion of the trade.

32. Meyer and Black, *Makers of Our Clothes*, 27.

33. Booth, *Life and Labour*, 4:282; Mudie-Smith, *Sweated Industries*, 71.

34. Mudie-Smith, *Sweated Industries*, 71–72; Booth, *Life and Labour*, 4:282–84.

35. J. R. MacDonald, ed., *Women in the Printing Trades* (London: P. S. King & Son, 1904), 5, 7, 17; *Report of the Commissioners Appointed to Inquire into the Working of the Factory and Workshops Acts*, Parliamentary Papers 1876, vol. 30, 133; F. Hunt, "Opportunities Lost and Gained: Mechanization and Women's Work in the London Bookbinding and Printing Trades," in *Unequal Opportunities*, ed. John, 73.

36. MacDonald, *Women in Printing*, 4; Mudie-Smith, *Sweated Industries*, 82.

37. MacDonald, *Women in Printing*, 4–5; Hunt, "Opportunities Lost and Gained," 86–87.

38. Mudie-Smith, *Sweated Industries*, 82; *Working of the Factory and Workshops Acts*, 126–27; MacDonald, *Women in Printing*, 101; C. Black, *Married Women's Work* (1915; reprint, London: Virago, 1983), 54.

39. *Working of the Factory and Workshops Acts*, 144.

40. A. August, "Patterns of Women's Union Membership: England and Wales at the Turn of the Twentieth Century" (Master's thesis, Columbia University, 1985), 35. Accord-

ing to the 1901 census general report, only 1.36% of women in printing and bookbinding worked at home.

41. MacDonald, *Women in Printing*, 55, 57.

42. This offers an interesting exception to the strategy of defining women's work as unskilled and thus paying low wages. In this case, the definition of these tasks as skilled and thus requiring a lengthy training period also allowed employers to hold down wage rates.

43. Hunt, "Opportunities Lost and Gained," 74–75, 86.

44. Though furniture manufacturing was also quite common in Globe Town, it appears that the small producers of the East End sweated trade did not upholster most of their furniture. Among men in the Globe Town furniture trades, only 3% worked in upholstery, while in Somers Town, 13% of men in the furniture trades worked in this branch.

45. *Report on the Sweating System*, 5800, 1387.

46. Booth, *Life and Labour*, 4:206.

47. *Minutes of Evidence of the Royal Commission on Labour*, Parliamentary Papers 1892, vol. 35, 323.

48. Ibid., 327; *Report on the Sweating System*, 3067, 7494–96.

49. F. Sheppard, *London, 1808–1870: The Infernal Wen* (Berkeley: University of California Press, 1971), 192. E. H. Whetham, "The London Milk Trade," *Economic History Review*, 2d ser., 17 (1964–65): 369–71.

50. Sheppard, *London, 1808–1870*, 191.

51. W. Collison, *The Apostle of Free Labour* (London: Hurst and Blackett, 1913), 2.

52. Whetham, "Milk Trade," 37–72.

53. Opposition to women's employment generally originated either in the opposition to women's participation in roles that were viewed as inappropriate or in male workers' fears of competition from female labor. See H. Benenson, "The 'Family Wage' and Working Women's Consciousness in Britain, 1880–1914," *Politics & Society* 19 (1991): 71–72.

54. On the changes in the organization of domestic work, and the debate over whether these developments are properly explained by "supply" or "demand" factors, see T. M. McBride, *The Domestic Revolution: The Modernization of Household Service in England and France 1820–1920* (London: Croom Helm, 1976), 111–13; E. Higgs, *Domestic Servants and Households in Rochdale, 1851–1871* (New York: Garland, 1986), 219–40; P. Horn, *The Rise and Fall of the Victorian Servant* (New York: St. Martin's, 1975), 151–52.

55. Malcolmson, *English Laundresses*, 28, 30–34.

56. Ibid., 33; *Royal Commission on Labour, Reports by the Lady Assistant Commissioners on the Conditions of Work in Various Industries*, Parliamentary Papers 1893–94, vol. 37, 21.

57. Foakes, *My Part of the River*, 16.

58. Black, *Married Women's Work*, 119. The neighborhood is not identified.

59. *Reports by the Lady Assistant Commissioners*, 21.

60. Malcolmson, *English Laundresses*, 41.

61. Higgs, *Domestic Servants*, 34.

62. Ibid., 48.

63. Ibid.

64. This includes 185 whose relationship to the household head was "servant," and one in each of the following relationships: "nurse," "housekeeper," "cook," and "maid."

65. These other servants in the households might include those employed outside the domestic sphere, but whose relationship to the household head was described as servant.

66. Across all the neighborhoods, 43% of heads of households including live-in female domestic servants worked in food processing, selling, or service.

67. I. Beeton, *Book of Household Management*, quoted by Horn, *Victorian Servant*, 50.

68. Horn, *Victorian Servant*, 113–15.

69. McBride, *Domestic Revolution*, 102.

70. C. Chinn, *They Worked All Their Lives: Women of the Urban Poor in England, 1880–1939* (Manchester: Manchester University Press, 1988), 105–6.

71. Clearly, however, the management of a poor household did not require all the same domestic skills as did cleaning a middle-class home. Polishing silver, for example, was not likely to fall among the ordinary tasks of a poor housewife.

72. Ross, *Love and Toil*, 120.

73. McBride, *Domestic Revolution*, 12.

74. Higgs, *Domestic Servants*, 43.

75. Horn, *Victorian Servant*, 66.

76. Ibid., 59–61.

77. E. Higgs, "Domestic Service and Household Production," in *Unequal Opportunities*, ed. John, 138.

78. Horn, *Victorian Servant*, 60.

79. Those manufacturing trades employing more than 80% women have been categorized as predominantly female.

80. Schmiechen, *Sweated Industries and Sweated Labor*, 57; *Third Report from the Select Committee of the House of Lords on the Sweating System with Minutes of Evidence and Appendices*, Parliamentary Papers 1889, vol. 13, 17456–57; Hall, *Industries of London*, 43–48.

81. *Report on the Sweating System*, 4000–4002; Mudie-Smith, *Sweated Industries*, 56; Meyer and Black, *Makers of Our Clothes*, 87.

82. Stedman Jones, *Outcast London*, 27 n. 42a.

83. Schmiechen, *Sweated Industries and Sweated Labor*, 24–27; Booth, *Life and Labour*, 4:90–91.

84. *Report on the Sweating System*, 1636–40.

85. Schmiechen, *Sweated Industries and Sweated Labor*, 27.

86. Booth, *Life and Labour*, 4:266; *Report on the Sweating System*, 5611–22.

87. *Second Report of the Royal Commission on Labour*, Parliamentary Papers 1892, vol. 36, 157; *Report on the Sweating System*, 2580; Booth, *Life and Labour*, 4:267.

88. J. White, *Rothschild Buildings: Life in an East End Tenement Block, 1887–1920* (London: Routledge and Kegan Paul, 1980), 226; Black, *Married Women's Work*, 44.

89. *Reports by the Lady Assistant Commissioners*, 10; Black, *Married Women's Work*, 44.

90. White, *Rothschild Buildings*, 226.

91. Morris, "Sweating," 102; Black, *Married Women's Work*, 93, 96; Schmiechen, *Sweated Industries and Sweated Labor*, 53.

92. M. E. Bulkley, *The Establishment of Legal Minimum Rates in the Boxmaking Industry* (London: G. Bell & Sons, 1915), 4; Booth, *Life and Labour*, 4:281, 279.

93. Black, *Married Women's Work*, 57; Booth, *Life and Labour*, 4:279; Mudie-Smith, *Sweated Industries*, 30.

94. Quoted by Bythell, *Sweated Trades*, 139–40. Matchbox workers were subject to the harmful effects of work with phosphorus, which could lead to necrosis or "phossy jaw." A. Wohl, *Endangered Lives: Public Health in Victorian Britain* (London: J. M. Dent & Sons, 1983), 269.

95. Mudie-Smith, *Sweated Industries*, 27–28; *Reports by the Lady Assistant Commissioners*, 94; Black, *Married Women's Work*, 33.

96. Barret, *Women's Oppression Today*, 181–82; P. Hudson and W. R. Lee, "Women's Work and the Family Economy in Historical Perspective," in *Women's Work and the Family Economy in Historical Perspective*, ed. P. Hudson and W. R. Lee (Manchester: Manchester University Press, 1990), 21. E. Jordan, "The Exclusion of Women from Industry in Nineteenth-Century Britain," *Comparative Studies of Society and History* 31 (1989): 289–93.

97. Green, *Artisans to Paupers*, 74–77.

98. *Royal Commission on the Poor Laws*, 323, 325.

99. Schwarz, *London*, 190–93.

100. Green, *Artisans to Paupers*, 80.

101. Hunt, "Opportunities Lost and Gained," 86.

102. For interesting analyses of the sexual division of labor, see Rose, *Limited Livelihoods*; L. Tilly, "Gender and Jobs in Early Twentieth-Century French Industry," *International Labor and Working Class History* 43 (1993); J. Lown, *Women and Industrialization: Gender at Work in Nineteenth-Century England* (Minneapolis: University of Minnesota Press, 1990); Jordan, "Exclusion of Women."

103. *Royal Commission on the Poor Laws*, 225.

104.- Exceptions to this rule included the part of the artificial-flower trade that produced for the millinery industry and box making. However, both these trades were closely linked to consumer demand, and were subject to seasonal fluctuations.

105. Mudie-Smith, *Sweated Industries*, 45, 56; Meyer and Black, *Makers of Our Clothes*, 29, 86.

106. *Working of Factory and Workshops Acts*, 132, 175, 180–82; *Report on the Sweating System*, 3737–38, 3464, 7952–56; *Second Report of the Royal Commission on Labour*, 158; *Reports of the Lady Assistant Commissioners*, 94; Morris, "Sweating," 97, 110; Black, *Married Women's Work*, 96.

107. Malcolmson, *English Laundresses*, 24; N. Vynne and H. Blackburn, *Women under the Factory Act* (London: Williams and Norgate, 1903), 98.

108. Black, *Married Women's Work*, 18.

109. MacDonald, *Women in Printing*, 80.

110. Booth, *Life and Labour*, 4:267.

111. Bythell, *Sweated Trades*, 60; H. Mayhew, *London Labour and the London Poor* (1861–62; reprint, New York: Dover, 1968), 2:301; Stedman Jones, *Outcast London*, 145, 101.

112. Booth, *Life and Labour*, 4:250.

113. As described above, these live-in "maids-of-all-work" faced an unrelenting series of tasks.

114. Schmiechen, *Sweated Industries and Sweated Labor*, 18.

115. Malcolmson, *English Laundresses*, 13–14.

116. Higgs, *Domestic Servants*, 79.

117. One exception to this pattern was the millinery trade, in which many workers still received time wages. This may reflect the fact that some millinery workers worked as sales clerks in shops as well as in production. Stedman Jones, *Outcast London*, 39.

118. *Report on the Sweating System*, 1478.

119. Bythell, *Sweated Trades*, 177–79; *Report on the Sweating System*, 9352; Black, *Married Women's Work*, 70.

120. Mudie-Smith, *Sweated Industries*, 71.

121. Schmiechen, *Sweated Industries and Sweated Labor*, 64.
122. Malcolmson, *English Laundresses*, 13–14.
123. MacDonald, *Women in Printing*, 116. Other firms seem to have offered slightly higher average wages.
124. Booth, *Life and Labour*, 4:90–92.
125. Bythell, *Sweated Trades*, 149.
126. Green, "Metropolitan Economy," 14.
127. Bythell, *Sweated Trades*, 74. Booth, *Life and Labour*, 4:279; Bulkley, *Minimum Rates*, 65–66.
128. F. Thompson, quoted in Malcolmson, *English Laundresses*, 33; See also Davin, *Growing Up Poor*, 47–48.
129. *Report on the Sweating System*, 1417.
130. Booth, *Life and Labour*, 4:266.
131. Meyer and Black, *Makers of Our Clothes*, 45; Morris, "Sweating," 110; *Working of the Factory and Workshops Acts*, 131–32, 180; *Report on the Sweating System*, 7952–56; *Reports by the Lady Assistant Commissioners*, 13; *Second Report of the Royal Commission on Labour*, 158.
132. The broad demographic differences between the neighborhoods, discussed above, are reflected in the employed female populations of each neighborhood. For example, Globe Town had the youngest population of employed women, while a relatively large proportion of employed women in Lisson Grove were between ages thirty-five and forty-four.
133. Definitive evidence of this pattern could only come from a study of particular women over the course of their lives.
134. Fifty-five percent of upholsteresses, 52% of mantle makers, and 50% of all employed women were under age thirty.
135. Of all employed women, 40% were under age twenty-five.
136. Only 22% of women in the silk trade were under age twenty-five, but 38% were fifty-five or older.
137. Homework was not regulated until the implementation of the Trade Boards Act of 1909. Schmiechen, *Sweated Industries and Sweated Labor*, 135–38, 174ff.

CHAPTER 4. RELENTLESS LABOR: WOMEN'S EMPLOYMENT
AND THE LIFE COURSE

1. D. Levine, "Industrialization and the Proletarian Family in England," *Past and Present* 107 (1985): 189; E. Richards, "Women in the British Economy since about 1700: An Interpretation," *History* 59 (1974): 350; E. Hobsbawm, "Man and Woman: Images on the Left," in *Workers: Worlds of Labor*, 94; P. Branca, *Women in Europe since 1750* (New York: St. Martin's, 1978), 33.
2. Chinn, *They Worked All Their Lives*, 99. See also Malcolmson, *English Laundresses*, 12–13; Bythell, *Sweated Trades*, 167; and J. Lewis, "The Working-Class Wife and Mother and State Intervention, 1870–1918," in *Labour and Love: Women's Experience of Home and Family, 1850–1940*, ed. J. Lewis (Oxford: Basil Blackwell, 1986), 102.
3. J. Lewis, "Introduction: Reconstructing Women's Experience of Home and Family," in *Labour and Love*, ed. Lewis, 19; and idem, "The Working-Class Wife," 102.
4. Harold Benenson offers another example of a group of women workers who rejected dominant notions of the role of married women. Benenson, "Family Wage."

5. T. K. Hareven, *Transitions: The Family and the Life Course in Historical Perspective* (New York: Academic Press, 1978); T. K. Hareven, *Family Time and Industrial Time: The Relationship between the Family and Work in a New England Industrial Town* (Cambridge: Cambridge University Press, 1982); G. Alter, *The Family and the Female Life Course: Women of Verviers, Belgium, 1849–1880* (Madison: University of Wisconsin Press, 1988).

6. Even those who have applied the life-course and family-economy approach most successfully have cited economic need or crisis as the key variable shaping married women's employment. Hareven, *Family Time and Industrial Time*, 208; Tilly and Scott, *Women, Work, and Family*, 126.

7. See the introduction; Higgs, "Women, Occupations and Work," 59–80.

8. If we include wives of household heads who took in boarders or lodgers, 27.8% of all married women were employed.

9. E. Roberts, "Women's Strategies, 1890–1940," in *Labour and Love,* ed. Lewis, 227.

10. Those aged fifteen or older have been considered adult for this study.

11. W. Seccombe, "The Western European Marriage Pattern in Historical Perspective: A Response to David Levine," *Journal of Historical Sociology* 3:1 (1990): 64.

12. L. Jamieson, "Limited Resources and Limiting Conventions: Working-Class Mothers and Daughters in Urban Scotland," in *Labour and Love,* ed. Lewis, 52–56.

13. G. Sen, "Sexual Division of Labor and the Working-Class Family: Toward a Conceptual Synthesis of Class Relations and the Subordination of Women," *Review of Radical Political Economics* 16 (1976): 76–86.

14. For example, Sonya Rose suggests that in one common pattern of married women's employment, they "sought employment during the times when there were more dependents than could be supported by a single wage earner." Rose, *Limited Livelihoods*, 76.

15. In order to determine the influence of other earners on wives' employment, the percentage of other household members who were employed has been used in this analysis. This is calculated by dividing the number of employed household members, not including the wife of the household head, by the number of household members, also excluding the wife of the household head.

16. This categorization of families is based on that used by Lees, *Exiles of Erin*, 260, adjusted to include a category for households with wives over age sixty-five.

17. This pattern does not change if we add wives in households that included lodgers to those considered employed. If we consider these wives to be employed, the percentages employed in each family type across all three neighborhoods were: Type 1—33.1%, Type 2—22.8%, Type 3—20.7%, Type 4—24.1%, Type 5—29.4%, Type 6—33.7%, Type 7—31.6%.

18. Ross, "Fierce Questions and Taunts," 576.

19. The Johns family fits type 5.

20. This region includes London and the three metropolitan counties of Essex, Middlesex, and Surrey.

21. Of wives born in and around London, 48.3% lived in this type of family, compared to 41.0% of those born outside this area. This reflects the fact that migration to these neighborhoods had slowed well before 1881 and migrants tended to be older than those born in London. Of wives born outside the London area, 35.7% lived in type 6 or 7 families, while only 20.4% of London-born wives did.

22. Davidoff and Hall, *Family Fortunes*, 380–88.

23. The figure of 20.1% of wives of employed household heads who were employed differs from the figures for married women as a whole, as it does not include wives of lodgers, boarders, sons of household heads, etc. Nor does it count married women whose husbands were absent on census night, or were unemployed.

24. David R. Green estimates that laborers working with skilled workers commonly earned two-thirds the wages of the skilled workers. Green, *Artisans to Paupers*, 67.

25. In this case as well, the domestic responsibilities of their wives rather than narrow economic factors shaped this pattern. Railway porters worked irregular hours, including at night, and this increased their wives' domestic work. For an analogous example, see M. P. Hanagan, *Nascent Proletarians: Class Formation in Post-Revolutionary France* (Oxford: Basil Blackwell, 1989), 140–41.

26. M. E. Bibby et al., *The Pudding Lady: A New Departure in Social Work* (London: Steads, 1910), 64.

27. E. Ross, "Labour and Love: Rediscovering London's Working-Class Mothers, 1870–1918," in *Labour and Love,* ed. Lewis, 79.

28. J. W. Scott and L. Tilly, "Women's Work and Family in Nineteenth-Century Europe," *Comparative Studies in Society and History* 16 (1976): 41–42.

29. *Report on the Sweating System*, 1549.

30. Quoted in M. Hewitt, *Wives and Mothers in Victorian Industry* (London: Rockliff, 1958), 194.

31. Ittman, *Work, Gender and Family*, 202–3, 207, 227.

32. R. Whipp, "Kinship, Labour and Enterprise: The Staffordshire Pottery Industry, 1890–1920," in *Women's Work and the Family Economy,* ed. Hudson and Lee, 187–89.

33. Thompson, *Rise of Respectable Society*, 175.

CHAPTER 5. "THE ILLS I HAD TO BEAR": GENDER, POWER, AND WELL-BEING

1. Foakes, *Between High Walls*, 72.

2. Foakes, *My Part of the River*, 19.

3. Valuable surveys of this literature can be found in J. Thomas, "Women and Capitalism: Oppression or Emancipation? A Review Article," *Comparative Studies in Society and History* 30 (1988): 534–49; and Bradley, *Men's Work, Women's Work*, chap. 2.

4. See, for example, W. Seccombe, "Patriarchy Stabilized: The Construction of the Male Breadwinner Wage Norm in Nineteenth-Century Britain," *Social History* 11 (1986): 53–76; and Richards, "Women in the British Economy," 356.

5. E. Shorter, "Women's Work: What Difference Did Capitalism Make?" *Theory and Society* 3 (1976): 520–21.

6. More nuanced versions of the pessimist position recognize that many working-class women earn wages in industrial capitalism, but that the division of labor keeps them in marginal positions in labor markets, enforcing their dependence on men and supporting gender inequality. The experience of poor London women supports this view. See J. Brenner and M. Ramas, "Rethinking Women's Oppression," *New Left Review* 144 (March–April 1984): 58–59.

7. An option for women outside the family structure would be to live with nonrelatives. It was, however, rare for a household to include only nonrelated individuals. Only 2.8% of households in the three areas fit this description.

8. Women's anxiety to get married was a pervasive theme in London music hall songs. See Stedman Jones, "Working-Class Culture," 226.

9. G. Sen, "Sexual Division of Labor," 78.

10. E. Roberts, *A Woman's Place: An Oral History of Working-Class Women, 1890–1940* (Oxford: Basil Blackwell, 1984), 39–45; Jamieson, "Limited Resources," 49–69.

11. Ross, "Fierce Questions and Taunts," 576.

12. Moral and emotional ties, the domestic work performed by their mothers and sisters, and the potential economic cushion during periods of slack work explain the tendency for young men to continue to live with their parents and contribute their earnings to the household budget. Jamieson points out the higher status and greater privileges accorded young men who lived with their parents. Jamieson, "Limited Resources," 60–61.

13. Booth, *Life and Labour*, 1:34–35.

14. H. Hartmann, "The Family as a Locus of Gender, Class, and Political Struggle: The Example of Housework," *Signs* 6 (1981): 373. G. Sen, "Sexual Division of Labor," 76. Of course, the focus on the economic benefits of marriage does not deny emotional and cultural motives for forming domestic relationships.

15. A. Sen describes this as women's less favorable "breakdown position," which detracted from their positions in the "cooperative conflicts" through which the terms of these relationships are set. A. Sen, "Gender and Cooperative Conflicts," in *Persistent Inequalities: Women and World Development*, ed. I. Tinker (Oxford: Oxford University Press), 132, 135. L. Tilly, "Gender and Jobs," 32.

16. Chinn, *They Worked All Their Lives*, 49.

17. Seccombe, "Patriarchy Stabilized," 58. S. Meacham, *A Life Apart: The English Working Class, 1890–1914* (Cambridge: Harvard University Press, 1977), 116, 84.

18. See K. Oppenheim Mason, "The Status of Women: Conceptual and Methodological Issues in Demographic Studies," *Sociological Forum* 1 (1986): 285–300.

19. See A. Sen, "Gender and Cooperative Conflicts," 123–49; idem, "Economics and the Family," *Asian Development Review* 1 (1983): 14–26; J. Kynch and A. Sen, "Indian Women: Well-Being and Survival?" *Cambridge Journal of Economics* 7 (1983): 363–80. I am grateful to Louise Tilly for her guidance on these issues.

20. *Marylebone Mercury*, 30 August 1879.

21. Acorn, *One of the Multitude*, 5ff.

22. *CKTSP Gazette*, 23 August 1884, 4 October 1884, 8 September 1888.

23. *Marylebone Mercury*, 30 August 1879; Ross, "Fierce Questions and Taunts," 580–85; idem, *Love and Toil*, 74.

24. James also repeatedly beat his wife, particularly during conflicts over this financial issue. *Marylebone Mercury*, 10 August 1878.

25. Children generally turned over their entire wages to their mothers, who then supplied them with spending money. E. Roberts, *A Woman's Place*, 42. Ross argues that the wages of older children offered mothers a brief period of relative prosperity, during which they might enjoy increased leisure opportunities. Ross, "Labour and Love," 87.

26. "Studies concerned with the impact of women's status on demographic or social phenomena would be wise to focus on resource control." Oppenheim Mason, "Status of Women," 297.

27. Blake, *Memories of Old Poplar*, 8.

28. Ross, "Survival Networks," 7.

29. Chinn, *They Worked All Their Lives*, 55.

30. Acorn, *One of the Multitude*, 5.

31. Pember Reeves, *Round About a Pound a Week*, 155.

32. Ross, "Fierce Questions and Taunts," 584–85; idem, *Love and Toil*, 77–78.

33. W. Seccombe, *Weathering the Storm: Working-Class Families from the Industrial Revolution to the Fertility Decline* (London: Verso, 1993), 154.

34. L. Oren, "The Welfare of Women in Laboring Families: England, 1860–1950," in *Clio's Consciousness Raised: New Perspectives on the History of Women*, ed. M. Hartman and L. W. Banner (New York: Harper and Row, 1974), 229–30. See also Pember Reeves, *Round About a Pound a Week*, 133; Chinn, *They Worked All Their Lives*, 15, 50–51; Dyhouse, *Girls Growing Up*, 8; D. J. Oddy, "Working-Class Diets in Late Nineteenth-Century Britain," *Economic History Review*, 2d ser., 23 (1970): 321.

35. Alice Linton, *Early Memories*, cited by Ross, "Fierce Questions and Taunts," 585.

36. J. Williamson, *Father Joe*, and E. M. Bunting et al., *A School for Mothers*, quoted by Ross, *Love and Toil*, 55.

37. Oren, "Welfare of Women," 230; M. Llewelyn Davies, ed., *Maternity: Letters from Working Women* (1915; reprint, New York: W. W. Norton, 1978), 5.

38. *Marylebone Mercury*, 5 July, 1879.

39. Oren, "Welfare of Women," 231; Ross, "Fierce Questions and Taunts," 586; Seccombe, *Weathering the Storm*, 155.

40. Pember Reeves, *Round About a Pound a Week*, 156.

41. Bibby et al., *Pudding Lady*, 7.

42. R. Church, *Over the Bridge: An Essay in Autobiography* (London: William Heinemann, 1955), 75.

43. This song, "Girls, We Would Never Stand It," by Marie Loftus, is quoted in Stedman Jones, "Working-Class Culture," 227.

44. E. Roberts, *A Woman's Place*, 148.

45. Blake, *Memories of Old Poplar*, 12.

46. Jamieson, "Limited Resources," 56, 53, 66. Dyhouse, *Girls Growing Up*, 11.

47. M. Tebbutt describes the impact of bug infestation, which drove the poor into the streets until late at night during the summer months. M. Tebbutt, *Women's Talk? A Social History of Gossip in Working-Class Neighborhoods, 1880–1960* (Aldershot, Hants, U.K.: Scolar Press, 1995), 89–91.

48. Booth Collection, B215:101, 141, B220:195, B225:89. Often more than half of those arrested for drunkenness were women. See *Marylebone Mercury*, 25 October 1879, 28 February 1880, 15 January 1881.

49. *CKTSP Gazette*, 29 March 1879. We have a record of this evening's activity because that night two of the Hopkins' children, infants aged five weeks and eighteen months, died in bed with their mother.

50. *Marylebone Mercury*, 3 May 1879.

51. *East London Observer*, 6 January 1883.

52. Booth Collection, A32:3; Stedman Jones, "Working-Class Culture," 205, 224ff.

53. *Eastern Argus*, 11 November 1882.

54. Booth Collection, B73:174; A38:14.

55. Blake, *Memories of Old Poplar*, 23.

56. W. Southgate, *That's the Way It Was: A Working Class Autobiography, 1890–1950* (London: New Clarion Press, 1982), 76.

57. Blake, *Memories of Old Poplar*, 23.

58. *CKTSP Gazette*, 1 December 1883.

59. Oren, "Welfare of Women," 239–40.

60. Ross, *Love and Toil*, 80–81, 140; Dyhouse, *Girls Growing Up*, 8–9.

61. Tebbutt describes women's leisure time as "infinitely more amorphous" than men's. *Women's Talk*, 58. See also Seccombe, *Weathering the Storm*, 131–32.

62. Wohl, *Endangered Lives*, 13.

63. Oren, "Welfare of Women," 229; Chinn, *They Worked All Their Lives*, 133–34.

64. Rickets, generally caused by vitamin D deficiency, "could result in a narrowing of the pelvis," making childbirth difficult and increasing complications. Wohl, *Endangered Lives*, 56–57, 130–31; S. R. Johansson, "Sex and Death in Victorian England," in *A Widening Sphere: Changing Roles of Victorian Women*, ed. M. Vicinus (Bloomington: Indiana University Press, 1977), 170.

65. Oren, "Welfare of Women," 233–34.

66. *CKTSP Gazette*, 2 July 1881.

67. Llewelyn Davies, *Maternity*, 33.

68. Ibid., 37, italics in original.

69. Ross, *Love and Toil*, 114–22.

70. While male mortality was generally higher than that of women, there is some debate about the impact of childbearing on women's mortality. See R. Woods, "Mortality Patterns in the Nineteenth Century," in *Urban Disease and Mortality in Nineteenth-Century England*, ed. R. Woods and J. Woodward (London: Batsford, 1984), 42; and Johansson, "Sex and Death," 170.

71. E. Roberts, *A Woman's Place*, 104.

72. J. Lewis, *The Politics of Motherhood: Child and Maternal Welfare in England, 1900–1939* (London: Croom Helm, 1980), 43.

73. Llewelyn Davies, *Maternity*, 9.

74. Ross, "Fierce Questions and Taunts," 578; D. Gittens, *Fair Sex: Family Size and Structure, 1900–39* (London: Hutchinson, 1982), 88.

75. Data on family size presented above suggest that women in Lisson Grove and Somers Town attempted to control their fertility more than did those in Globe Town.

76. A. McLaren, "The Sexual Politics of Reproduction in Britain," in *The European Experience of Declining Fertility, 1850–1970*, ed. J. Gillis, L. Tilly, and D. Levine (Cambridge, Mass.: Blackwell, 1992), 89–90; McLaren, *Birth Control*, 244–46.

77. Llewelyn Davies, *Maternity*, 15.

78. Chinn, *They Worked All Their Lives*, 149; Llewelyn Davies, *Maternity*, 15.

79. W. Seccombe, "Men's 'Marital Rights' and Women's 'Wifely Duties': Changing Conjugal Relations in the Fertility Decline," in *European Experience of Declining Fertility*, ed. Gillis, Tilly, and Levine, 72–73, and W. Seccombe, "Starting to Stop: Working-Class Fertility Decline in Britain," *Past and Present* 126 (1990): 155.

80. Chinn, *They Worked All Their Lives*, 142.

81. Ross, "Fierce Questions and Taunts," 594.

82. Llewelyn Davies, *Maternity*, 27–28.

83. Even Chinn, who argues that some women enjoyed a position of great authority in working-class households, admits that in sexual relations "the subservience of women to men in marriage is at its most apposite." Chinn, *They Worked All Their Lives*, 142.

84. Ross, "Fierce Questions and Taunts," 590–93.

85. A. S. Jasper, *A Hoxton Childhood* (London: Barrie & Rockliff, 1969), 17–18.

86. *CKTSP Gazette*, 29 August 1885 and 5 September 1885.

87. *Marylebone Mercury*, 26 May 1883.

88. This was accepted as the proper contribution for a good husband, and even those

men earning relatively high wages would not necessarily turn over more than this to their wives.

89. Ross, "Fierce Questions and Taunts," 582.

90. Ibid., 593.

91. *Marylebone Mercury*, 24 March 1883 and 7 April 1883.

92. T. Morgan in T. Thompson, *Edwardian Childhoods* (London: Routledge and Kegan Paul, 1981), 22.

93. Acorn, *One of the Multitude*, 2; Ross, "Fierce Questions and Taunts."

94. *CKTSP Gazette*, 26 June 1880.

95. *Marylebone Mercury*, 2 October 1880.

96. Ibid., 9 June 1883.

97. *CKTSP Gazette*, 17 September 1887. Sherman was bound over to keep the peace with his wife, and released.

98. Ibid., 14 June 1879.

99. *Marylebone Mercury*, 9 June 1883.

100. Ibid., 25 June 1881.

101. *CKTSP Gazette*, 9 June 1888.

102. Ross, "Fierce Questions and Taunts," 593.

103. *Marylebone Mercury*, 30 August 1879.

104. Ross, "Fierce Questions and Taunts," 591–92.

105. *Marylebone Mercury*, 21 July 1883.

106. Ross, "Fierce Questions and Taunts," 592.

107. Chinn, *They Worked All Their Lives*, 52, 19.

108. Ibid., 13, 19, 44.

109. E. Roberts, *A Woman's Place*, 110.

110. Ross, "Labour and Love," 85.

111. Chinn, *They Worked All Their Lives*, 165.

112. Oppenheim Mason, "Status of Women," 290.

113. Meacham, *A Life Apart*, 64, 116; L. Davidoff, "Mastered for Life: Servant and Wife in Victorian and Edwardian England," *Journal of Social History* 7 (1974): 422.

114. P. Ayers and J. Lambertz, "Marriage Relations, Money, and Domestic Violence in Working-Class Liverpool, 1919–1939," in *Labour and Love,* ed. Lewis, 197.

115. *Marylebone Mercury*, 1 April 1882. Catherine pleaded before the court for her husband's release.

116. Ross, *Love and Toil*, 150.

117. Jamieson, "Limited Resources," 67.

118. *CKTSP Gazette*, 26 May 1888.

119. Foakes, *Between High Walls*, 6.

120. Tebbutt, *Women's Talk*, 49, 77.

121. Llewelyn Davies, *Maternity*, 7.

122. Chinn, *They Worked All Their Lives*, 23.

123. Lewis, "Reconstructing Women's Experience," 15.

124. Chinn, *They Worked All Their Lives*, 29.

125. Jamieson, "Limited Resources," 62–63, 67; Chinn, *They Worked All Their Lives*, 12, 51.

126. J. Lewis, *Women in England, 1870–1950: Sexual Divisions and Social Change* (Bloomington: Indiana University Press, 1984), 66.

127. E. Roberts, "Working Wives and Their Families," in *Population and Society in*

Britain, 1850–1980, ed. T. Barker and M. Drake (New York: New York University Press, 1982), 162.

128. Chinn, *They Worked All Their Lives*, 45.

129. A. Sen, "Gender and Cooperative Conflicts," 132, 135; L. Tilly, "Gender and Jobs," 44; M. Young and P. Willmott, *The Symmetrical Family: A Study of Work and Leisure in the London Region* (Harmondsworth, U.K.: Penguin, 1973), 86; Hartmann, "Family as the Locus," 372, 391.

130. The argument here does not dispute Chinn's descriptive findings about life among the urban poor. Most of his material agrees with patterns discovered in London neighborhoods. But this chapter does question Chinn's interpretation of these findings as indicating a "hidden matriarchy." Chinn, *They Worked All Their Lives*, 12–13, 44.

131. Brenner and Ramas, "Rethinking Women's Oppression," 58–59. For analogous cases in which women's wage earning failed to undercut patriarchy, see Ittman, *Work, Gender and Family*, 196, and L. Tilly, "Beyond Family Strategies," 125.

132. R. L. Smith and D. M. Valenze, "Mutuality and Marginality: Liberal Moral Theory and Working-Class Women in Nineteenth-Century England," *Signs* 13:2 (1988): 285.

CONCLUSION: "THE AIM OF EVERY GIRL"

1. Sims, *How the Poor Live*, 90.

2. Ross, *Love and Toil*, 137.

3. At times, this required conflict within the family, as when wives quarreled with their husbands over the amount of their contribution to the household budget or even stole from their husbands. Yet these resources were devoted to the family's budget, not the wife's personal needs.

4. L. Tilly, "Comments on the Yans-McLaughlin and Davidoff Papers," *Journal of Social History* 7 (1974): 452–59; Smith and Valenze, "Mutuality and Marginality," 282–98.

5. Chinn, *They Worked All Their Lives*, 42.

6. Green and Parton, "Slums and Slum Life," 79–80.

7. Some single women could remain with their parents, or live with adult siblings, but these arrangements also required significant self-sacrifice on the part of the single woman. See Jamieson, "Limited Resources," 60, 64; and D. Gittens, "Marital Status, Work and Kinship, 1850–1930," in *Labour and Love,* ed. Lewis, 250.

8. Foakes, *My Part of the River*, 22–24.

9. Dyhouse, *Girls Growing Up*, 19, 31.

10. The fact that this effort contributed to the unequal burden of labor that formed an essential aspect of the patriarchal organization of their households does not detract from these women's admirable commitment to their duties.

11. Ross, "Survival Networks," 4–27.

12. David Levine describes working-class women who "triumphed through an exercise of will and sheer moral courage." D. Levine, *Reproducing Families: The Political Economy of English Population History* (Cambridge: Cambridge University Press, 1987), 201.

13. Ross, *Love and Toil*, 166–69.

14. *CKTSP Gazette*, 31 January 1885.

15. On definitions of "political," see L. Tilly and P. Gurin, "Women, Politics and Change," in *Women, Politics and Change,* ed. L. Tilly and P. Gurin (New York: Russell Sage Foundation, 1990), 2.

16. See A. Vickery, "Golden Age to Separate Spheres? A Review of the Categories and Chronology of English Women's History," *Historical Journal* 36 (1993): 383–414.

17. For the development of domesticity in the early nineteenth century, see Davidoff and Hall, *Family Fortunes*, chap. 3. For the persistence of these prescriptions, see C. Dyhouse, "Mothers and Daughters in the Middle-Class Home, c. 1870–1914," in *Labour and Love,* ed. Lewis, 27–47.

18. Walkowitz, *City of Dreadful Delight,* 67.

APPENDIX 1. METHODOLOGICAL APPENDIX

1. Booth, *Descriptive Map.*

2. The area to the south of Drummond Crescent and west of Church Way belonged to the Southampton Estate. However, the construction of Seymour Street and Euston Station separated this small plot from the rest of the estate and linked it with the land owned by Lord Somers.

3. The distinctly more affluent character of these blocks is confirmed by Booth, *Descriptive Map.*

4. *Census of 1881.*

APPENDIX 2. "POSSIBLE SERVANTS"

1. Higgs, *Domestic Servants,* 45–46.

2. Four stepdaughters have been included in the "normal nuclear family" categories.

3. Higgs, *Domestic Servants,* 46.

4. This includes eleven of the possible servants who were the heads of households.

5. Higgs cites the large number of retailer and farmer households that included possible servants in Rochdale. Higgs, *Domestic Servants,* 47.

6. This does not include the households headed by domestic servants.

Bibliography

THE MANUSCRIPT CENSUS

The enumerators' books for the 1881 census are available on microfilm at the Public Record Office census archive. The sections used in this study include:

RG 11 151–54
RG 11 198–203
RG 11 415–16
RG 11 420
RG 11 422–23
RG 11 480

ARCHIVAL COLLECTIONS

Charles Booth Collection. British Library of Political and Economic Science. London School of Economics.
British Library Map Collection. British Library.
Camden Local History Library Collection. Swiss Cottage.
Greater London Record Office.
Heal Collection. Camden Local History Library. Swiss Cottage.
Holborn Local History Collection. Holborn Library.
Marylebone Local History Collection. Marylebone Library.
Tower Hamlets Local History Library Collection. Mile End.

GOVERNMENT PUBLICATIONS

London County Council. Minutes of Proceedings.
Parliamentary Papers:
    1852–53, vol. 85. *Census of Great Britain, 1851.*
    1863, vol. 53. *Census of England and Wales for the Year 1861.*

1876, vol. 30. *Report of the Commissioners Appointed to Inquire into the Working of the Factory and Workshops Acts.*

1883, vols. 79, 80. *Census of England and Wales, 1881.*

1887, vol. 71. *Tabulations of the Statements of Men Living in Certain Selected Districts of London in March 1887.*

1888, vol. 20. *Report of the Select Committee of the House of Lords on the Sweating System.*

1889, vol. 13. *Third Report from the Select Committee of the House of Lords on the Sweating System with Minutes of Evidence and Appendices.*

1892, vol. 35. *Minutes of Evidence of the Royal Commission on Labour.*

1892, vol. 36. *Second Report of the Royal Commission on Labour.*

1893–94, vol. 37. *Royal Commission on Labour, Reports by the Lady Assistant Commissioners on the Conditions of Work in Various Industries.*

1893–94, vol. 105. *Census of England and Wales, 1891.*

1902, vol. 120. *Census Returns of England and Wales, 1901.*

1903, vol. 84. *Census Returns of England and Wales, 1901.*

1909, vol. 37. *Report of the Royal Commission on the Poor Laws and the Relief of Distress.*

1912–13, vol. 111. *Census Returns of England and Wales, 1911.*

Registrar General. *Quarterly Reports of Marriages, Births and Deaths.*

St. Marylebone. "Annual Reports of the Medical Officer of Health."

St. Pancras. "Annual Reports of the Medical Officer of Health."

St. Pancras Health Department. "Housing of the Working Classes Act, 1890, Minutes of Evidence." 1893.

OTHER PRIMARY SOURCES

The A to Z of Victorian London. Lympne Castle, Kent, U.K.: Harry Margary, 1987.

Acorn, G. [pseud.]. *One of the Multitude: An Autobiography of a Resident of Bethnal Green.* London: William Heinemann, 1911.

Besant, W. *East London.* New York: The Century Company, 1901.

Bibby, M. E., E. G. Colles, F. Petty, and J. F. J. Sykes. *The Pudding Lady: A New Departure in Social Work.* London: Steads, 1910.

Bingham, F. *The Metropolitan Borough of Bethnal Green: The Official Guide.* London: Borough of Bethnal Green, 1921.

Black, C. *Married Women's Work.* 1915. Reprint, London: Virago, 1983.

Blake, J. *Memories of Old Poplar.* London: Stepney Books, 1977.

Booth, C. *Charles Booth's Descriptive Map of London Poverty.* 1889. Reprint, London: London Topographical Society, 1984.

———. *Life and Labour of the People in London.* 17 vols. London: Macmillan, 1904.

Bulkley, M. E. *The Establishment of Legal Minimum Rates in the Boxmaking Industry.* London: G. Bell & Sons, 1915.

Camden and Kentish Towns, Hampstead, Highgate, Holloway and St. Pancras Gazette

Church, R. *Over the Bridge: An Essay in Autobiography*. London: William Heinemann, 1955.

Clinch, G. *Marylebone and St. Pancras*. London: Truslove and Shirley, 1890.

Collison, W. *The Apostle of Free Labour*. London: Hurst and Blackett, 1913.

East London Observer

Eastern Argus

Ezard, E. *Battersea Boy*. London: William Kimber, 1979.

Foakes, G. *Between High Walls: A London Childhood*. London: Shepheard-Walwyn, 1972.

———. *My Part of the River*. London: Shepheard-Walwyn, 1974.

Gaspey, W. *Tallis' Illustrated London*. London: John Tallis & Co., 1851.

Gavin, H. *Sanitary Ramblings: Being Sketches and Illustrations of Bethnal Green, a Type of the Conditions of the Metropolis and other Large Towns*. London: Churchill, 1848.

Hollingshead, J. *Ragged London in 1861*. London: Smith, Elder, and Co., 1861.

Jasper, A. S. *A Hoxton Childhood*. London: Barrie & Rockliff, 1969.

Kelly, F. *The Post-Office London Directory for 1881*. London: Kelly & Co., 1881.

Krausse, A. S. *Starving London*. London: Remington & Co., 1886.

Llewelyn Davies, M., ed. *Maternity: Letters from Working Women*. 1915. Reprint, New York: W. W. Norton, 1978.

MacDonald, J. R., ed. *Women in the Printing Trades*. London: P. S. King & Son, 1904.

Marylebone Mercury

Mayhew, H. *London Labour and the London Poor*. 4 vols. 1861–62. Reprint, New York: Dover, 1968.

Meyer, C., and C. Black. *Makers of Our Clothes*. London: Duckworth, 1909.

Miller, F. *Saint Pancras Past and Present: Being Historical, Traditional, and General Notes of the Period*. London: F. Miller, 1874.

Mudie-Smith, R. *Sweated Industries: A Handbook of the "Daily News" Exhibition*. 1903. Reprint, New York: Garland, 1980.

Pember Reeves, M. *Round About a Pound a Week*. 1913. Reprint, London: Virago, 1979.

Samuel, R. *East End Underworld: Chapters in the Life of Arthur Harding*. London: Routledge and Kegan Paul, 1981.

Sims, G. R. *How the Poor Live and Horrible London*. New York: Garland, 1984.

Smith, T. *A Topographical and Historical Account of the Parish of St. Mary-le-bone*. London: John Smith, 1833.

Southgate, W. *That's the Way It Was: A Working Class Autobiography 1890–1950*. London: New Clarion Press, 1982.

Swan, W. "The Journal of William Swan." In *The Journals of Two Poor Dissenters, 1786–1880*. London: Routledge & Kegan Paul, 1970.

Thompson, T. *Edwardian Childhoods*. London: Routledge & Kegan Paul, 1981.

Vynne, N., and H. Blackburn. *Women under the Factory Act*. London: Williams and Norgate, 1903.

Wheatley, H. B. *London Past and Present: Its History, Associations and Traditions*. London: J. Murray, 1891.

SECONDARY SOURCES

Alexander, S. "Women's Work in Nineteenth-Century London: A Study of the Years 1820–1850." In *The Rights and Wrongs of Women*, edited by A. Oakley and J. Mitchell. Harmondsworth, U.K.: Penguin, 1976.

Alter, G. *Family and the Female Life Course: Women of Verviers, Belgium, 1849–1880*. Madison: University of Wisconsin Press, 1988.

Anderson, M. *Family Structure in Nineteenth Century Lancashire*. Cambridge: Cambridge University Press, 1979.

———. "Household Structure and the Industrial Revolution: Mid-Nineteenth-Century Preston in Comparative Perspective." In *Household and Family in Past Time*, edited by P. Laslett with R. Wall. Cambridge: Cambridge University Press, 1972.

Armstrong, W. A. "A Note on the Household Structure of Mid-Nineteenth-Century York in Comparative Perspective." In *Household and Family in Past Time*, edited by P. Laslett with R. Wall. Cambridge: Cambridge University Press, 1972.

August, A. "The Other Side of 'Outcast London': Women in Three Poor Neighborhoods." Ph.D. diss., Columbia University, 1993.

———. "Patterns of Women's Union Membership: England and Wales at the Turn of the Twentieth Century." Master's thesis, Columbia University, 1985.

Ayers, P., and J. Lambertz. "Marriage Relations, Money, and Domestic Violence in Working-Class Liverpool, 1919–1939." In *Labour and Love: Women's Experience of Home and Family, 1850–1940*, edited by J. Lewis. Oxford: Basil Blackwell, 1986.

Bales, K. "Charles Booth's Survey of *Life and Labour of the People in London* 1889–1903." In *The Social Survey in Historical Perspective, 1880–1940*, edited by M. Bulmer, K. Bales, and K. Kish Sklar. Cambridge: Cambridge University Press, 1991.

Barker, T. C., and M. Robbins. *A History of London Transport*. 2 vols. London: George Allen and Unwin, 1963.

Barrett, M. *Women's Oppression Today: The Marxist/Feminist Encounter*. Rev. ed. London: Verso, 1988.

Benenson, H. "The 'Family Wage' and Working Women's Consciousness in Britain, 1880–1914." *Politics and Society* 19 (1991): 71–108.

Bradley, H. *Men's Work, Women's Work: A Sociological History of the Sexual Division of Labour in Employment*. Minneapolis: University of Minnesota Press, 1989.

Branca, P. *Women in Europe since 1750*. New York: St. Martin's, 1978.

Brenner, J., and M. Ramas. "Rethinking Women's Oppression." *New Left Review* 144 (1984): 33–71.

Bythell, D. *The Sweated Trades: Outwork in Nineteenth-Century Britain*. New York: St. Martin's, 1978.

Chinn, C. *They Worked All Their Lives: Women of the Urban Poor in England, 1880–1939*. Manchester: Manchester University Press, 1988.

Clarke, L. *Building Capitalism: Historical Change and the Labour Process in the Production of the Built Environment*. London: Routledge, 1992.

Daunton, M. J. "Housing." In *The Cambridge Social History of Britain, 1750–1950*. Vol. 2,

People and their Environment, edited by F. M. L. Thompson. Cambridge: Cambridge University Press, 1990.

Davidoff, L. "Mastered for Life: Servant and Wife in Victorian and Edwardian England." *Journal of Social History* 7 (1974): 406–28.

———. "The Separation of Home and Work? Landladies and Lodgers in Nineteenth- and Twentieth-Century England." In *Fit Work for Women*, edited by S. Burman. London: Croom Helm, 1979.

Davidoff, L. and C. Hall. *Family Fortunes: Men and Women of the English Middle Class, 1780–1850*. Chicago: University of Chicago Press, 1987.

Davin, A. *Growing Up Poor: Home, School and Street in London, 1870–1914*. London: Rivers Oram Press, 1996.

Dyhouse, C. *Girls Growing Up in Late Victorian and Edwardian England*. London: Routledge & Kegan Paul, 1981.

———. "Mothers and Daughters in the Middle-Class Home, c. 1870–1914." In *Labour and Love: Women's Experience of Home and Family, 1850–1940*, edited by J. Lewis. Oxford: Basil Blackwell, 1986.

Dyos, H. J. *Exploring the Urban Past: Essays in Urban History by H. J. Dyos*. Edited by D. Cannadine and D. Reeder. Cambridge: Cambridge University Press, 1982.

Fishman, W. J. *East End 1888: Life in a London Borough among the Labouring Poor*. Philadelphia: Temple University Press, 1988.

Garside, P. L. "London and the Home Counties." In *The Cambridge Social History of Britain, 1750–1950* Vol. 1, *Regions and Communities*, edited by F. M. L. Thompson. Cambridge: Cambridge University Press, 1990.

George, M. D. *London Life in the Eighteenth Century*. 2d ed. Chicago: Academy Chicago, 1966.

Gillis, J. *For Better, For Worse: British Marriages, 1600 to the Present*. Oxford: Oxford University Press, 1985.

Gittens, D. *Fair Sex: Family Size and Structure, 1900–1939*. London: Hutchinson, 1982.

———. "Marital Status, Work and Kinship, 1850–1930." In *Labour and Love: Women's Experience of Home and Family, 1850–1940*, edited by J. Lewis. Oxford: Basil Blackwell, 1986.

Green, D. R. *From Artisans to Paupers: Economic Change and Poverty in London, 1790–1870*. Aldershot, Hants, U.K.: Scolar, 1995.

———. "The Metropolitan Economy: Continuity and Change 1800–1939." In *London: A New Metropolitan Geography*, edited by K. Hoggart and D. R. Green. London: Edward Arnold, 1991.

Green, D. R., and A. G. Parton. "Slums and Slum Life in Victorian England: London and Birmingham at Mid-Century." In *Slums*, edited by S. M. Gaskell. Leicester, U.K.: Leicester University Press, 1990.

Hall, P. G. *The Industries of London since 1861*. London: Hutchinson, 1962.

Hanagan, M. P. *Nascent Proletarians: Class Formation in Post-Revolutionary France*. Oxford: Basil Blackwell, 1989.

Hanjal, J. "Age at Marriage and Proportions Marrying." *Population Studies* 7 (1953): 111–36.

Hareven, T. K. *Family Time and Industrial Time: The Relationship between the Family and Work in a New England Industrial Town.* Cambridge: Cambridge University Press, 1982.

⸻. "The History of the Family and the Complexity of Social Change." *American Historical Review* 96 (1991): 95–124.

⸻, ed. *Transitions: The Family and the Life Course in Historical Perspective.* New York: Academic, 1978.

Hartmann, H. "The Family as the Locus of Gender, Class, and Political Struggle: The Example of Housework." *Signs* 6 (1981): 366–94.

Hennock, E. P. "The Measurement of Urban Poverty: From the Metropolis to the Nation, 1880–1920." *Economic History Review,* 2d ser., 40 (1987): 208–27.

Hewitt, M. *Wives and Mothers in Victorian Industry.* London: Rockliff, 1958.

Higgs, E. *Domestic Servants and Households in Rochdale 1851–1871.* New York: Garland, 1986.

⸻. "Domestic Service and Household Production." In *Unequal Opportunities: Women's Employment in England, 1800–1918,* edited by A. V. John. Oxford: Basil Blackwell, 1986.

⸻. "Women, Occupations and Work in the Nineteenth Century Censuses." *History Workshop Journal* 23 (1987): 59–80.

Hobsbawm, E. *Industry and Empire: From 1750 to the Present Day.* Harmondsworth, U.K.: Penguin, 1969.

⸻. *Workers: Worlds of Labour.* New York: Pantheon, 1984.

Holmes, M. *Somers Town: A Record of Change.* London: London Borough of Camden Libraries and Arts Department, 1985.

Horn, P. *The Rise and Fall of the Victorian Servant.* New York: St. Martin's, 1975.

Hudson, P., and W. R. Lee. "Women's Work and the Family Economy in Historical Perspective." In *Women's Work and the Family Economy in Historical Perspective,* edited by P. Hudson and W. R. Lee. Manchester: Manchester University Press, 1990.

Hunt, F. "Opportunities Lost and Gained: Mechanization and Women's Work in the London Bookbinding and Printing Trades." In *Unequal Opportunities: Women's Employment in England, 1800–1918,* edited by A. V. John. Oxford: Basil Blackwell, 1986.

Ittman, K. *Work, Gender and Family in Victorian England.* New York: New York University Press, 1995.

Jamieson, L. "Limited Resources and Limiting Conventions: Working-Class Mothers and Daughters in Urban Scotland." In *Labour and Love: Women's Experience of Home and Family, 1850–1940,* edited by J. Lewis. Oxford: Basil Blackwell, 1986.

Johansson, S. R. "Sex and Death in Victorian England." In *A Widening Sphere: Changing Roles of Victorian Women,* edited by M. Vicinus. Bloomington: Indiana University Press, 1977.

Johnson, P. *Saving and Spending: The Working-Class Economy in Britain, 1870–1939.* Oxford: Clarendon Press, 1985.

Jordan, E. "The Exclusion of Women from Industry in Nineteenth-Century Britain." *Comparative Studies in Society and History* 31 (1989): 273–96.

Joyce, P. "Work." In *The Cambridge Social History of Britain, 1750–1950* Vol. 2, *People and their Environment,* edited by F. M. L. Thompson. Cambridge: Cambridge University Press, 1990.

Kynch, J., and A. Sen. "Indian Women: Well-Being and Survival." *Cambridge Journal of Economics* 7 (1983): 363–80.

Lampard, E. "The Urbanizing World." In *The Victorian City: Images and Realities,* edited by H. J. Dyos and M. Wolff. London: Routledge & Kegan Paul, 1973.

Laslett, P. "Mean Household Size in England since the Sixteenth Century." In *Household and Family in Past Time,* edited by P. Laslett with R. Wall. Cambridge: Cambridge University Press, 1972.

Lees, L. *Exiles of Erin: Irish Migrants in Victorian London.* Ithaca: Cornell University Press, 1979.

Levine, D. "Industrialization and the Proletarian Family in England." *Past and Present* 107 (1985): 168–203.

———. *Reproducing Families: The Political Economy of English Population History.* Cambridge: Cambridge University Press, 1987.

Lewis, J. "Introduction: Reconstructing Women's Experience of Home and Family." In *Labour and Love: Women's Experience of Home and Family, 1850–1940,* edited by J. Lewis. Oxford: Basil Blackwell, 1986.

———. *The Politics of Motherhood: Child and Maternal Welfare in England, 1900–1939.* London: Croom Helm, 1980.

———. *Women in England, 1870–1950: Sexual Divisions and Social Change.* Bloomington: Indiana University Press, 1984.

———. "The Working-Class Wife and Mother and State Intervention, 1870–1918." In *Labour and Love: Women's Experience of Home and Family, 1850–1940,* edited by J. Lewis. Oxford: Basil Blackwell, 1986.

Lown, J. *Women and Industrialization: Gender at Work in Nineteenth-Century England.* Minneapolis: University of Minnesota Press, 1990.

Mackenzie, G. *Marylebone: Great City North of Oxford Street.* London: Macmillan, 1972.

Malcolmson, P. *English Laundresses: A Social History, 1850–1930.* Urbana: University of Illinois Press, 1986.

Mathias, P. *The First Industrial Nation: An Economic History, 1700–1914.* 2d ed. London: Methuen, 1983.

McBride, T. M. *The Domestic Revolution: The Modernisation of Household Service in England and France 1820–1920.* London: Croom Helm, 1976.

McKibben, R. "Why Was There No Marxism in Great Britain?" In *The Ideologies of Class: Social Relations in Britain, 1880–1950.* Oxford: Clarendon Press, 1990.

McLaren, A. *Birth Control in Nineteenth-Century England.* New York: Holmes and Meier, 1978.

———. "The Sexual Politics of Reproduction in Britain." In *The European Experience of Declining Fertility, 1850–1970,* edited by J. Gillis, L. Tilly, and D. Levine. Cambridge, Mass.: Blackwell, 1992.

Meacham, S. *A Life Apart: The English Working Class, 1890–1914.* Cambridge: Harvard University Pres, 1977.

Middleton, C. "Women's Labour and the Transition to Pre-Industrial Capitalism." In *Women and Work in Pre-Industrial England*, edited by L. Charles and L. Duffin. London: Croom Helm, 1985.

Moch, L. P. *Moving Europeans: Migration in Western Europe since 1650*. Bloomington: Indiana University Press, 1992.

Modell, J., and T. K. Hareven. "Urbanization and the Malleable Household: An Examination of Boarding and Lodging in American Families." In *Family and Kin in Urban Communities, 1700–1939*, edited by T. K. Hareven. New York: New Viewpoints, 1977.

Morris, J. "The Characteristics of Sweating: The Late-Nineteenth-Century London and Leeds Tailoring Trade." In *Unequal Opportunities: Women's Employment in England, 1800–1918*, edited by A. V. John. Oxford: Basil Blackwell, 1986.

Newman, L. T. "It All Began with J. C. Bach: A History of Piano Making in Camden." *Camden History Review* 1 (1973): 30–32.

Oddy, D. J. "Working-Class Diets in Late Nineteenth-Century Britain." *Economic History Review*, 2d ser., 23 (1970): 314–23.

Oppenheim Mason, K. "The Status of Women: Conceptual and Methodological Issues in Demographic Studies." *Sociological Forum* 1 (1986): 284–300.

Oren, L. "The Welfare of Women in Laboring Families: England, 1860–1950." In *Clio's Consciousness Raised: New Perspectives on the History of Women*, edited by M. S. Hartman and L. Banner. New York: Harper and Row, 1974.

Owen, D. *The Government of Victorian London, 1855–1889: The Metropolitan Board of Works, the Vestries and the City Corporation*. Cambridge: Harvard University Press, 1982.

Pevsner, N. *The Buildings of England: London, Except the Cities of London and Westminster*. Harmondsworth, U.K.: Penguin, 1952.

Phillips, A., and B. Taylor. "Sex and Skill: Notes towards a Feminist Economics." *Feminist Review* 6 (1980): 79–88.

Richards, E. "Women in the British Economy since about 1700: An Interpretation." *History* 59 (1974): 337–57.

Roberts, E. *A Woman's Place: An Oral History of Working-Class Women, 1890–1940*. Oxford: Basil Blackwell, 1984.

———. "Women's Strategies, 1890–1940." In *Labour and Love: Women's Experience of Home and Family, 1850–1940*, edited by J. Lewis. Oxford: Basil Blackwell, 1986.

———. *Women's Work, 1840–1940*. London: Macmillan, 1988.

———. "Working-Class Standards of Living in Barrow and Lancaster, 1880–1914." *Economic History Review*, 2d ser., 30 (1977): 306–21.

———. "Working Wives and Their Families." In *Population and Society in Britain, 1850–1980*, edited by T. Barker and M. Drake. New York: New York University Press, 1982.

Roberts, R. S. "Rereadings: Gavin, H., *Sanitary Ramblings*." *East London Papers* 8 (1965): 110–18.

Rose, S. *Limited Livelihoods: Gender and Class in Nineteenth-Century England*. Berkeley: University of California Press, 1992.

Ross, E. "'Fierce Questions and Taunts': Married Life in Working-Class London." *Feminist Studies* 8 (1982): 575–602.

———. "Labour and Love: Rediscovering London's Working-Class Mothers, 1870–1918."

In *Labour and Love: Women's Experience of Home and Family, 1850–1940*, edited by J. Lewis. Oxford: Basil Blackwell, 1986.

————. *Love and Toil: Motherhood in Outcast London, 1870–1918*. Oxford: Oxford University Press, 1993.

————. "Survival Networks: Women's Neighbourhood Sharing in London before World War I." *History Workshop Journal* 15 (1983): 4–27.

Sabin, A. K. *The Silk Weavers of Spitalfields and Bethnal Green: With a Catalogue and Illustrations of Spitalfields Silks*. London: South Kensington Museum, 1931.

Samuel, R. "Workshop of the World: Steam Power and Hand Technology in Mid-Victorian Britain." *History Workshop Journal* 3 (1977): 6–72.

Schmiechen, J. A. "State Reform and the Local Economy: An Aspect of Industrialization in Late Victorian and Edwardian London." *Economic History Review*, 2d ser., 28 (1975): 413–28.

————. *Sweated Industries and Sweated Labor: The London Clothing Trades, 1860–1914*. Urbana: University of Illinois Press, 1984.

Schwarz, L. D. *London in the Age of Industrialisation: Entrepreneurs, Labour Force and Living Conditions, 1700–1850*. Cambridge: Cambridge University Press, 1992.

Scott, J., and L. Tilly. "Women's Work and the Family in Nineteenth-Century Europe." *Comparative Studies in Society and History* 16 (1976): 36–64.

Seccombe, W. "Men's 'Marital Rights' and Women's 'Wifely Duties': Changing Conjugal Relations in the Fertility Decline." In *The European Experience of Declining Fertility, 1850–1970*, edited by J. Gillis, L. Tilly, and D. Levine. Cambridge, Mass.: Basil Blackwell, 1992.

————. "Patriarchy Stabilized: The Construction of the Male Breadwinner Wage Norm in Nineteenth-Century Britain." *Social History* 11 (1986): 53–76.

————. "Starting to Stop: Working-Class Fertility Decline in Britain." *Past and Present* 126 (1990): 151–88.

————. *Weathering the Storm: Working-Class Families from the Industrial Revolution to the Fertility Decline*. London: Verso, 1993.

————. "The Western European Marriage Pattern in Historical Perspective: A Response to David Levine." *Journal of Historical Sociology* 3 (1990): 50–74.

Sen, A. "Economics and the Family." *Asian Development Review* 1 (1983): 14–26.

————. "Gender and Cooperative Conflicts." In *Persistent Inequalities: Women and World Development*, edited by I. Tinker. Oxford: Oxford University Press, 1990.

Sen, G. "The Sexual Division of Labor and the Working-Class Family: Toward a Conceptual Synthesis of Class Relations and the Subordination of Women." *The Review of Radical Political Economics* 16 (1976): 76–86.

Sheppard, F. *London, 1808–1870: The Infernal Wen*. Berkeley: University of California Press, 1971.

Shorter, E. *The Making of the Modern Family*. New York: Basic Books, 1975.

————. "Women's Work: What Difference Did Capitalism Make?" *Theory and Society* 3 (1976): 513–27.

Smith, R. L., and D. M. Valenze. "Mutuality and Marginality: Liberal Moral Theory and Working-Class Women in Nineteenth-Century England." *Signs* 13 (1988): 277–98.

Snaith, S. *Bethnal Green, 1851–1951*. London: Bethnal Green Public Libraries, 1951.

Stedman Jones, G. *Outcast London: A Study in the Relationship between Classes in Victorian Society*. 2d ed. New York: Pantheon, 1984.

———. "Working-Class Culture and Working-Class Politics in London, 1870–1900: Notes on the Remaking of a Working Class." In *Languages of Class: Studies in English Working Class History, 1832–1982*. Cambridge: Cambridge University Press, 1983.

Stonebridge, A. J. D. *St. Marylebone: A Sketch of Its Historical Development*. London: N.p., 1952.

Tebbutt, M. *Women's Talk? A Social History of Gossip in Working-Class Neighborhoods, 1880–1960*. Aldershot, Hants, U.K.: Scolar, 1995.

Thomas, J. "Women and Capitalism: Oppression or Emancipation? A Review Article." *Comparative Studies in Society and History* 30 (1988): 534–39.

Thompson, F. M. L. "Nineteenth-Century Horse Sense." *Economic History Review*, 2d ser., 29 (1976): 60–81.

———. *The Rise of Respectable Society: A Social History of Victorian Britain 1830–1900*. Cambridge: Harvard University Press, 1988.

Tilly, C. "Transplanted Networks." Working Paper no. 35, Center for Studies of Social Change, New School for Social Research, 1986.

Tilly, L. "Beyond Family Strategies, What?" *Historical Methods* 20 (1987): 123–25.

———. "Comment on the Yans-McLaughlin and Davidoff Papers." *Journal of Social History* 7 (1974): 452–59.

———. "Gender and Jobs in Early Twentieth-Century French Industry." *International Labor and Working-Class History* 43 (1993): 31–47.

Tilly, L., and J. Scott. *Women, Work, and Family*. New York: Holt, Rinehart and Winston, 1978.

Tilly, L., and P. Gurin, eds. *Women, Politics and Change*. New York: Russell Sage Foundation, 1990.

Tomes, N. "'A Torrent of Abuse': Crimes of Violence between Working-Class Men and Women in London, 1840–1875." *Journal of Social History* 11 (1978): 328–45.

Treble, J. H. *Urban Poverty in Britain*. New York: St. Martin's, 1979.

Vale, G. F. *Old Bethnal Green*. London: Blythendale, 1934.

Vicinus, M. *Independent Women: Work and Community for Single Women, 1850–1920*. London: Virago, 1985.

Vickery, A. "Golden Age to Separate Spheres? A Review of the Categories and Chronology of English Women's History." *The Historical Journal* 36 (1993): 383–414.

Walkowitz, J. R. *City of Dreadful Delight: Narratives of Sexual Danger in Late-Victorian London*. Chicago: University of Chicago Press, 1992.

———. *Prostitution and Victorian Society: Women, Class and the State*. Cambridge: Cambridge University Press, 1980.

Waller, P. J. *Town, City, and Nation: England, 1850–1914*. Oxford: Oxford University Press, 1983.

Warner, F. *The Silk Industry of the United Kingdom: Its Origin and Development*. London: Drane's, 1921.

Weightman, G., and S. Humphries. *The Making of Modern London, 1815–1914*. London: Sidgwick & Jackson, 1983.

Whetham, E. H. "The London Milk Trade." *Economic History Review*, 2d ser., 17 (1964–65): 369–80.

Whipp, R. "Kinship, Labour and Enterprise: The Staffordshire Pottery Industry, 1890–1920." In *Women's Work and the Family Economy in Historical Perspective*, edited by P. Hudson and W. R. Lee. Manchester: Manchester University Press, 1990.

White, J. *Rothschild Buildings: Life in an East End Tenement Block, 1887–1920*. London: Routledge and Kegan Paul, 1980.

———. *The Worst Street in North London: Campbell Bunk, Islington, between the Wars*. London: Routledge and Kegan Paul, 1986.

Whitehead, J. *The Growth of St. Marylebone and Paddington: From Hyde Park to Queen's Park*. London: Jack Whitehead, 1989.

Wilson, A. *London's Industrial Heritage*. Newton Abbot, Devon, U.K.: David and Charles, 1967.

Wohl, A. *Endangered Lives: Public Health in Victorian Britain*. London: J. M. Dent & Sons, 1983.

———. *The Eternal Slum: Housing and Social Policy in Victorian London*. London: Edward Arnold, 1977.

Woods, R. "Mortality Patterns in the Nineteenth Century." In *Urban Disease and Mortality in Nineteenth-Century England*, edited by R. Woods and J. Woodward. London: Batsford, 1984.

Young, M., and P. Wilmott. *The Symmetrical Family: A Study of Work and Leisure in the London Region*. Harmondsworth, U.K.: Penguin, 1973.

Index

DATE DUE

DEMCO 38-296